Praise for *Understanding Prayer*

Few people have taught more about seeking God in prayer than Sam Storms, in the difference between praying with God and not just to him. I'm not sure whether his books stand out more for their biblical and theological rigor or their devotional passion! Either way, Sam has had a huge impact on both my walk with the Lord and my ministry. *Understanding Prayer* is no exception. I felt my faith igniting again as I read it. Chapter 6 on praying with Paul for the lost wrecked me! There is no shortage of books on prayer, but this one is special.

—J.D. Greear, PhD, pastor, The Summit Church, Raleigh-Durham, NC

Sam Storms has written an excellent book on prayer. One of the things that sets this book apart is that it is not theoretical. Sam is a man of prayer. He has learned so much about prayer not only through his study of the Scriptures but through spending many hours in prayer. I think this book has the potential to improve the prayer life of many people. It is a privilege to recommend it.

—Dr. Jack Deere, author, *Why I'm Still Surprised by the Power of the Spirit*

Sam Storms is one of God's best gifts to the church today. In Sam we find superb exegesis and compelling communication. All in the person of a godly, Christlike man. When such a man tackles a subject as profound—and elusive—as prayer, then this is a book not to miss.

—Jeff Wells, senior pastor and elder, WoodsEdge Community Church

Sam Storms is a theologian, but he's far more than just an academic. Over the past three years, I've had the privilege of experiencing his deep passion for prayer as his "prayer partner" every Friday, as well as in weekly prayer meetings at our church. In *Understanding Prayer*, readers will benefit not only from his theological insight but also from his experience as a lifelong friend of God. Sam takes us through every prayer in the New Testament, teaching us how to pray like Jesus and the apostles. You'll be inspired by their examples, as well as by the stories of prayer warriors and mystics throughout church history. If you're looking to deepen both your under-standing and passion for prayer, this book is a must-read!

—Michael Rowntree, lead pastor, Convergence Church OKC

T0356728

UNDERSTANDING
PRAYER

UNDERSTANDING
PRAYER

BIBLICAL FOUNDATIONS
AND PRACTICAL GUIDANCE
FOR SEEKING GOD

SAM STORMS

ZONDERVAN
REFLECTIVE

ZONDERVAN REFLECTIVE

Understanding Prayer
Copyright © 2025 by Sam Storms

Published in Grand Rapids, Michigan, by Zondervan. Zondervan is a registered trademark of The Zondervan Corporation, L.L.C., a wholly owned subsidiary of HarperCollins Christian Publishing, Inc.

Requests for information should be addressed to customercare@harpercollins.com.

Zondervan titles may be purchased in bulk for educational, business, fundraising, or sales promotional use. For information, please email SpecialMarkets@Zondervan.com.

ISBN 978-0-310-17112-6 (audio)

Library of Congress Cataloging-in-Publication Data

Names: Storms, C. Samuel, 1951- author.
Title: Understanding prayer : biblical foundations and practical guidance for seeking God / Sam Storms.
Description: Grand Rapids, Michigan : Zondervan Reflective, [2025] | Includes index.
Identifiers: LCCN 2024039484 (print) | LCCN 2024039485 (ebook) | ISBN 9780310171102 (paperback) | ISBN 9780310171119 (ebook)
Subjects: LCSH: Prayer--Biblical teaching. | Bible. New Testament--Criticism, interpretation, etc. | BISAC: RELIGION / Christian Living / Prayer | RELIGION / Christian Ministry / Discipleship
Classification: LCC BS2545.P67 S76 2025 (print) | LCC BS2545.P67 (ebook) | DDC 248.3/2--dc23/ eng/20240925
LC record available at https://lccn.loc.gov/2024039484
LC ebook record available at https://lccn.loc.gov/2024039485

Cover design: Lucas Art & Design
Cover photo: © Ermine; Stillfx / Deposit Photos
Interior typesetting: Sara Colley

Printed in the United States of America

25 26 27 28 29 LBC 5 4 3 2 1

To Carol Ham
(Woods Edge Church, Spring, TX)

Thanks, Carol, for your tireless commitment to
interceding for the body of Christ!

Contents

Part 4: Learning about Prayer from James

Part 5: Concluding Thoughts

Acknowledgments

Those who deserve my gratitude for all they have done to make this project possible are far too many to include in this brief acknowledgment. But I must express my heartfelt gratitude to a few of them.

I begin with Ryan Pazdur of Zondervan and his commitment to this book and his constant encouragement along the way. Ryan is a blessing not only to Zondervan but to the entire body of Christ for his devotion to bringing solid biblical and immensely practical resources to the church at large.

I also want to thank Adam Barr for his rigorous editing of this book. Adam has made what I hope is a good book even better.

It would be a mistake if I were to fail to mention several people who themselves believe in the power of prayer and demonstrated such by their constant intercession on my behalf. I should begin with my wife, Ann, my two daughters, Melanie and Joanna, and my sister, Betty Jane. They each pray for me daily and I can't imagine where I would be or whether this book would ever have seen the light of day without their bringing me to the throne of grace on a regular basis.

I should also mention Kendra Argo, Diane Wyche, Loretta Miller, and Valerie Oldfield, four ladies who consistently intercede on my behalf. All of you are a tremendous blessing to me and I can't thank you enough for your passionate devotion to supporting me through your prayers and petitions on my behalf.

Introduction

To be perfectly honest, I used to be *really* lousy at prayer. By God's grace I've made some progress and am, at present, just lousy! I may be a bit hard on myself in saying that, but when I compare my prayer life to what I read in Scripture, I see how far short I fall in coming confidently to the throne of grace. My prayer (yes, I do pray, even if not well) is that I will grow in my commitment to prayer. In one sense, this book is a confession of my own incompetence and an attempt to motivate my own soul to seek the Lord more passionately and persistently.

In saying I used to be "really lousy" at prayer I do not mean I never prayed. I prayed sporadically, with little confidence that God was listening, and even less assurance that he might actually do what I asked. In moving from "really" lousy to just "lousy" I have come to see the vital importance of prayer and find myself more diligent and devoted to seeking God in the way Scripture mandates.

This book is substantially different from others you've read on prayer. It is an attempt to unpack the meaning and power of prayer by looking closely at the prayers recorded in Scripture (primarily in the New Testament) and the exhortations to fervently bring our requests to God. I can't anticipate how you'll respond to the content and focus of the many prayers found in Scripture, but I'm not embarrassed to confess that my reaction was embarrassment. The things I regularly pray for don't find a counterpart in the prayers of the psalmists or Paul or Luke or other biblical authors. Their priorities and values in life are noticeably different from and more God-centered than mine. I can only pray that God will use their experience to challenge and transform my own.

I have another confession to make. I came close to quitting this project almost before it began. My frustrations with my prayers weighed heavily on my heart, and I didn't want to write a book urging you to do what I failed to do myself. Simply put, the potential for hypocrisy loomed before my eyes. But the more I dove into the deep end of the prayer pool in Scripture, the more my heart was convicted, and my soul was energized to make necessary adjustments in my life.

I have one word of advice as you navigate through this book. It's entirely possible and perhaps even helpful for you to pick and choose what you read. Most of the chapters are stand-alone treatments of particular prayers in the Bible and can be read without regard for what precedes or follows. There are a few exceptions to this, such as the chapters on prayer in the book of James. But feel free to read as you feel led, rather than sequentially, focusing on whatever you find most appealing. I pray you will be as encouraged as I was when you see how vitally important this spiritual discipline is not only for our personal growth but also for the way God has determined to accomplish his purposes on earth.

Although I know a few men and women who are remarkably energized in prayer and have little to no difficulty in seeking God on their own behalf and for the sake of others, most Christians with whom I interact lament that they don't pray the way they should. I deeply empathize with those feelings of guilt and failure. Would we not agree that prayer is a more mysterious and frustrating endeavor in our spiritual walk with Christ? You may be an outlier who rarely struggles to pray confidently, passionately, persistently, and with a long list of fruitful answers. If so, I'm sure you can find more helpful books to read than this one.

But for those of you who understand why the disciples fell asleep at the wheel (so to speak) when Jesus needed them most (Matt. 26:36–46), and why the apostle Paul asked believers in Rome to "strive together" with him in prayer (Rom. 15:30), and why he felt it necessary to urge others to "continue steadfastly in prayer" and to be "watchful in it" (Col. 4:2), and why he described Epaphras as "struggling" in his prayers on behalf of the church he planted in Colossae (Col. 4:12), you can appreciate the battle we all face and the powerful temptation to quit praying. Quitting is the only easy thing about praying, and it sometimes feels justified. It doesn't take much energy to throw in the towel and devote yourself to some other spiritual discipline.

I hope that something I say in this book will stir your heart to remain engaged with the Lord and steadfast in your prayer life.

A Brief Word about the Subtitle

If you're wondering why I envision prayer as *Seeking God* as the subtitle suggests, I take that from Zechariah 8:21, which reads: "Let us go at once to entreat the favor of the LORD and to seek the LORD of hosts." The KJV translation renders it this way: "Let us go speedily to pray before the LORD, and to seek the LORD of hosts." I concur with Jonathan Edwards that "praying before the Lord" and "seeking the Lord of hosts" must be looked upon as "synonymous expressions."[1] Edwards goes further:

> But certainly that expression of "seeking the Lord," is very commonly used to signify something more than merely, in general, to seek some mercy of God: it implies, that God himself is the great good desired and sought after; that the blessings pursued are God's gracious presence, the blessed manifestations of him, union and intercourse with him; or, in short, God's manifestations and communications of himself by his Holy Spirit.[2]

In sum, what we pray for when we seek after God is simply, but gloriously, more of God himself. This final text from Jeremiah sealed my decision about the subtitle to the book:

> Then you will call upon me and come and pray to me, and I will hear you. You will seek me and find me, when you seek me with all your heart. (Jer. 29:12–13)

In sum, calling upon God and coming to God and praying to God are what it means to "seek" after God with all our heart.

One more encouragement before we begin.

We all know the frustration of trying to contact someone in an emergency, only to hear a busy signal or be put on hold. At best, we are instructed

---

1. Jonathan Edwards, *Apocalyptic Writings*, ed. Stephen J. Stein (New Haven, CT: Yale University Press, 1977), 315.

2. Edwards, *Apocalyptic Writings*, 315.

to leave a message after the beep. But not so with God. I'm still struggling to come to grips with the fact that God always listens the first time I speak to him. Never a busy signal. Never a voice message. I'm never told that he'll take my call in approximately 30 minutes, nor does an angel instruct me to hang up and that he'll get back to me as soon as possible, with the assurance that I won't lose my place in line.

There is no way to overstate the glory and privilege of prayer. There aren't enough superlatives in the English language to scratch the surface of the wonder involved when it comes to communicating with the Creator of the universe! Pause momentarily and ponder this truth: you and I are repeatedly invited in Scripture to talk to *God*! Not to a neighbor, a Hollywood star, an NFL all-pro quarterback, a senator, or even the president of our country. But, to *God*! We who are weak, finite, and broken have immediate and unhindered access to him who is omnipotent, infinite, and transcendently perfect in every conceivable way. Nothing can compare with the awesome experience of communicating directly with the God who has Genesis 1 on his resume! And yet that is precisely what prayer is all about: talking with God, voicing our fears, lamenting our condition, laying our requests at his feet, all with the rock-solid assurance from God himself that he never turns a deaf ear to the cries of his kids. If that doesn't whet your spiritual appetite to dig deeply into what follows, I don't know if anything ever could. Be encouraged by the words of David as you join me in this journey into the heart of God:

> I sought the LORD, and he answered me
> and delivered me from all my fears.
> Those who look to him are radiant,
> and their faces shall never be ashamed.
> This poor man cried, and the LORD heard him
> and saved him out of all his troubles. (Ps. 34:4–6)

CHAPTER 1

Why Pray, or Does Prayer Really Change Things?

Almost every time I speak on the subject of prayer, the first question from someone in the audience is, "Does prayer really change things?" It seems as if the answer to that question determines whether people will devote themselves to prayer or not. If the answer is no, they conclude: Why bother praying? If the answer is yes, they press back with other questions: How does it change things? What things does it change?

So, let's take a little time to explore what this question entails. We need to think about what prayer is and why God commands it so consistently and pervasively in Scripture. There's no way to deny that prayer is essential to Christian living, but why? Surely God would not have made this a staple of our existence if it was nothing more than a meaningless ritual to occupy our time. I fear, though, that such is precisely what many think. They've bumped into what feels like a concrete ceiling, their prayers bouncing back upon their heads without fruit or even the courtesy of an answer.

The best way to answer this question is to take a moment and carefully consider what the Bible says about the power of prayer. This will better position us to determine in what sense it may be said that prayer "changes" things if, in fact, it does. But before I do that, briefly consider the importance of prayer. I can think of no better place to see this than in Isaiah 30:18–19. Although it applied most directly to the nation of Israel during the time of the old covenant, the principle is still relevant:

> Therefore the LORD waits to be gracious to you,
> and therefore he exalts himself to show mercy to you.

> For the LORD is a God of justice;
>> blessed are all those who wait for him. . . .
>
> He will surely be gracious to you at the sound of your cry. As soon as he hears it, he answers you.

But why does the Lord "wait" to be "gracious" to us? If he is really gracious and kind and wants to bless us, well, in the words of the Nike commercial, "Just do it!" If God longs to show us mercy and pour out his power, why does he wait until he hears "the sound of your cry" in prayer? Why must he first "hear" it before he blesses us?

I will answer those questions in a moment, but for now, what you need to know is that God orchestrates it this way so that he might be glorified in the most visible and public way. We read in Proverbs 15:8 that "the sacrifice of the wicked is an abomination to the LORD, but the prayer of the upright is acceptable to him." Why is it his delight? Why does it draw attention to his greatness? How does it glorify him? I think the answer is that more than anything else, prayer highlights the depths of our poverty and helplessness and magnifies the riches and resources of God's gracious supply. God is determined to disclose how desperately dependent on him we are for everything in life, and suspending his blessings on our asking for them is an excellent way to do it.

Otherwise

Think with me about what we see in Scripture regarding the necessity of prayer. Or put more simply, "Why must we pray? Why is this a matter of such urgency?" There are answers scattered throughout God's Word. For example, we must pray because *otherwise, God will not be glorified.* Here is how Jesus put it: "Whatever you ask in my name, this I will do, that the Father may be glorified in the Son" (John 14:13).

We must pray because *otherwise, you and I will not experience the fullness of joy that Jesus lived, died, and rose again to give us.* Again, Jesus declared: "Until now you have asked nothing in my name. Ask, and you will receive, that your joy may be full" (John 16:24). We must pray because *otherwise we will go without.* James goes straight to the point: "You do not have, because you do not ask" (James 4:2b). Never be deceived into thinking that God will give you apart from prayer what he has promised to give you only through prayer.

We must pray because *otherwise, the gospel will not succeed.* Look at Paul's request of the Thessalonians: "Finally, brothers, pray for us, that the word of the Lord may speed ahead and be honored" (2 Thess. 3:1). He made a similar request of the church in Colossae: "At the same time, pray also for us, that God may open to us a door for the word, to declare the mystery of Christ" (Col. 4:3a).

We must pray because *otherwise, when we attempt to preach the gospel, we are more likely to bring confusion rather than clarity.* I only quoted to you the first half of Colossians 4:3. Here is the complete request that Paul made of them: "At the same time, pray also for us, that God may open to us a door for the word, to declare the mystery of Christ, on account of which I am in prison—*that I may make it clear,* which is how I ought to speak" (Col. 4:3–4).

We must pray because *otherwise, we will remain enslaved to fear and cowardice and fail to preach the gospel at all.* It is nothing short of shocking that Paul made this request of the church in Ephesus: "[Pray also] for me, that words may be given to me in opening my mouth boldly to proclaim the mystery of the gospel, for which I am an ambassador in chains, that I may declare it boldly, as I ought to speak" (Eph. 6:19–20). We must pray because *otherwise, the lost will not be converted to Christ.* In speaking of his Jewish kinsmen, Paul said: "Brothers, my heart's desire and prayer to God for them is that they may be saved" (Rom. 10:1).

We must pray because *otherwise, the church will experience hardship and face obstacles that hinder the fulfillment of our calling as God's people.* This is what Paul had in view when he said, "I urge that supplications, prayers, intercessions, and thanksgivings be made for all people, for kings and all who are in high positions, that we may lead a peaceful and quiet life, godly and dignified in every way" (1 Tim. 2:1–2).

We must pray because *otherwise, the sick will not be healed.* James said it in several ways in the fifth chapter of his letter. "Is anyone among you suffering? Let him pray" (James 5:13a). "Is anyone among you sick? Let him call for the elders of the church, and let them pray over him, anointing him with oil in the name of the Lord" (James 5:14). And again, "confess your sins to one another and pray for one another, that you may be healed" (James 5:16).

Finally, we must pray because *otherwise, the demonized and oppressed will not be set free.* Concluding his discussion of our battle with demonic forces,

Paul exhorted the church to pray "at all times in the Spirit, with all prayer and supplication. To that end, keep alert with all perseverance, making supplication for all the saints" (Eph. 6:18). When Jesus finally delivered a young boy of a demon, he explained to his disciples that "this kind (of demon) cannot be driven out by anything but prayer" (Mark 9:29).

The necessity and urgency of prayer is stated with perfect clarity by Jesus in Luke 11:9–10 (cf. Matt. 7:7–11). There he says,

> And I tell you, ask, and it will be given to you; seek, and you will find; knock, and it will be opened to you. For everyone who asks receives, and the one who seeks finds, and to the one who knocks it will be opened.

Let's turn that around and look at it from a slightly negative point of view. Jesus is saying, "If you *don't* ask, it *won't* be given to you, and if you *don't* seek, you *won't* find it, and if you *don't* knock, it *won't* be opened." Do you believe that? If so, you understand now the urgency of intercession if we are ever to attain the goals God has given us to pursue.

But how can we be so certain that God will hear our prayers and provide us with what we need in response to them? We can know, because immediately following what Jesus just said about persistent asking, seeking, and knocking, he said this:

> What father among you, if his son asks for a fish, will instead of a fish give him a serpent; or if he asks for an egg, will give him a scorpion? If you then, who are evil, know how to give good gifts to your children, how much more will the heavenly Father give the Holy Spirit to those who ask him! (Luke 11:11–13)

The first thing to note here is that every problem in prayer is traceable to a misconception about God. When you understand the depths of God's goodness, prayer becomes easy and exciting. This doesn't mean that Jesus is giving us an unconditional promise, as if God will always give us whatever we ask. Here is how John Stott explains it:

> It is absurd to suppose that the promise, "Ask, and it shall be given you" is an absolute pledge with no strings attached; that "Knock, and it will be opened to you" is an "Open, Sesame" to every closed door without exception; and

that by the waving of a prayer wand any wish will be granted and every dream will come true. The idea is ridiculous. It would turn prayer into magic, [it would turn] the person who prays into a magician like Aladdin, and [it would turn] God into our servant who appears instantly to do our bidding like Aladdin's genie every time we rub our little prayer lamp.[1]

We'll see repeatedly in the many prayers of Scripture that God is good, willingly giving marvelous blessings to his children. He is also wise, knowing what gifts to give and when they are most needed.

So, what kind of father is our heavenly Father? He is not the careless and extravagant sort who gives his child whatever they want just to get them out of his hair. Far less is he the cruel and stingy sort who withholds what is most urgently needed. Here is how D. A. Carson describes our heavenly Father:

Sadly, many of God's children labor under the delusion that their heavenly Father extracts some malicious glee out of watching his children squirm now and then. Of course, they are not quite blasphemous enough to put it in such terms; but their prayer life reveals they are not thoroughly convinced of God's goodness and the love he has for them. Jesus' argument is *a fortiori*: If human fathers, who by God's standards of perfect righteousness can only be described as evil, know how to give good gifts to their children, *how much more* will God give good gifts to them who ask him? We are dealing with the God who once said to his people, "Can a mother forget the baby at her breast and have no compassion on the child she has borne? Though she may forget, I will not forget you!" (Isa. 49:15).[2]

I can't think of any words more encouraging than those three that occur in Luke 11:13—"*How much more.*" The force of our Lord's logic is overwhelming. It is unbreakable. It is undeniable. He argues from the lesser to the greater. Surely, we who are evil, selfish, and absorbed with our own needs and desires are still quick to provide our children with good gifts that will bless them. If so, and none would deny it to be so, *how much more* will your heavenly Father,

---

1. John Stott, *Christian Counter-Culture: The Message of the Sermon on the Mount* (Downers Grove, IL: InterVarsity Press, 1978), 188.

2. D. A. Carson, *The Sermon on the Mount: An Evangelical Exposition of Matthew 5–7* (Grand Rapids: Baker, 1978), 111.

who is good, giving, and absorbed with your needs and the multitude of ways in which he might bless us, give the Holy Spirit to all who come to him in prayer and ask for his presence and power!

If you haven't yet comprehended the force of our Lord's logic, pause and consider it again. Despite man's evil nature, it is inconceivable that a father would turn a deaf ear to his child's request for food. If a hungry boy were inclined to ask his otherwise sinful and selfish father for food, surely he would not refuse this request, far less would he taunt and torture him by substituting something similar in appearance but altogether different and even dangerous. If a child asks for a loaf of bread, his father won't deceive or mock him by giving instead a stone of like size and color, will he? If the child hungers for a fish or an egg, surely his father will not try to pass off a snake or a scorpion in its place, will he? Although this man may well be evil, he will certainly come to the aid of his earthly child.

How much more, then, shall our heavenly Father, who not only is not evil but is infinitely good, generous, wise, and powerful, give us those things we most desperately need? By just as much as the goodness of one's heavenly Father exceeds that of his earthly father, so does his willingness to give in response to our prayers. "God must not be thought of," says Carson, "as a reluctant stranger who can be cajoled or bullied into bestowing his gifts . . . [or] as a malicious tyrant who takes vicious glee in the tricks he plays . . . [or] even as an indulgent grandfather who provides everything requested of him."[3] Rather, he is our loving Father, all-wise, overflowing with goodness, whose chief concern is the welfare of those who have his heart.

A Summary of the Urgency and Power of Prayer[4]

We see the urgency of prayer yet again in 2 Corinthians 1:8–11 where Paul confidently declared that the God who already delivered him from a life-threatening affliction would do so yet again (v. 10). God's purpose in Paul's suffering had worked: he no longer looked to himself but now trusted wholly in the "God who raises the dead" (v. 9). I can hear some conclude from this:

---

3. D. A. Carson, *Matthew*, The Expositor's Bible Commentary (Grand Rapids: Zondervan, 1984), 187.
4. Some of my comments on 2 Corinthians 1 have been adapted from my book, *A Sincere and Pure Devotion to Christ: 100 Daily Meditations on 2 Corinthians*, vol. 1, 2 Corinthians 1–6 (Wheaton, IL: Crossway, 2010), 35–38.

"Well, what then is the point of prayer? If Paul is so confident that God '*will* deliver' (v. 10) him, it matters little, if at all, whether the Corinthians pray. God's going to do what he will do irrespective of their prayers for Paul or, conversely, their indifference toward him. Whatever will be, will be."

That may well be your conclusion, but it wasn't Paul's! No sooner has he spoken with assurance of God's gracious intentions toward him than he enlists the intercessory prayers of the Corinthians on his behalf. What is it that Paul asks them to ask God? Undoubtedly, he encourages them to ask God to do what God has declared is his desire and character to do! Does that sound odd? Perhaps, but there it is in black and white.

God will deliver us, says Paul (v. 10a). We have put our hope in him "that he will deliver us again" (v. 10b). Therefore, based on this assurance, flowing out of this confidence, we beseech you Corinthians to "help us" (v. 11a) by praying for our welfare. Verse 11 reads as follows:

> You also must help us by prayer, so that many will give thanks [to God] on our behalf for the blessing granted us [by God] through the prayers of many.

It has been argued that the opening line of verse 11 should be rendered with a conditional force: "*If* you help us by your prayers," or "Provided that you, for your part, help us by interceding on our behalf." If we follow this suggestion, and I think we should, it would reinforce the emphasis Paul consistently places on prayer as a contributing factor to the success of his ministry (see below on Philem. 22; Phil. 1:19; Rom. 15:30–32).

He desired that news of his rescue from death be the impetus for the saints in Corinth to join together in prayer on his behalf, in response to which he hoped God would deliver him yet again should similar perils arise. If a "blessing" (ESV) or "favor" (NASB) was to be granted Paul, these believers *must* intercede on his behalf. And not only would he prosper as a result, but God would also be glorified by the many thanksgivings uttered for the blessings he bestowed on Paul through prayer.

Do you see how prayer is always a win for all concerned? Look at *the dynamics of intercession*, how it works for the benefit of everyone involved:

The ones who pray (in this case, the Corinthians) experience the
    joy of being an instrument in the fulfillment of God's purposes

and delight in beholding how God works in response to their
intercessory pleas (cf. Rom. 10:14–15).

The one who is prayed for (in this case, the apostle Paul) experiences
the joy of being delivered from peril, sustained in trial, or made the
recipient of some otherwise unattainable blessing.

The one to whom prayer is offered (in every case, God) experiences the
joy of being thanked, and thus glorified, for having intervened in a
way that only God can bless, deliver, or save his people.

Thus, what we read here in 2 Corinthians 1:11 is like the emphasis found
elsewhere in Paul's writings. On two occasions, he indicated that whether
or not he was released from prison may well depend on prayer. Although the
power to set him free appeared to rest with the civil authorities, they were
but instruments used by God to accomplish his purpose in Paul's life (cf.
Prov. 21:1), a purpose God had determined to fulfill through prayer offered
on Paul's behalf by the saints.

In his letter to Philemon, Paul wrote, "At the same time, prepare a guest
room for me, for I am hoping that *through your prayers* I will be graciously
given to you" (v. 22; italics mine). The word here translated "given" means "to
graciously grant a favor." Combined with the fact that it is passive in voice,
this indicates Paul envisioned his physical welfare and eventual whereabouts
to be in God's hands. And it is God, Paul hoped, who had determined to
act in response to the petitions of his people, specifically Philemon and his
household, to secure his release.

Paul was uncertain of the outcome. He hoped to be set free but knew
that it rested with God. The civil authorities were mere intermediaries who
could be moved to do God's bidding through the petitions of God's people.
Is it too much to say that Paul had no hope without their prayers? Is it too
much to say that Paul may have remained in that prison if Philemon and his
family had not prayed? Perhaps God had purposed to secure Paul's release
through another means should the saints have faltered in their prayers for
him. Perhaps. But not to pray on that assumption would have been presumptuous and sinful on the part of Philemon and his household.

We find a similar scenario described in Philippians 1. Paul is again confident of his impending release from prison and ultimate vindication. Yet he
also says, "for I know that *through your prayers* and the help of the Spirit of

Jesus Christ this will turn out for my deliverance" (Phil. 1:19; italics mine). Paul evidently believed that God had purposed to secure his deliverance through the prayers of the Christians at Philippi and the gracious provision of the Holy Spirit.

Paul's appeal to the Roman Christians is especially poignant:

> I appeal to you, brothers, by our Lord Jesus Christ and by the love of the Spirit, to strive together with me in your prayers to God on my behalf, that I may be delivered from the unbelievers in Judea, and that my service for Jerusalem may be acceptable to the saints, so that by God's will I may come to you with joy and be refreshed in your company. (Rom. 15:30–32)

I address this "appeal" in considerable detail later in this book. Let me briefly say that the apostle was convinced God had suspended the success of his mission on the prayers of his people. Without those prayers, Paul was at a loss. His anxiety about a threat from the unbelieving Jews in Judea was well-founded (cf. Acts 20–21). Therefore, "his request for continued prayers was not merely a tactical maneuver to engage their sympathy, but a call for help in what he knew to be a matter of life and death."[5]

His plan to come to Rome and enjoy the fellowship of these saints was also dependent on prayer (cf. 1 Thess. 3:10–13). In Romans 15:32, Paul suspends his impending journey on "God's will." He refused to presume on God's determinate purpose, never suggesting that he will make it to Rome whether or not they choose to pray for him. He eventually made it to Rome, although his arrival there was not in the manner he expected (see Acts 21:17–28:16). The important thing to note is that Paul believed prayer was a means employed by God in the effectual fulfillment of his will.

Andrew Brunson's Release from a Turkish Prison and the Prayers of God's People

A modern-day version of release from prison through the faithful intercessory prayers of God's people concerns Andrew Brunson.[6] Andrew ministered in

---

5. Gordon P. Wiles, *Paul's Intercessory Prayers: The Significance of the Intercessory Prayer Passages in the Letters of St. Paul* (London: Cambridge University Press, 1974), 269.
6. You can read the incredible story in Andrew Brunson, with Craig Borlase, *God's Hostage: A True Story of Persecution, Imprisonment, and Perseverance* (Grand Rapids: Baker, 2019).

Turkey for twenty-three years and was the pastor of the Izmir Resurrection Church. He was arrested in October of 2016 and charged with aiding terrorism. Andrew's wife, Norine, was also arrested but was released after thirteen days in custody.

Although then President Donald Trump was instrumental in securing Brunson's release after nearly two years in prison, I am entirely persuaded that it was God's doing in response to the continual prayers being brought to the throne of grace by thousands of Christians worldwide. Bridgeway Church in Oklahoma City, where I served as lead pastor for fourteen years, met every Wednesday from noon to 1:00 p.m. and interceded passionately for Andrew's release. We learned of hundreds of such prayer meetings, devoting extended seasons of prayer, asking God to sovereignly intervene and make a way for Andrew's release. I believe that just as the prayers by the Philippians and Philemon led to Paul's deliverance, Andrew Brunson was set free in consequence of the countless prayers offered on his behalf.

From a purely human point of view, it appeared that Andrew's fate rested in the hands of the Turkish government. I am confident that the Turkish government rested in the hands of a supremely sovereign God who answers the prayers of his people. Yes, prayer is powerful. Yes, prayer changes things!

The Indispensable Role of Prayer

Simply put, *we must never presume that God will grant us apart from prayer what he has ordained to grant us only by means of prayer.* We may not have the theological wisdom to fully decipher how prayer functions in relation to God's will, but we must never cast it aside on the arrogant and unbiblical assumption that it is ultimately irrelevant to God's purpose for us and others.

Here's the bottom line: If we don't ask, God doesn't give. If God doesn't give, people don't receive. If people don't receive, God won't be thanked. And if God is not thanked, God is not glorified.

Permit me for a moment to remind us all again of the simply stunning, utterly breathtaking reality that undergirds everything Paul says in Romans 15, Philippians 1, and Philemon 1. He is telling us, without the slightest tinge of insincerity or rush of sensationalism, that *God has designed and ordained this universe so that he will act and intervene on our behalf when we ask him to.* Do you find that difficult to believe? That truth, apart from which nothing here makes any sense at all, is that God has promised to do marvelous things for his children that we cannot do for ourselves. And no less true is the fact that if we do *not* pray as instructed, he likely will *not* do what we need done.

Does it not blow your mind when you hear Jesus say something like: "Ask, and it will be given to you; seek, and you will find; knock, and it will be opened to you" (Matt. 7:7)? Do you and I really take James seriously when he tells us, "You do not have, because you do not ask" (James 4:2)? *The all-powerful, all-wise, all-loving God who called this universe into existence out of nothing wills for your prayers to be the occasion of his acting on your behalf.*

What "Things" Does Prayer Change?

If prayer doesn't change things, what will you make of the interaction between God and Moses? Their conversation in Exodus 32 is nothing short of stunning. When God told Moses to stop praying for him to be merciful to the Israelites for building the golden calf, he said:

> "Now therefore let me alone, that my wrath may burn hot against them and I may consume them, in order that I may make a great nation of you."
>
> But Moses implored the LORD his God and said, "O LORD, why does your wrath burn hot against your people, whom you have brought out of the land of Egypt with great power and a mighty hand? . . . Turn from your burning anger and relent from this disaster against your people. Remember Abraham, Isaac, and Israel, your servants, to whom you swore by your own self, and said to them, 'I will multiply your offspring as the stars of heaven, and all this land that I have promised I will give to your offspring, and they shall inherit it forever.'" *And the LORD relented from the disaster that he had spoken of bringing on his people.* (Ex. 32:10–14; emphasis mine)

Moses prayed to God not to carry through on his threatened judgment against Israel. And God "relented" from what he had said concerning his response to their idolatry. I don't know how to account for this other than to conclude that the prayer request of Moses "changed" how God would react to his people.

The power of prayer is seen again in Joshua 10, where God intervened in the routine operation of nature to secure victory for his people. The most amazing thing about this famous incident in Joshua isn't that God performed a miracle of nature to assist Israel in its battle against the Canaanites. The most amazing thing is that God "heeded the voice of a man" (v. 14). It is as if God said to Joshua: "I'm going to put myself under the command of a man! I am in no man's debt. I don't owe Joshua or anyone else anything. I am free and sovereign to do as I please. But in this case, what pleases me most is to do whatever Joshua asks me to do!"

I think we're ready now to try and provide an answer to the lingering question: Does prayer change things?

It's been a while, but I still recall the controversy that erupted in 1984 when Hurricane Gloria was barreling down on Virginia Beach, Virginia, the site of Pat Robertson's ministry headquarters. Robertson stirred the media pot when he suggested that the hurricane may have been diverted from its course because of his prayers. We don't know if he was correct in this, but whatever one may think of Robertson, we can't rule out the possibility that it was true. Of course, who knows who else might have been praying with equal if not greater fervency for the hurricane to change its course? Perhaps some little-known grandmother who lived nearby was on her knees before the throne of grace. Perhaps thousands of Christian men and women in Virginia and around the country were all praying the same prayer. We do not and cannot know whose (if anyone's) prayers God may have answered to exert his control over this phenomenon of nature.

The December 12, 1986, edition of *Christianity Today* featured an interesting letter to the editor. The Rev. Larry D. Kelley of Highland Baptist Church in Junction City, Kansas, was puzzled by the inconsistency of certain reporters who criticized Robertson for his claims about prayer and the hurricane. "Reporters," wrote Kelley, "do not snicker at prayer breakfasts held in Washington, nor prayer at a Presidential inauguration. It is obvious they feel it is acceptable to pray—but not to become fanatical by claiming it has any effect!" Whether Robertson's prayer was the reason why God diverted the hurricane is beside the point. The point is that God can and often does answer the prayers of his people to effect monumental, as well as mundane, changes in the affairs of this world.

Okay, then, does that mean prayer really does change things after all? Some respond to this by saying, "No, *prayer* doesn't change things; God does." Of course, that's true. Prayer is just prayer. It is an empty ritual, a meaningless flow of words apart from God. Prayer is powerful because God is powerful, and prayer is the means through which divine power is released and channeled into our lives.

Others prefer to say, "No, prayer doesn't change *things*; prayer changes the person who prays." Again, this too is true. Prayer does change us insofar as we learn humility and grow in love for those on whose behalf we intercede. Often, the greatest change in the person praying is the subordination of their will to God's. But we're selling prayer short if we think its primary purpose is to produce changes in us. Prayer is not self-referential, as if it were no more than a divinely prescribed self-help therapy.

The best way to answer the question, "Does prayer change things?" is to determine what we mean by *things*. If the things in view are the course and circumstances of life as eternally decreed by God in his secret and sovereign counsel, the answer is "No, prayer does not change those things." Prayer cannot change these things if by that one means that prayer can cause God to rescind a decree or force him to take back what he has planned. But we must not forget that prayer is one element in all God has decreed. And we must always be careful never to base or suspend our prayers on what we speculate may or may not be God's sovereign and secret purpose. Our prayer lives are to be governed by God's revealed and preceptive will, his moral will, which is to say the "will" of God for our lives as stated explicitly in Scripture. The Bible sets the parameters for our prayers, not what we think God has or should have decreed from eternity past.

God has sovereignly decreed when and how his Son, Jesus Christ, will return to this earth, and no amount of prayer, regardless of how fervent, will alter that fact. The day of divine reckoning for the wicked and unrepentant will come, regardless of who or how many may pray that it be deleted from God's calendar for the future. According to Psalm 139:16 and Job 14:5, the length of our days on this earth is determined and decreed by God. We shall not die one second before or after the divinely appointed time. No amount of prayer will alter that fact. And yet, God may have also decreed that, in response to the prayers of his children, Mr. Smith is to live to be 85 years, 3 months, and 6 days old, rather than dying when he is 75.

My point is that apart from prophesied events such as Christ's return and the final judgment or other events that are explicitly identified in Scripture, we do not know what God has decreed for human history in general or for our lives in particular. We do know that God commands us to pray because he is pleased to suspend certain blessings on the prayers of his people. Consequently, from a human perspective, it is true that "prayer changes things." If we fail to pray, we may well forfeit those "things" that God has said may be ours if we ask him for them. Perhaps a better way of expressing the idea is to say that prayer "implements" or "facilitates" things, but that's a bit awkward, to say the least. But surely God uses prayer to implement things he has decreed and commanded. When God decreed in eternity past that in 1984 Virginia Beach should be spared the devastating impact of Hurricane Gloria, he may have done so in conjunction with the decree that the prayers of his people be the reason why he did it. In this instance, the prayers of God's people may have been the way God had determined to implement his will concerning where and when, if at all, Hurricane Gloria was to strike the shore.

Although this may not be an answer that satisfies everyone's curiosity, we must put aside the vain notion that we can perfectly harmonize the relationship between God's sovereign foreordination of all "things" and the responsible activity of human beings, one aspect of which is prayer. No amount of theologizing will ever fully satisfy our desire to reconcile these two biblical verities. We must, therefore, gladly acknowledge God's sovereignty over all of life at the same time we passionately ask him to intervene in human affairs to change the course of affairs.

PART 1

PRAYER IN THE LIFE AND MINISTRY OF JESUS

CHAPTER 2

Principles on Prayer from the Life of Jesus

W hat would Jesus do? That question echoed pervasively throughout the evangelical world a few years ago. Bumper stickers and bracelets were emblazoned with the initials WWJD. People everywhere were asking how Jesus would respond to all manner of questions and challenges. Of course, it is to be expected that Christians would look to Jesus as their model. We turn to him for guidance on how to deal with demonic opposition and oppression. We find in him an example of how to address hypocrisy and legalism. When we are tempted sexually, Jesus provides truth about what is right and wrong and strength to remain pure. We see in Jesus how God would have us cope with poverty, racial prejudice, and issues of public justice. Jesus is our example of compassion when we're confronted with diseases and debilitating afflictions. In him, we find the revelation of God's character and the countless reasons why he can be trusted.

All this being the case, is there any reason we wouldn't look to Jesus as a model for prayer? I can think of none. One of his disciples asked Jesus for instruction in how to pray (Luke 11:1). Our Lord was happy to oblige him. We have every reason to ask the same question. "Jesus, why do you pray? How, when, where, and for what do you pray?" The answer to those questions is the focus of this chapter.

The Sovereign Savior on His Knees

There's something extraordinarily mysterious about the prayer life of Jesus. Although fully human (John 1:14), Jesus is simultaneously the second person of the triune Godhead. He is in perfect fellowship with the Father and the Spirit. What they know and do, he knows and does. So, why then does he so often pray to the Father? What need is there for this? We know that Jesus came to accomplish the Father's will (John 5:30; 6:38–40) and always does what the Father desires and never sins. So, what possible reason could he have for praying to the Father?

The answer to this question is found in the truth that although he was fully divine during his earthly sojourn, Jesus lived and taught and served others as a man, depending on the power of the indwelling Holy Spirit. Although still omniscient as the Son of God, he suspended the exercise of this divine attribute so that he might live a fully human life, operating within the same limitations that we do as humans. He, therefore, would naturally seek wisdom from the Father (Luke 2:40, 52) and insight into what the Father is doing.

When people ask, "Since Jesus was God, what can I possibly learn from his prayer life?" I remind them that in his self-renunciation (Phil. 2:6–11), he voluntarily suspended the exercise of whatever divine attributes that were inconsistent with living as a human being. He didn't lose or forfeit or divest himself of any divine attribute. When the Son of God became incarnate as a man (John 1:14), he didn't commit divine suicide. But he did resolve to live and minister as a man in constant dependence upon the presence and power of the Holy Spirit with whom he was filled (Luke 4:1, 14, 18–19; John 3:34).

We know that before he chose the twelve disciples, he withdrew to a mountain, "and all night he continued in prayer to God" (Luke 6:12). But why? What could he possibly be asking from the Father? Could it be that he sought wisdom and guidance in knowing whom to choose to be his apostles? Undoubtedly, yes! Following his long night of prayer, the first thing he did was to choose twelve from his disciples, "whom he named apostles" (Luke 6:13).

You might be inclined to wonder what possible relevance all of this has for us. Jesus is Jesus, after all, and we are not. He was both God and man, and we are but men and women. His example is designed to encourage us as we pray. In his prayers, we see a human seeking guidance, power, insight, and sustaining strength from the Father. Jesus models how to pray for all we need to carry out God's calling on our lives. Just as Jesus drew strength from the Holy Spirit, so should we. Just as Jesus sought his Father's input, counsel, and guidance, so should we.

I'm not suggesting that we should always pray for precisely the same things that Jesus asked from his Father. For example, in his prayer from John 17, Jesus prayed that God would "glorify" him so that he might glorify God (John 17:1). He prayed, "Father, glorify me in your own presence with the glory that I had with you before the world existed" (John 17:5). Clearly, none of us existed before the world did as the eternal Son of God. But there is still much we can learn from observing how Jesus prayed.

We see something of the nature of prayer in the physical postures that Jesus employed. When he healed a man who was deaf and couldn't speak, he looked "up to heaven" (Mark 7:34; see also Mark 6:41). I find it fascinating that our postures today are so vastly different from those we read about in Scripture. Today, we tell others to bow their heads, close their eyes, often with the expectation that their hands will remain hanging limply at their side or folded with interlocking fingers. But in Scripture, one often prays with their heads turned toward heaven, eyes wide open, and hands lifted high (Ps. 28:2; 63:4; 134:2; 141:2; Lam. 2:19).

But Jesus also kneeled when he prayed, as when he sought strength from the Father in the garden of Gethsemane (Luke 22:41). He not only frequently knelt, but he also fell face down on the ground to pray (Matt. 26:39), a clear expression of his heartfelt dependence on the Holy Spirit. Peter is also found kneeling to pray for the resuscitation of Dorcas (Acts 9:40), as did Paul when he bid his farewell to the elders at Ephesus (Acts 20:36).

There is in much of the evangelical world a tragic de-emphasis on the importance of our bodies when it comes to prayer and praise. In a sense, we are modern-day Gnostics, who in the early years of the church's existence minimized, indeed, often demonized the physical dimension of our existence. But our bodily postures are designed to express or reflect our soul's passions. Posture in prayer matters, not in the sense that any physical position magically ensures an answer to our requests. Looking upward to heaven indicates that we turn from reliance on earthly powers and trust wholly in the power of God. Kneeling is an expression of honor and reverence for God. Raised hands signify acknowledgment that God alone is our source of strength and testifies to our hunger and willingness to receive whatever he chooses to give. Falling face down is a manifestation of utter desperation, a repudiation of self-reliance, an open confession of our weakness and dependence on God and his gracious supply.

As for the proper time to pray, no time is the wrong time. Still though, we read in Mark 1:35 that Jesus, "rising very early in the morning, while it was still dark, . . . departed and went out to a desolate place, and there he prayed." Not wishing to be interrupted or distracted, Jesus would often retreat to "desolate places" (Luke 5:16) to pray alone (see Matt. 14:23; Luke 9:18). We see much the same practice in Luke 6:12 where Jesus "went out to the mountain to pray, and all night he continued in prayer to God" (cf. Mark 6:46).

Gratitude was also an essential element in the prayers of Jesus. We see this in Matthew 11:25–27 and Luke 10:21. In the former text, Jesus gives thanks to the Father for his sovereign determination to hide spiritual truths from those who thought themselves too "wise and understanding" to need revelation from God. Their pride and arrogance shut them off from the revelation of the only pathway to salvation. He also thanks the Father for revealing his saving mercy "to little children," a reference not to chronological age but to those known for their humility and hunger for everything God might choose to give them.

Our Lord's prayer of thanksgiving in Luke 10 is remarkably similar to the one in Matthew 11 but took place on a different occasion. In the Lukan text, Jesus has just commended the ministry of the seventy-two and invested in them authority "over all the power of the enemy" (Luke 10:19). It was then, "in that same hour" (v. 21), that "he rejoiced in the Holy Spirit" and spoke virtually the same words that we saw earlier in Matthew 11. The unique feature in this prayer of thanksgiving, found nowhere else, is that his joyful gratitude to the Father for accomplishing his "gracious will" (v. 21b) was energized by "the Holy Spirit" (v. 21a). Jesus lived, ministered, taught, and prayed as a man, with all the limits of human nature, reliant upon the Spirit's indwelling and empowering presence. Even Jesus' emotional life ("he rejoiced") was awakened and energized by the Holy Spirit.

One of our Lord's more surprising expressions of prayer is when he told Peter that he would pray for his restoration following his threefold denial of Jesus (Luke 22:31–32). This is remarkable for several reasons. First, Jesus doesn't say he would pray that Peter wouldn't deny him in the first place. That might seem to us to be the expected petition from our Lord. If he could pray successfully that Peter be repentant and restored after his threefold denial, he surely could have prayed with no less success that Peter be preserved from ever doing such a horrible and ridiculous thing in the first place. But there was evidently a purpose in God's mind that could only be accomplished by letting Peter go his own sinful and self-protective way. Perhaps it was a lesson for us all to see what happens when our self-reliance and arrogance opens a door for Satan to "sift" us "like wheat" (Luke 22:31b).

The second important thing about this prayer is that Jesus doesn't tell Peter that he will ensure that his faith will not fail. Instead, he informs his friend that he will ask God the Father to uphold Peter in faith and fellowship. There have been countless occasions in my life when I knew friends and family members were under severe pressure to succumb to Satan's temptations. On those occasions, I found in Jesus a model to guide my own intercession on their behalf, pleading with the Father to preserve them spiritually and, should they sin, to bring them to repentance.

Thirdly, the fruit of Peter's restoration, the result of our Lord's intercessory prayer for him, is that he would then be in a position to "strengthen" the other disciples (v. 32). Evidently Peter would be better equipped to encourage and exhort them in the face of failure in the aftermath of his own. This could not have happened had Jesus simply declared that he planned on preventing Peter from sinning in the first place.

We can learn several additional lessons from Jesus' prayer life. First, it is important not to impose on others a rigid rule for when, how, and where to pray. There is considerable variation in the prayer practice of Jesus, and no one way, posture, or method guarantees the answer from God that we desire. It reminds me of a scene from the comic strip *Peanuts*, where Linus is preparing himself for bed. He appears to be deep in thought as he moves his hands in differing configurations. Lucy, his sister, enters the room only to find Linus on his knees, in prayer. "I think I've made a new theological discovery," declares Linus. "What is it?" Lucy asks. "If you hold your hands upside down, you get the opposite of what you pray for!"

A second lesson for us is that Jesus valued both praying *with* his disciples (Luke 9:28) and praying *alone*, in isolation, far from the noise of crowds and the demands placed on him by others. It would do us all well to regularly find a time and place where we can be alone with God, uninterrupted and undistracted by the presence of others. In fact, it may be most effective to pray *for* others in the *absence* of others! In this way, our petitions for them can be honest and detailed without worrying about what they might think or do.

Third, as best I can tell, Jesus never explicitly prayed for anyone to be healed! In virtually every instance where the sick and demonized approached him, he simply commanded them to be healed. He drove out demons with a word. This doesn't suggest that we shouldn't pray for the sick to be healed. This is clear from James 5, a passage we'll examine later in this book. The only possible exceptions to this habit of Jesus are the raising of Lazarus and the incident recorded in Mark 9. In the case of Lazarus, we read that "Jesus lifted up his eyes and said, 'Father, I thank you that you have heard me. I knew that you always hear me, but I said this on account of the people standing around, that they may believe that you sent me'" (John 11:41–42). Could this be a reference to Jesus praying that God would raise Lazarus from the dead? Perhaps, but we can't be certain.

In the case of Mark 9, you will recall the frustration of the disciples who were unable to heal a young boy who was mute and demonized. When they saw Jesus set him free, they asked, "Why could we not cast it out?" (Mark 9:28). To this, Jesus replied, "This kind cannot be driven out by anything but prayer" (Mark 9:29). Does this suggest that it was only because Jesus himself prayed that this extraordinarily powerful demon was cast out? Or is he simply referring to what his disciples must always do in such cases? Again, it's hard to be dogmatic. Even if these two instances reflect the prayer practice of Jesus, they are clearly the exception to the norm.

One additional lesson we can learn from how Jesus prayed is that he sought his Father before crucial occasions. This doesn't mean we should only pray in times of crisis or when life-changing decisions must be made. But it surely suggests that in such circumstances, prayer is vitally important. Thus, we see Jesus praying at his baptism in the river Jordan. We have no way of knowing what he asked of the Father. The text only says that Jesus "was praying" as he was being baptized by John (see Luke 3:21). Perhaps his request was that the Father would strengthen him by the Spirit to faithfully carry out his ministry (see Acts 10:38).

I've already pointed out that Jesus prayed intensely through the night before selecting from his twelve apostles (Luke 6:12). It would have been unthinkable for our Lord to do this apart from seeking his heavenly Father's will. We also know that Jesus prayed before the miracle of feeding five thousand men (Mark 6:41; who knows how large the crowd was once women and children were included?) and before he fed the four thousand (Mark 8:6–7). Jesus also prayed with gratitude to the Father when he instituted the Lord's

Supper (Mark 14:22–23) and prayerfully entrusted himself to the Father on the cross (Mark 15:34).

I can't escape the feeling that, considering these numerous instances where Jesus is explicitly described as praying, he prayed moment by moment throughout his life and ministry. Is there any reason why we should not follow suit? No.

For What Does Jesus Instruct Us to Pray?

In the next chapter, we'll examine the so-called Lord's Prayer (mistakenly so named because Jesus, the Lord, would never have prayed to be "forgiven" of any sins committed). But there are a few occasions in the Gospels where Jesus gives explicit instruction regarding the content of our requests. We'll only examine two specific cases.

In the Sermon on the Mount, Jesus instructed his followers to love their enemies and to "pray for those who persecute you" (Matt. 5:44; see Rom. 12:14). You might think that the prayer would be for them to cease their persecution, but I suspect that Jesus had something more redemptive in mind. Certainly, he wants us to pray for the conversion of our enemies. Our fleshly temptation is to summarily dispense them into hell, that they might suffer for their sins. But we who ourselves deserved to suffer in this way have been mercifully forgiven. Similarly, we should pray that the Spirit regenerates their hearts and leads them to faith and repentance. Whatever Jesus had in mind when he issued this exhortation, I'm certain he envisioned our prayers for their spiritual welfare.

Jesus also encouraged us to pray for more of the Holy Spirit, for more of his work in our hearts, for more of his power for ministry, for more of his enlightenment that we might more clearly see and understand the blessings that are ours, that we might be ever more progressively conformed to the image of Jesus (Luke 11:13). The striking thing about this prayer is that it is the one example given of what happens when we continue to ask and to seek and to knock in prayer. Our "heavenly Father" is infinitely good and generous and knows how to give good gifts to his children, preeminent among which is the Holy Spirit.

The somewhat surprising thing about this prayer in Luke 11 is that it is repeated in Matthew 7, but with one remarkable difference. While Luke assures us that the Father will give the Holy Spirit to those who ask, Matthew says he will grant us "good things" (Matt. 7:11). He doesn't specify what "things" he has in mind, but I can well imagine it would include whatever we need to resist sin, seek Christ, enjoy his presence, grow in intimacy, ward off the fiery missiles of the enemy, love others with the love with which we have been loved, and the list could go on endlessly. The apostle Paul asked this glorious rhetorical question in Romans 8:32: "He who did not spare his own Son but gave him up for us all, how will he not also with him graciously give us all things?" These "things" that come with faith in Christ are not earthly fame or fortune but whatever is needed to enhance our delight in God and to empower us in our war with the world, the flesh, and the devil.

Whatever "things" you most desperately need to sustain your walk with God and your ever-increasing joy in Jesus, the Father will supply abundantly. But you must ask! You have to pray! We can never expect God to do for us apart from prayer what he has said he will do only in response to our prayer.

CHAPTER 3

Praying "In Jesus' Name": Magical Incantation or Pathway to Power?

> Whatever you ask in my name, this I will do, that the Father may be glorified in the Son. If you ask me anything in my name, I will do it. (John 14:13–14)

There are numerous reasons why non-Christians struggle to believe the Christian faith. I won't burden you by listing them. But when it comes to Christians themselves—believers in Jesus—there are typically only two. If you should ask a born-again-justified-by-faith-in-Jesus man or woman what their greatest struggle is when it comes to Christianity, they will most likely point to one of two things.

Some will say *suffering*. Why does God orchestrate life for his beloved children so that they have to suffer as they do? We can understand why those who hate God might suffer. But why do those who love him seem to suffer equally and just as painfully? Suffering is a stumbling block for all of us, to some degree or other.

But the second struggle many Christians will mention, often before suffering, is the perplexity posed by *prayer*. Why does God say yes to some requests but no to others? Why does it seem God often doesn't answer us at all? Why does God suspend so many of his blessings on our asking him for them? What does it mean to pray "in Jesus' name"?

I can't answer all those questions in this one chapter. But I hope at least to provide you with an answer to the last one: What does it mean to pray "in Jesus' name"? Can we really believe what Jesus says here in John 14:14 when he declares: "If you ask me anything in my name, I will do it"? For many, this is an especially painful point. You prayed fervently and frequently for someone you loved to be healed. You prayed "in Jesus' name," yet they died. You repeatedly asked God to provide you with a new and more fulfilling career, but you remain stuck in a boring and low-paying job. So, what could this passage possibly mean?

Four Essentials to Effective Prayer

When we examine the entire Farewell Discourse of Jesus in John 13–17, we find several requirements for effective prayer. We can't simply explore one passage and ignore the others. They are designed to convey a unified approach to the theology and practice of prayer.

(1) Prayer in Christ's Name (John 14:13–14)

The first essential element in effective praying is coming to the Father and making our requests in Christ's name. *Twice* in verses 13–14 Jesus says you must pray "*in my name.*" What does that mean? Is Jesus telling us that attaching the words *in Christ's name* at the end of each prayer will guarantee a positive answer? If that were the case, the words *in Christ's name* or *in the name of Jesus* would function like an incantation, no different from what the owner of a magic lamp would do when he says "Abracadabra" and a genie suddenly appears to grant him three wishes.

It's important to note that one need not even repeat the words "in Christ's name" to pray "in Christ's name." Praying in Christ's name is less a form of precise words and more an attitude, a belief, an overall theology that says all I have is because of him and through him. It expresses utter dependence. Thus, you can pray "in Christ's name" while remaining altogether silent.

When you pray "in Christ's name," you are declaring the only reason why God should bother to listen. The only way you can draw near to the throne of grace is that you trust in the finality of Christ's work on the cross, his resurrection, and his ascension to the Father's right hand.

We must never treat Christ's name as a formula that automatically or mechanically generates a positive answer. It is not a superstitious conclusion or a lucky rabbit's foot to hang on the end of a prayer.

Numerous other Christian activities are done "in Christ's name." Demons are cast out in his name (Luke 10:17), which is to say, through his authority and power. Miracles are performed in his name (Acts 3:6; 4:10; 16:18), which I take to mean through his power and for his glory. Baptism is administered in the name of Jesus (Acts 10:48), church discipline is enforced in the name of Jesus (1 Cor. 5:4), and the gospel is preached in his name (Acts 9:27–28). Jesus later says in John 14:26 that the Father will send the Holy Spirit "in my name." In 2 Thessalonians 3:6, Paul writes: "Now we command you, brothers, in the name of our Lord Jesus Christ..." He tells us in 1 Corinthians 6:11 that we are sanctified and justified "in the name of the Lord Jesus Christ." In fact, Paul tells us in Colossians 3:17 that whatever we do, in word or deed, we are to do it "in the name of the Lord Jesus."

When it comes to prayer, it simply means approaching the throne of grace fully aware of who we are: unworthy sinners whose only claim on God is because of Jesus' virtue and merit. It is to pray conscious of the fact that we are in vital union with him.

It also means we must pray in harmony with his person or character, consistently with all we know to be true of him. We should never ask for something that is contrary to the purpose for which he came to earth or inconsistent with what we know he desires.

It means to pray in line with his own objectives and goals. It is to pray as if you were that person. It is to pray according to his will. It is to pray based on the authority that Christ himself has given us.

Simply put, to pray in Christ's name is to have his fame preeminent in your heart, not your own. It is to pray cognizant of his immeasurable worth and the sufficiency of his work on the cross in paying for your sins. Run every prayer through the filter of Christ's name: will it honor him, promote his kingdom, make him more famous, and enable me to live more effectively for his glory? Is it in harmony with his mind and revealed will?

We pray in Jesus' name because we have no rights or claim to anything good apart from who Jesus is and what God has done for us through him. We are accepted by God because of Jesus. We are clothed in righteousness because of Jesus. We have access to the throne of grace because of Jesus. The same goes for every blessing and good thing that we enjoy. It is only because of Jesus. Do you pray with that in your mind? You should. You must.

But doesn't Jesus prohibit in John 16:23 what he commands in 14:14?

In John 14:13–14 he twice uses the Greek word *aiteō*, which means "to make a request for something" or "to petition someone for a favor." Another word, *erōtaō*, has the sense of "to interrogate" or "to ask a question" or "to seek information" from someone. Both words are used in John 16:23. The NASB makes this clear:

> In that day you will not question (*erōtaō*) Me about anything. Truly, truly, I say to you, if you ask (*aiteō*) the Father for anything in My name, He will give it to you.

The shift in terms may only be stylistic. But if a distinction is to be maintained, John 16:23 is not concerned with prayer to Jesus. It refers to the disciples' asking for information, not favors in their relationship with Jesus (see John 16:19, where *erōtaō* is used in a similar way). To this point in their relationship with Jesus the disciples had not prayed to him at all, but they had asked him many questions (John 13:6, 25, 36ff.; 14:5, 8, 22; 16:19). But "in that day" (16:23) that is to say, once Jesus has been raised and the Holy Spirit has been given to them, they will no longer need to ask the questions they used to ask, questions that reflected their ignorance and confusion. They will soon enjoy complete understanding.

So Jesus is not suggesting a day is coming when they will pray only to the Father and never to the Son. Rather, the day is coming when the Spirit's presence, on the one hand, will make unnecessary their interrogation of Christ, while on the other hand, it will introduce the marvelous blessing of prayer to the Father in Christ's name.

(2) Prayer for the Father's Glory (John 14:13–14)

Merely praying "in Christ's name" isn't enough. Jesus also says that his purpose in answering our prayers is so "*that the Father may be glorified in the Son*" (v. 13). Jesus says much the same thing later in John 15:7–8,

> If you abide in me, and my words abide in you, ask whatever you wish, and it will be done for you. By this my Father is glorified, that you bear much fruit and so prove to be my disciples.

Is what you are asking for something that, if God were to give it to you, he and he alone would be honored and praised and glorified and seen by others to be the highest treasure of your heart? Jesus clearly roots and grounds all effective prayer in God. Prayer that is not God-centered will not be answered.

This helps us understand the meaning of the word *whatever* in John 14:13 and the word *anything* in verse 14. Do these words mean that whatever we ask, and anything we ask, regardless of its content and irrespective of its outcome, we'll receive? No. The *whatever* and *anything* are qualified by their capacity or tendency to glorify God the Father.

If I pray, in Christ's name, "Lord, promote my name and fame beyond yours," will God answer that with a yes? No. The reason is obvious. It doesn't glorify God; it glorifies me. Or if you pray, "Lord, would you please grant me an exemption and allow me to watch pornography regularly without damaging my relationship with my spouse or with you," do you think God will answer by saying yes simply because I ask for this "in Christ's name"? No. Or if you should pray, "Lord, I ask you in the name of Jesus that you would blind the eyes of the auditor so that I may embezzle money that I promise to give the church," do you think God will say yes? No, he most assuredly will not!

Prayer exists to make God look good. Prayer exists so that our lives reflect his grace and goodness, and he would be honored. No prayer will be granted if it fails to show that God is supremely beautiful.

I believe this is what David meant in Psalm 37:4: "Delight yourself in the LORD, and he will give you the desires of your heart." Be God-centered, said David. Make God and his will and his fame your desire and focus. If you do that, your desires will always be the sort that God will happily and abundantly fulfill. When God's glory and beauty are preeminent in your heart and mind, your desires will be God-centered. You will only ask for things that bring glory to his name. When you ask for God to fulfill some "desire" in your heart and he says no, I suggest it is because your "delight" is in yourself, not God.

That is why Jesus began the Lord's Prayer in Matthew 6:9 with these words: "Our Father in heaven, hallowed be your name." That is to say, Father, my chief aim, my foremost desire, my all-consuming goal in all I ask is that it would promote your name, not mine.

Perhaps the best way of summing up this point is to say: *If you want God to respond to your interests, you must first be devoted to his.* When God's name and fame are the center of our universe and all else in life orbits around him, he is pleased to answer our requests. Why? Because those requests will be the only sort that serve to keep him central and supreme in all of life. This is just another way of saying what we see in 1 John 5:14–15—

> And this is the confidence that we have toward him, that if we ask anything according to his will he hears us. And if we know that he hears us in whatever we ask, we know that we have the requests that we have asked of him.

We must never pray to gratify our own personal desires unless fulfilling them serves the greater goal of glorifying God. When our hearts are so transformed that we sincerely desire only what God desires and only what honors him, we can pray with complete confidence. And if we pray and God says no, it can only be that, contrary to what we may have believed, the answer to that prayer would not, in fact, have served to bring honor and praise to God.

So, one crucial key to effective praying is *alignment*: the alignment of our hearts, minds, and deepest desires with God's. Once our hearts are aligned with his, we will never ask anything he wouldn't delight to give us.

Thus far, we have seen that for prayer to be effective, it must be in Christ's name and for God's glory and praise. We come now to a third essential element in effective praying.

(3) Abiding in Christ (John 15:7–8)

> If you abide in me, and my words abide in you, ask whatever you wish, and it will be done for you. By this my Father is glorified, that you bear much fruit and so prove to be my disciples. (John 15:7–8)

We are all familiar with the importance of abiding in Christ, but how many of us actually know what it means? It is clearly an essential element for successful prayer, so let's unpack this experience to ascertain what Jesus had in mind. I can think of at least four things involved in abiding, all beginning with the letter 'R' (to help you remember them!).

(1) Remain!

What does it mean to remain in Jesus? First, it means you *don't wander away* or drift aimlessly in thought or deed. You stay connected in your heart, soul, mind, and body with the person of Jesus. When times get hard and the world, the flesh, and the devil tempt you to look for other sources of comfort, you say no, I will remain in Jesus. I will remain within the orbit of his loving influence. I will continue to look to him for all I need emotionally, spiritually, financially, physically, and in every other sense.

To remain or abide in Jesus means that you exercise control over your thought life. Through the power of the Spirit, you cry out to him to keep your mind on who Jesus is, what he has done for us, and what he has promised to do throughout eternity. By the Spirit's power, you resist any temptation to let your thoughts wander off to some other rival beauty, rival god, or alternative therapy you are tempted to think can do what Jesus can't for you.

There is a verse in the book of Jude that means much the same thing. Jude says, "Keep yourselves in the love of God" (v. 21). He doesn't mean to do things to make God love you. No. God already loves you! Now, take steps to keep that truth alive in your heart. Avoid anything that would undermine your confidence in God's love. Avoid any thought or action that would anesthetize your soul to the joy of being delighted in by God! One of the primary ways that you keep yourselves in the love of God is by abiding, remaining, or staying intimately connected to Jesus in every way.

(2) Rest!

Does this mean physical rest or spiritual rest? Yes! But primarily it means spiritual, emotional rest. It is basically synonymous with trusting Jesus. Believe that he is sufficient. Believe that he will provide all you need. Stop striving by conniving! Put an end to all your speculations and fleshly plans and worldly schemes to do for your soul what you fear God either can't or won't do for you. The best way to do this is by remembering the many promises in God's Word. Don't just remind yourself. Believe them! If you doubt them, cry out to God repeatedly in prayer that he would enable you by his Spirit to believe they are true. Don't crank it up in your own power but seek God to supply you with the strength and energy you need to rest.

(3) Reflect

This flows directly out of the first two. What I mean by "reflect" is to think deeply and meditate on the truths and promises you've asked God to help you believe are true.

Don't forget that Jesus didn't merely talk about us abiding in him in John 15. He also spoke of his abiding in us: "Abide in me, *and I in you*" (v. 4).[1] He likewise goes on to say in verse 7, "If you abide in me, *and my words abide in you*, ask whatever you wish, and it will be done for you." What does it mean for the words of Jesus to "abide" in us? It means we take them seriously, reflect on them often, obey them when they give us commands, believe them when they come in the form of promises. To have the words of Jesus "abide in us" means we trust the truth of what he says over against everything that anyone else says to us. His words are "abiding" in me when I'm thinking on them, memorizing them, obeying them, soaking my soul in them, and believing them to be true and trustworthy.

To "abide" in Christ is to live in such a way that his "words" abide in us. All we think about is what Jesus has said about who he is, what he has done for us, and what he now requires that we do in obedience to his commands. We feed on his words. We drink deeply from the well of his words. His voice, as preserved for us in Scripture, is the source of our strength and the foundation of our existence and the joy of our hearts.

If we "abide" in him in this way and his "words" abide in us, our minds will be conformed to his mind. Our will shall be one with his will. Our desires will never deviate from what we know he desires from us. We would never think of asking for something that only serves us but doesn't serve to glorify and honor him. To abide in Jesus means that we are being changed inwardly so that what we want in life is what he wants for us.

This also means that our lives will bear the fruit of good deeds and a way of living each day that conforms to his will. We see this both here in John 15:7–8 and again down in 15:16. Let's look closely at both texts:

> If you abide in me, and my words abide in you, ask whatever you wish, and it will be done for you. By this my Father is glorified, that you bear much fruit and so prove to be my disciples. (John 15:7–8)

---

1. I added the italics to Bible quotations in this paragraph.

> You did not choose me, but I chose you and appointed you that you should go and bear fruit and that your fruit should abide, so that whatever you ask the Father in my name, he may give it to you. (John 15:16)

Look closely at the opening words of John 15:8—"By this" the Father is glorified. By "what"? I think Jesus is directing our attention back to what was just said in verse 7. He is saying that when we abide in him, and his words abide in us, we will be certain to ask only for those things that glorify the Father. And when we pray in that way, we may rest assured that God will answer us. When God is shown to be kind and generous and abundant in his giving to us, in response to our prayers, he is glorified.

We see much the same thing in 1 John 3:22. There we read, "And whatever we ask we receive from him, because we keep his commandments and do what pleases him." Bearing fruit for Jesus is the same as keeping his commandments and doing whatever it is that pleases him.

One final word about abiding in Christ. As long as we are in this world and remain in our fallen bodies where the principle of sin operates, we will never perfectly abide in Christ. It will always be a matter of degree. So don't despair when you fail to abide or when your trust and confidence turn to another. Confess, repent, and cry out to the Spirit to restore your heart to its true resting place: in Christ alone.

Thus, abiding in the vine means receiving, believing, and trusting in the words of Jesus. It means receiving the love of Jesus for the Father and his people and the joy that Jesus has in the Father and in us. It means sharing with others the joy, the love, and the words of Jesus. This is very similar to Paul saying in Galatians 3 and 5 that the fruit of the Spirit is love and joy as we hear and trust the promises of Christ (Gal. 3:2; 5:22–23).

(4) Rejoice

I use this word to describe the fourth way to abide because we must respond to the first three. We must respond to all God is for us in Jesus by worshiping him. We must respond to all that God has promised to be for us now and forever in Jesus by thanking, celebrating, and adoring him. Many think that abiding means lying down and doing nothing. No! Abiding is an active decision of the will. We choose to remain and to rest and to reflect and then to rejoice in worship, praise, and exultation.

Consider a well-known passage in Philippians 4:11–13, where I believe Paul is talking about abiding in Jesus:

> Not that I am speaking of being in need, for I have learned in whatever situation I am to be content. I know how to be brought low, and I know how to abound. In any and every circumstance, I have learned the secret of facing plenty and hunger, abundance and need. I can do all things through him who strengthens me.

Most of us have no problem with living in abundance. But if you try to do so without abiding in Jesus, you will end up trusting in your abundance instead of Christ. Even in abundance, Paul refused to trust what he owned. His heart was always riveted and fixated on Jesus. What Paul is saying here is identical with what we read in the Psalms:

> I say to the LORD, "You are my Lord;
>   I have no good apart from you." (Ps. 16:2)

> Whom have I in heaven but you?
>   And there is nothing on earth that I desire besides you. (Ps. 73:25)

One final word: Abiding, remaining, and resting in Jesus do not primarily relate to physical relaxation. Yes, you must rest physically! But you can abide in Jesus while changing diapers, doing the dishes, mowing the lawn, serving others, or paying bills. Abiding is fundamentally a posture of the heart, not the body.

We come now to the fourth and final requirement for effective prayer. It is found in John 16:23–24.

(4) So That Our Joy May Be Full (John 16:23–24)

> In that day you will ask nothing of me. Truly, truly, I say to you, whatever you ask of the Father in my name, he will give it to you. Until now you have asked nothing in my name. Ask, and you will receive, that your joy may be full.

I want us to focus on the last words in verse 24—"*[so] that your joy may be full*." Ask yourself: What brings me the greatest joy? If your answer is more money, sin, gadgets, fame, or respect, don't hold your breath waiting for God to answer your prayers.

But if your greatest joy is the presence, power, and praise of God in and through your life, you can rest assured that God will answer your prayers so that this joy may be rich and unceasing. Consider what the psalmist said in Psalm 16:11 and Psalm 90:14:

> You make known to me the path of life;
>> in your presence there is fullness of joy;
>> at your right hand are pleasures forevermore. (Ps. 16:11)

> Satisfy us in the morning with your steadfast love,
>> that we may rejoice and be glad all our days. (Ps. 90:14)

The joy that comes from answered prayer is the presence of God, the nearness of God, the experience of his power, and the assurance of his steadfast love. God wants to answer your prayers so that your joy in him would be complete. But if you ask for things that undermine that joy, things that redirect the focus and trust of your heart away from God and toward the world, it's doubtful if you will receive what you ask.

God will not give us anything in prayer that will diminish our joy in Jesus. We may think our joy would increase if God would only give us whatever we want. But he knows better than we do. He knows that some things, though good enough in themselves, will only serve to distract us from focusing on Jesus and undermine our capacity to enjoy him to the fullest.

Conclusion

Let me close with two questions for you to consider and a couple of practical suggestions.

First, do you really want God to say yes to all your prayers? Before you answer, think! I don't. I've prayed for some incredibly stupid, selfish, and self-destructive things during my life. Of course, I probably didn't know then that they were stupid, selfish, and self-destructive. But as time passed, it became obvious to me this was precisely the case.

It may be that you've asked God for a different (and what you thought was a better and higher-paying) job. But God said no. He obviously wanted you to stay put. Only later did you come to see that the job you prayed for was not better, did not serve to glorify God, and would have damaged your career and your Christian life, even though it may have paid better.

I'm only speaking for myself here, but I suspect most of you will agree with me after a little thought. I would much prefer that God respond to my prayers according to his will, wisdom, and best intentions instead of responding according to my will. Do you not believe that the wisest, kindest, and most loving God would do a better job of deciding what is best for you than you would yourself? I do.

Second, is it really the case that God ever actually says no to our prayer requests? Your immediate response to such a question is probably, "Yes, he often says no!" In which case, I encourage you to reflect on J. I. Packer's answer.

> God's yes is regularly a case of [God saying to us] "your thinking about how I could best meet this need was right"; his no is a case of [his saying to us] "not that, for this is better"—and so is really a yes in disguise!—and his wait (which we infer from the fact that though we have asked for action, nothing yet has changed) is a case of [God saying] "wait *and see*; I will deal with this need at the best time in the best way. Whether or not you will be able to discern my wisdom when I do act, that is what in fact I am going to do. Keep watching, and see what you can see."[2]

Packer continues:

> We have it on firm scriptural authority that the Father's response to requests faithfully, humbly, hopefully, expectantly made by his own children, out of a pure heart and an honest desire for God's glory, is never going to be a flat no. One way or another God's response will be a positive response, though it may be "I am adjusting the terms of your prayer to give you something better than you asked for." Or it may be, "I know that this isn't the moment in which answering your prayer would bring you

---

2. J. I. Packer and Carolyn Nystrom, *Praying: Finding Our Way Through Duty to Delight* (Downers Grove, IL: IVP Books, 2006), 173–74. Italics in original.

and others most blessing, so I'm asking you to wait." Or it may be, "I am answering your prayer, but you don't know the strategy I'm working on, and it doesn't at the moment feel or look like an answer at all. Nonetheless, it is. Keep praying, keep trusting, and keep looking for what, down the road, I may be able in wisdom to let you see."[3]

Here I close with a few practical suggestions.

First, don't leave prayer to chance or convenience. In other words, *plan to pray.* Set aside a time to pray. Make it an unbreakable priority in your life. If you say to yourself, "Well, I know prayer is important, and I'll just trust God to alert me to the best and most appropriate time to pray," you likely will rarely, if ever, pray. If you say, "Well, I'm incredibly busy right now, so I'll wait until my schedule lightens up. Perhaps circumstances will take a turn for the good and I'll find an extra fifteen minutes in my day to pray."

No. If you leave prayer to chance or commit to praying only when it is convenient, you will probably never pray. Set a time and place and stay true to it.

Second, *combine praise with your prayer.* Spend time in worship first. Spend time with your favorite music and adore God, worship God, enjoy God, and reflect on all he is for you and has done for you in Jesus. Prayer will often flow more naturally out of a heart that has first been filled with the wonder of who God is. If you want a good example of this, read David's praise of God in 1 Chronicles 29:10–17, followed by his prayer to God in 29:18–19.

Third, *pray with an open Bible.* If you struggle to pray, pray the prayers already found in the Bible. Read aloud and make these prayers your own: Matthew 6:9–13; Ephesians 1:15–23; 3:14–21; Philippians 1:3–11; and Colossians 1:9–14. Take biblical promises and turn them back into prayer. Read slowly through the Psalms and make the psalmist's prayers your own.

Fourth, if you genuinely don't know what to ask for, ask God to lay his burdens on your heart. Be attentive to his voice. Trust him to reveal to you the things he wants you to ask him to do.

---

3. Packer and Nystrom, *Praying,* 177.

CHAPTER 4

Can We Pray the Lord's Prayer "Inoffensively"?

Matthew 6:7–15

B ack in 2015 a short video clip of people praying the Lord's Prayer was supposed to be seen before the new *Star Wars* movie, *The Force Awakens*. I was alerted to this video by a pastor friend of mine, Andrew Wilson, in England. He pointed out in a blog he wrote that leading movie theaters in the UK have banned this short rendition of the Lord's Prayer because they believe it to be "offensive." The fear was that "it could offend or upset people of other faiths or none" (Wilson).

Wilson describes how people in the UK have responded to this decision. The response, he notes, "has been fairly predictable: secularists cheering because they think it is offensive, and Christians lamenting because they don't. Personally," notes Wilson, "I think the advert is great, and that the brouhaha will cause more people to watch it in the end anyway. But as to whether it is offensive, I have to come out and say it: the secularists are right. The Lord's Prayer is not mild, inoffensive, vanilla, listless, nominal, wishy-washy or wallpapery. If you don't worship the God and Father of the Lord Jesus Christ, it is, in fact, deeply subversive, upsetting, and offensive, from the first phrase to the last."

I completely agree with Andrew on this point. I suspect that this catches many of you by surprise. After all, *what could possibly be offensive about the Lord's Prayer?* The former Archbishop of Canterbury, Justin Welby, who is the first man to appear in the video, was surprised that anyone would find it offensive. Here is what he said:

I find it extraordinary that cinemas rule that it is inappropriate for an advert on prayer to be shown in the week before Christmas when we celebrate the birth of Jesus Christ. Billions of people across the world pray this prayer on a daily basis. I think they would be astonished and deeply saddened by this decision.... This advert is about as "offensive" as a carol service or church service on Christmas Day.

With all due respect to the former head of the Church of England, I must disagree with Justin Welby. When one looks closely at the Lord's Prayer, it is impossible to avoid the inflammatory and dogmatic spirit in which Jesus intended it. It is shot through and through with exclusivism. By exclusivism, I refer to the belief that there is only one true God, that he can be known only through a relationship of faith in Jesus Christ, that his will alone must prevail in our lives, and that those who stand in unbelief and opposition to the coming of his kingdom will be judged.

That the prayer might "offend" people of a different opinion or different religious conviction is unavoidable. I hope they are offended by it! I hope they are frozen in their tracks as they stop to think deeply about what Jesus was saying. I hope that the Holy Spirit would grant them enough insight and understanding that they would realize that one cannot casually reject the God who is addressed in this prayer. I hope and pray that they would see that the God to whom this prayer is addressed is not Allah or any other alleged "deity."

The apostle Paul has already alerted us that the Christian gospel of what God the Father has accomplished for sinners in and through God the Son, Jesus Christ, will be offensive to everyone! In fact, it is precisely through the offense of the gospel that people are awakened from their spiritual slumber and brought to faith in Jesus. Paul said this in his first letter to the Corinthians:

For the word of the cross is folly to those who are perishing, but to us who are being saved it is the power of God. For it is written,

"I will destroy the wisdom of the wise,
and the discernment of the discerning I will thwart."

> Where is the one who is wise? Where is the scribe? Where is the debater of this age? Has not God made foolish the wisdom of the world? For since, in the wisdom of God, the world did not know God through wisdom, it pleased God through the folly of what we preach to save those who believe. For Jews demand signs and Greeks seek wisdom, but we preach Christ crucified, a stumbling block to Jews and folly to Gentiles, but to those who are called, both Jews and Greeks, Christ the power of God and the wisdom of God. For the foolishness of God is wiser than men, and the weakness of God is stronger than men. (1 Cor. 1:18–25)

God wants to "offend" the mind of the nonbeliever. He aims to upset them, to challenge them, and to remind them as lovingly but as forcefully as possible that if they do not repent of their idolatry and turn from their false gods, they will perish, eternally.

We live in strange times, as I'm sure all of you know. The question many are asking is: "How do I respond to the non-Christian world, in particular to the Muslim world? How should I think about their 'faith' and this so-called 'god' whom they refer to as Allah? When I pray, how should my prayers be shaped considering their presence in our society?"

Now, let there be no mistake: Jesus was not thinking specifically of Muslims or people of some other religion—or even atheists—when he taught his disciples and us to pray in this manner. But what he taught us to pray has direct and immediate application to our attitude toward those who reject Jesus Christ. It speaks specifically to our beliefs as Christians and thus provides us with guidelines for how we should think of and relate to non-Christian people. So, let's look closely at what our Lord said.

The Context

In Matthew 6:7–8 we are told not to babble on with meaningless and repetitious phrases, as if God were impressed by such mindless verbosity. The reason is that *God knows what we need before we ask him.* But if God knows all our problems and needs *before* we ask, why ask at all? We must remember that, generally speaking, God has determined not to fulfill our needs unless we ask him to. I've said it before, we must not presume that God will provide for us apart from our prayers what he has ordained to provide for us only through our prayers. Our petitions are how God has purposed to give us what he already knows we need. There is something important to God about asking him for things he knows we need. It would seem, on the surface, to be quicker and more efficient (and obviously less strenuous on all concerned) if God were simply to bypass prayer and get on with the giving! But that is not his way. He finds particular honor and glory in being the One to whom we must humbly come to receive what we need.

A related issue is this question: "What can I possibly tell a God who knows everything?" Some answer: "Nothing." Jesus answers: "Anything!" The doctrine of divine omniscience compels us to be totally honest with God in prayer.[1] When dealing with someone whose knowledge of you is limited, you can pretend, manipulate, deceive, and even lie to them. In other words, *ignorance often generates hypocrisy*. Omniscience, on the other hand, demands honesty. What good is it to pretend or playact with someone who already knows your heart and motivation? Thus, we need never worry about finding ourselves in a desperate condition and discovering that God was caught short. Augustine once said, "God does not ask us to tell him our needs that he may learn about them, but in order that we may be capable of receiving what he is preparing to give."

The Outline of the Lord's Prayer

Although we don't see this in Matthew's version of the prayer, in Luke 11:1ff. Jesus gives us this model prayer in response to a request by one of his disciples. "Lord, teach us to pray." My guess is that Jesus meant for this prayer to provide us with an outline or sketch of the broad themes that should occupy us when we pray. In other words, each request is like a topic statement that can and should be filled out with much more detail and content. For example, it would be a mistake to think that we've said all we should say about God's kingdom in three words: "Your kingdom come." The same may be said of the remaining five petitions.

As for the structure of the prayer, I think you can see that it is made up of six clearly defined petitions or requests: three relating to God and three

---

1. "We say that we believe God to be omniscient; yet a great deal of prayer seems to consist of giving Him information" (C. S. Lewis, *Letters to Malcolm: Chiefly on Prayer* [Boston: Mariner, 2012], 19).

relating to us. The first three pertain to God's name, his reign, and his will, respectively. The focus is on sanctification, sovereignty, and submission. The first petition conceives of God as our Father, the second of God as our King, and the third of God as our Master.

The second set of three petitions concerns our bread, our debts, and our enemy, the devil. We pray for provision, pardon, and protection.

(1) God's Name (Sanctification)

When I wrote this chapter, the internet was flooded with laughter and scoffing at a particular episode of the popular TV game show *Jeopardy!*. As you know, the contestants are given the answer and are required to provide the question. In the category, *Adjectives*, the answer given was, "Matthew 6:9 says, 'Our Father, which art in heaven,' this 'be thy name.'" Not one of the three participants knew the word was "hallowed"! I assume you would have answered correctly, but if not, let's ensure we know what it means.

It is the name of God, Yahweh, the Father of our Lord Jesus Christ and our Father as well, that is to be "hallowed" (v. 9b). It isn't the name of Allah or any other alleged 'god' but the name of our heavenly Father that is the focus of our prayers.

Contrary to what many today are saying, Allah is not the same as the Christian God. In fact, there is no Allah. Allah is a name used to describe a vacuum, nothing. Islam explicitly denies that God is triune, that he exists eternally as Father, Son, and Holy Spirit. They explicitly deny that God has a Son. The New Testament repeatedly declares that if you deny the Son, you also deny the Father. If you do not love the Son, believe in the Son, and obey the Son, you do not know God (see John 8:18–19, 24, 39–42). The apostle John put it as pointedly as anyone possibly could:

> Who is the liar but he who denies that Jesus is the Christ? This is the antichrist, he who denies the Father and the Son. No one who denies the Son has the Father. Whoever confesses the Son has the Father also. (1 John 2:22–23)

You cannot know God, worship God, or have a saving relationship with God unless you acknowledge and believe in Jesus Christ as his only Son, whom he sent to be a sacrifice for sinners. And to this one and only God, Jesus tells us to pray.

And what are we to pray? "Hallowed be your name" (Matt. 6:9b). There are two things here for us to note. First, there is a shocking contrast in this petition. We are instructed to pray to a "Father" who is in "heaven." To speak of God in "heaven" draws attention to his transcendence, otherness, and glorious difference from us. He fills the universe with his powerful presence. He is high and lifted up, far beyond our wildest imagination. We are, in comparison with him, as Isaiah says in the 40th chapter of his prophecy, mere grasshoppers; we are a drop from a bucket, a speck of dust on the scales.

And yet we are to address him as our "Father"! How can this be? How can the one and only God who created heaven and earth and rules over all affairs in providential power be our "Father"? *Father* is a word of intimacy. It points to God's nearness to us and our dearness to him. It is a word of relationship, love, joy, and fellowship. So, be stunned by this! Let this truth take your breath away: *The God who called the universe into existence out of nothing is not simply your God, not simply your Lord, not simply your Master, but your Father!*

The word translated "hallowed" renders a verb used elsewhere in the New Testament to refer to sanctification. To be "sanctified" first and primarily means to be set apart, consecrated, and acknowledged as different from all others. To pray that God's name be "hallowed" is to pray that his name be acknowledged as holy and majestic and that he be glorified as infinitely greater than and beyond all that we see in creation. In using the word *sanctification* with regard to God's name, Jesus is not saying that God is sinful and defiled and needs to be made pure. Rather, he is saying that our prayer should be that God take whatever necessary steps to be acknowledged *and worshiped as unfathomably great and grand.*

Think about how offensive this is, unavoidably so. To pray that God would act to make great and glorious his own name necessarily entails his defeat and destruction of anything and everyone that opposes him. It is to pray: "Oh God, heavenly Father, may *your* name be recognized and revered by all nations; may you take steps to suppress any opposition to *your* glory and your greatness." Quite simply, this is an incendiary, unavoidably offensive request!

(2) God's Reign (Sovereignty)

We are also to pray that the "kingdom" of God our Father might "come" (v. 10a). The kingdom of God is both present and future. It is already here but has not yet been consummated. God's sovereign rule is already revealed through Jesus bringing us forgiveness, adopting us into his family, and giving us hope for a glorious and eternal future with him. But the kingdom is also still in the future. It has not yet been consummated. It will come in power when Christ returns to judge his enemies, vindicate his people, and establish a new heaven and new earth.

Thus, when we pray, "Your kingdom come," we ask God to work by spreading the gospel of Jesus throughout the earth, bringing souls to saving faith in him. It is also to pray that Jesus Christ would physically and personally return to consummate his sovereign and kingly rule. When he does, he will crush all remaining unbelief; he will destroy all earthly power that resists him; he will dethrone his enemies and overturn empires and his rule will be pervasive and permanent.

Therefore, to pray for God's kingdom to come is to pray that all the enemies of Jesus Christ be defeated. Is that offensive to others? It certainly should be if they are paying attention.

(3) God's Will (Submission)

The third petition is that we pray: "Your will be done, on earth as it is in heaven" (v. 10b). The "will" of God that Jesus has in mind is what we call his revealed will or his preceptive will or his moral will. This is what God "wills" or "wants" to happen here on earth in the lives of men and women. We cannot know God's secret or sovereign will unless Scripture explicitly tells us. But God's moral precepts or his desire for how we should live is made clear to us in Scripture. It is to be our prayer, says Jesus, that what God has declared *should* happen does happen.

Our prayer is that God's will on earth be as fully and finally obeyed as that will is honored and obeyed in heaven, among the angels and those believers who have died and are now with Christ in heaven. This, then, is a prayer that only those things which honor God be done. And if we are to pray that only God's will be done, we are necessarily and unavoidably also asking that the will of all his enemies be thwarted.

(4) Our Bread (Provision)

In the second set of three petitions, Jesus turns his attention to us and our immediate needs. The first concerns our "bread" or the daily provision we need. The word *daily* is found in the New Testament only here and in Luke 11:3. Most believe it means that we are to petition God for whatever food and other physical needs are necessary for the coming day. But we who live in an age of grocery stores and refrigeration are inclined to take our daily bread for granted. In Jesus' day, however, many people purchased one day's food at a time, never quite sure if tomorrow's supply would run short.

Martyn Lloyd-Jones' comments here are worthy of careful consideration. He asks,

is there not something extraordinary and wonderful about the connection between this request and the previous requests? Is not this one of the most wonderful things in the whole of Scripture, that the God who is the Creator and Sustainer of the universe, the God who is forming his eternal kingdom and who will usher it in at the end, the God to whom the nations are but as 'the small dust of the balance'—that such a God should be prepared to consider your little needs and mine even down to the minutest details in this matter of daily bread! But that is the teaching of the Lord everywhere. He tells us that even a sparrow cannot fall to the ground without our Father, and that we are of much greater value than many sparrows. He says that "the very hairs on your head are all numbered." If only we could grasp this fact that the almighty Lord of the universe is interested in every part and portion of us! There is not a hair of my head that he is not concerned about, and the smallest and most trivial details in my life are known to him on his everlasting throne. This is something you find only in Scripture. You go straight from "Thy will be done in earth, as it is in heaven," to "Give us this day our daily bread." But that is the way of God, "the high and lofty One that inhabiteth eternity, whose name is Holy"; who nevertheless, as Isaiah tells us, dwells with him also "that is of a contrite and humble spirit." That is the whole miracle of redemption; that is the whole meaning of the incarnation which tells us that the Lord Jesus Christ takes hold of us here on earth and links us with the almighty God of glory. The kingdom of God, and my daily bread![2]

---

2. D. Martyn Lloyd-Jones, *Studies in the Sermon on the Mount*, vol. 2 (Grand Rapids: Eerdmans, 1974 [1971]), 70.

In essence, this request declares that we are utterly and altogether dependent on God for everything we have. We aren't ultimately dependent on the government, the stock market, or anyone other than God himself. And his promise is that he will more than amply provide. As Jesus himself will say at the close of Matthew 6, "But seek first the kingdom of God and his righteousness [that's the first half of the Lord's Prayer, the first three petitions], and all these things [such as our daily bread] will be added to you" (v. 33).

Nothing that concerns us is a matter of indifference to God. He bears our problems on his heart. As Peter would later say, "Cast all your anxieties on him because he cares for you" (1 Peter 5:7 NIV).

(5) Our Debts (Pardon)

Of the six petitions in this prayer, this one alone is blessed with an extended commentary. At the close of the prayer, Jesus returns in Matthew 6:14–15 with additional explanation: "For if you forgive others their trespasses, your heavenly Father will also forgive you, but if you do not forgive others their trespasses, neither will your Father forgive your trespasses."

What does this petition mean? Some have tried to restrict its relevance to the Old Testament, but salvation preceding the cross was no more conditioned upon obedience than it is now. Salvation always has been and always will be by faith alone. Furthermore, this prayer is given to and is meant to be prayed by *believers*. It is our heavenly *Father* to whom we pray. This is not the prayer of a lost sinner seeking eternal pardon. The forgiveness in view here is not that initial remission of sins that inaugurates the Christian life. Jesus is not referring to that once-for-all forgiveness for which we pray but once. Rather, this prayer is one of confession on the part of a child who seeks from their heavenly Father not the creation of a relationship but the restoration of it. The goal of this prayer is not salvation but the renewal of its joy and power and the spiritually reinvigorating experience of comfort and consolation.

We see this principle in the parable of the unmerciful servant (Matt. 18:23–35), where a man expects forgiveness but refuses to extend similar mercy to those in his debt. The point was that "God forgives only the penitent and that one of the chief evidences of true penitence is a forgiving spirit. Once our eyes have been opened to see the enormity of our offense against God, the injuries which others have done to us appear by comparison extremely trifling."[3] In other words, *how can I expect God to do mercifully for me what I callously refuse to do for my brother?* C. S. Lewis put it thusly:

> My resource is to look for some action of my own which is open to the same charge as the one I'm resenting. If I still smart to remember how A let me down, I must still remember how I let B down. If I find it difficult to forgive those who bullied me at school, let me, at that very moment, remember, and pray for, those I bullied.[4]

So, are we to forgive all those who sin against us, even those who abuse and manipulate and criticize us? Yes. So, are we to forgive those who seek our death and destruction by bombs and beheadings and other terrorist attacks? Yes. So let us pray: "Father, as we suffer at the hands of our enemies, remind us that the only thing we truly and rightfully deserve is eternal damnation, and because you have forgiven our sins through Christ, we will never, ever experience it!"

(6) Our Enemy (Protection)

How do we reconcile the notion of God leading us into temptation with what James wrote: "Let no one say when he is tempted, 'I am being tempted by God,' for God cannot be tempted with evil, and he himself tempts no one" (James 1:13). If we interpret the word *temptation* to mean a trial or test to which our faith is often subjected, we must acknowledge that God does indeed lead us into such an experience (see 1 Cor. 10:13; James 1:2–4; consider the experience of Abraham). We are to consider such tests or trials as occasions for "all joy" (1:2). They are tests that the Lord employs to cultivate in us perseverance, proven character, and hope (Rom. 5:1–5; 1 Peter1:6–7).

The way to interpret this petition in the Lord's Prayer is by addressing both parts: not only the "lead us not into temptation" but also the "deliver us from evil." The strong adversative *"but"* implies that what we desire in the second half of the verse is the antithesis of what we seek to evade in the first half. In other words, rather than leading us into temptation, we ask God to deliver us from evil. The second half of the petition defines positively what the

---

3. John Stott, *Christian Counter-Culture: The Message of the Sermon on the Mount* (Downers Grove, IL: InterVarsity Press, 1978), 149–50.

4. Lewis, *Letters to Malcolm*, 27–28.

first half states negatively. The temptation into which we ask God not to lead us is exposure to the seductive appeals of "the evil one" (the definite article is present), that is, "Satan" himself. It is he from whom we desire to be delivered.

Robert Stein believes that behind the words *lead us not* is an Aramaic expression which "rather than asking God not to lead the Christian into temptation, is asking him not to allow him to succumb to temptation."[5] Thus, whereas Stein takes the word *temptation* in its negative sense, he understands the petition to be a request that God enable us to resist it when it comes. "*Let us not succumb or yield or give into temptation*," therefore, is the preferable way of interpreting the prayer.

"For Yours Is the Kingdom and the Power and the Glory, Forever, Amen!"

Although this concluding doxology is not present in the best Greek manuscripts that we possess, it may well have been an original conclusion to the prayer. And even if it isn't part of the original manuscript, its theology is perfectly consistent with everything Jesus and the apostles have taught us.

Indeed, this may well be, at one and the same time, both the most glorious and most "offensive" statement in the entire prayer. *Yours* is the kingdom, says Jesus. The kingdom belongs to no other. There is no other 'god' whose rule and reign will prevail throughout eternity. *Yours* is the power, says Jesus. All other 'gods' are figments of the imagination. They are devoid of power. No one can stand against you and your purposes. And *yours* is the glory, says Jesus. No one else will ever be praised and honored and magnified.

Can you now see why I described this prayer as *exclusive*? Don't yield to the pressure to be inclusive simply to avoid offending people who disagree with you. You can only love them and display your care for their temporal and eternal welfare by pointing them to the one and only God and his Son Jesus Christ, to whom belong glory, honor, power, and praise. Only in relationship with our great triune God—Father, Son, and Holy Spirit—do we find eternal life.

And if that isn't offensive, you haven't been paying attention. But oh, what a glorious offense it is!

---

5. Robert H. Stein, *Difficult Passages in the Gospels* (Grand Rapids: Baker, 1984), 73.

CHAPTER 5

Persisting in Prayer without Pestering God

> Well, let's now at any rate come clean. Prayer is irksome. An excuse to omit it is never unwelcome. When it is over, this casts a feeling of relief and holiday over the rest of the day. We are reluctant to begin. We are delighted to finish. While we are at prayer, but not while we are reading a novel or solving a cross-word puzzle, any trifle is enough to distract us. (C. S. Lewis, *Letters to Malcolm*, 113)

When you say, "I'm finished," what precisely do you mean? Is it an expression of triumph, a cry of delight and satisfaction for completing a task or surviving a test? Or is it a declaration of defeat and discouragement? Perhaps it comes from a feeling of frustration and futility, finally realizing that there's no value in pressing on. So, when you bring your time of prayer and intercession to a close, what do you have in mind when you say, "I'm finished"?

I've often said that the easiest thing about prayer is quitting. The challenge is to press through whatever justification you think you have for throwing in the towel. Trust me, I've been there! Seeing no results, or at least not the ones I had hoped for, I've thrown my hands in the air while secretly shouting, "Prayer is a joke! There's no point in this! I quit!"

That's not easy for me to admit. I want to be perceived as a devoted prayer warrior. I know what God's Word says and desperately want to be obedient. But there always seem to be more productive things to do with my time and energy. I suspect the apostle Paul knew this tendency in his own heart and in the Christians living in Ephesus as well, which is why he urged them to be, praying at all times in the Spirit, with all prayer and supplication. To that end, keep alert with all perseverance, making supplication for all the saints. (Eph. 6:18)

The reason for Paul's exhortation is not hard to understand. In the preceding verses, he has warned us of the incessant onslaught from our spiritual enemy, Satan (Eph. 6:10–17). Satan and his demons are not repelled by legislative decree, force of arms, or loud and boisterous shouting on the part of zealous Christians. These combatants cannot be touched by bullets or bombs. They fall before the power of truth, righteousness, peace, faith, and, perhaps above all else, prayer. We quit praying at risk of our spiritual lives.

Did you get a feel for the urgency in Paul's words? We are to pray "at all times," never thinking that because life may be going well for us, with plenty of money in the bank, that our enemy has given up and gone home (or to hell!). The absence of painful adversity is no indication that Satan has agreed to a spiritual ceasefire. Often, when we are at external and physical ease, we think we can put prayer on pause. We say to ourselves, "Satan must have realized he can't win and has turned his attention to someone else. So, I can now better use my time for other tasks." Were that the case, I hardly think Paul would have used the language we find in Ephesians 6. "Continue steadfastly in prayer," he wrote to the Colossians (Col. 4:2). "Pray without ceasing," wrote Paul to the Thessalonians (1 Thess. 5:17). He didn't mean that we are to do nothing else but pray, but that we are to do nothing without praying. Prayer must be a constant, recurring experience.

I'm certain someone will push back against this, saying, "How can I pray without ceasing when I'm at work or with friends or watching my kid's soccer game?" For prayer to be fervent and faithful, it doesn't have to be lengthy and out loud. God delights to hear the prayerful sighs of our hearts or the groans that erupt from deep within our souls. Short, pungent prayers thrust heavenward are as effective as extended, sustained periods of vocal prayer. You'd be surprised how powerful these direct, solitary, instantaneous utterances of the heart in a busy and nerve-racking day can be.

But is it okay for us to pray persistently for the same thing? Doesn't that reveal a lack of faith on our part? If we truly believe God is both good and able to grant our requests, why not just ask once and then entrust the outcome to his care? No one wants to be guilty of nagging! Whenever I hear this objection, I think of Paul's prayers for himself. He prayed three times that God would remove his thorn in the flesh (2 Cor. 12:8–9). "Clearly these were not casual prayers," notes D. A. Carson, "carelessly offered at the spur of the moment, but three separate and sustained periods of intercession directed to Jesus himself."[1] There's no indication that Paul prayed once, then concluded that if God really loved him and intended to answer his prayer, he need not ask again. Paul didn't believe that repeating his petition was a defect in his faith. There's no hint that he prefaced his second and third requests with something like this: "Here I am again, Lord, asking for the same thing. Please forgive my lack of faith for not believing that once was enough, but the torment of this thorn is more than I can bear."

I strongly suspect Paul's faith in God's power and compassion energized his persistence. If Paul prayed once and then quit, it would have been evidence that he lacked faith in God's promises and power. And don't ever think that Jesus refused to respond to Paul's request. The apostle assumed that it was God's will to entirely remove the thorn (whatever it was!), but he soon discovered that instead, the Lord intended to grant his request by granting him more grace to endure it.

Jesus understood all too well the temptation to quit, which is why he told his disciples "a parable to the effect that they ought always to pray and not lose heart" (Luke 18:1). Furthermore,

> He said, "In a certain city there was a judge who neither feared God nor respected man. And there was a widow in that city who kept coming to him and saying, 'Give me justice against my adversary.' For a while he refused, but afterward he said to himself, 'Though I neither fear God nor respect man, yet because this widow keeps bothering me, I will give her justice, so that she will not beat me down by her continual coming.'" (Luke 18:2–5)

We need to understand a critically important principle right from the start. Virtually every mistake we make in prayer is due to a misunderstanding of the nature of God. We see this vividly illustrated in the story Jesus tells.

As you can see, two people play the principal roles in this parable, and

---

1. Donald A. Carson, *From Triumphalism to Maturity: An Exposition of 2 Corinthians 10–13* (Grand Rapids: Baker, 1984), 147.

they stand at opposite ends of the social, educational, and economic spectrum. Consider first this judge. Only two things are said of him: he did not fear God nor respect man. No, better still, this isn't what others say about him. This is his own personal confession! What a way to be remembered. He couldn't care less what God or other people thought about him. He doesn't deny this assessment of his character. He openly affirms it!

This judge wasn't unique in this regard. Insolent and impious judges were common in ancient times (and sadly, are often prevalent in our own day). Knowing this, Jehoshaphat spoke to the judges whom he appointed:

> Consider what you do, for you judge not for man but for the LORD. He is with you in giving judgment. Now then, let the fear of the LORD be upon you. Be careful what you do, for there is no injustice with the LORD our God, or partiality or taking bribes. (2 Chron. 19:6–7)

The judge in our story could have used this counsel, for he was utterly devoid of shame, a man whose conscience had become dull and insensitive, lacking the sense of honor to which someone might appeal in the pursuit of justice. His heart was as hard as a rock. He was apparently incapable of recognizing the evil in his actions. Even if he did see the wickedness of his decisions, he couldn't have cared less. People could have stood outside his house (or courtroom) and shouted, "Shame! Shame!" and he would have remained unmoved. He has no sense of shame.

The reason why Jesus exposes this man's character is to highlight the improbability of anyone, least of all a helpless and dependent widow, ever receiving a fair and equitable hearing in his court. The odds against her getting justice are astronomical. She couldn't even appeal to him "for God's sake," as he was utterly indifferent to God and cared only for his own sake.

Let's not forget who this woman is. She is not a prominent figure in the community. The judge likely didn't even know her name or bother to ask her. Along with the orphan, the widow in Scripture represents the innocent, powerless, and dependent. She is oppressed with no recourse other than the Lord. Her problem was not unlike that of many widows, then and now. Her legal rights were being violated. We hear almost every day on the news of yet another elderly woman or man being scammed out of their life savings by some unscrupulous con artist. They have no one to protect them or fight for their vindication. This widow in our story could not afford legal counsel. She was evidently without friends or relatives to intercede for her or stand beside her as she made her plea. She was altogether alone.

Some think her request of him is that he execute punishment on her oppressor. Others insist that she merely asked to receive what was rightfully hers under the law. In either case, the judge was unmoved. He wasn't impressed with her as a person and didn't want to be bothered by someone so insignificant who was in no position to benefit him. He knew he couldn't profit monetarily from hearing her case. A few have even suggested that his refusal to vindicate her cause had been purchased by a bribe from her oppressor.

Whatever the cause for his resistance, Jesus informed us that "for a while he refused" (Luke 18:4) to help her. He is even portrayed as conceding the accuracy of the judgment passed on his character. We tend to get defensive when we are accused of being insensitive. "No, that's not me. I'm not indifferent to God and other people." But not this judge! His confession in verse 4 tells us that his character didn't change. He makes no bones of the fact that he is unashamed in his hard-heartedness. It almost seems as if he's proud of being shameless. His ultimate decision to give the widow what she asked was not the result of any transformation in him. It was her character, not his, that ultimately brought her vindication. Nowhere do we read that the judge responded to her by saying, "Oh, my. I've been such a jerk. I've been so calloused and uncaring. Shame on me. I repent." Her persistence didn't transform him. He's just as shameless at the end as he was at the start. This guy remained a jerk throughout the process!

The judge himself declared that he would acquiesce to her demands for only one reason: she kept "bothering" (v. 5) him and he feared that she would "beat" him "down by her continual coming" (v. 5). The word translated "beat down" conveys a sense of pugilistic violence (cf. 1 Cor. 9:27). It could even be translated as "blacken the eye." I don't think the judge was afraid she might be provoked to attack him physically. And it certainly can't mean he feared she would destroy his reputation. Remember, he cared nothing about what others thought of him. It was her persistence that wore him down.

We now come to the point of the parable and its application to the practice of prayer. Jesus is reasoning from the lesser to the greater. The contrasts are shocking and constitute the message of the parable. The contrasting parallel is of an evil judge and a good and gracious God, on the one hand, and a strange, unknown, helpless widow and us, God's chosen children, on the other. Many have missed the parable's point by thinking that God is like the judge and we are like the widow. No! God is *not* like the judge, and we are *not* like the widow.

Unlike the judge, God is good and gracious. *Unlike* the widow, we are God's beloved and adopted children. His point is that if a wicked and shameless judge grants the request of a helpless and hopeless widow, *how much more* shall a gracious and loving Father grant the requests of his precious and forgiven child? If she, through persistence, obtained from the judge what she desired, how much more shall we, through persistence, receive from God what we need?

Some may still wonder how we are to differentiate between being persistent in prayer, on the one hand, and falling prey to vain repetition, on the other. Jesus himself exhorted us not to "heap up empty phrases" as if we think we "will be heard" for our "many words" (Matt. 6:7). How do we deal with this tension? D. A. Carson's explanation is extremely helpful:

> In the particular example before us, if we absolutize Matthew 6:7 [babbling like pagans, for they think they will be heard because of their many words], the logical conclusion is that followers of Jesus must never pray at length, and seldom if ever ask for anything since God knows their needs anyway. If instead we absolutize Luke 18:1–8, we will reason that if we are serious with God we will not only pray at length, but we may expect the blessings we receive to be proportionate to our loquacity. However, if we listen to both passages with a little more sensitivity, we discover that Matthew 6:7f. is really not concerned with the length of prayers, but with the attitude of heart which thinks it is heard for its many words. Likewise, we find that Luke 18:1–8 is less concerned with mere length of prayers than with overcoming the quitting tendency among certain of Christ's followers. These Christians, finding themselves under pressure, are often in danger of throwing in the towel. But they must not give up.[2]

In other words, the principal issue is the attitude of our hearts, the motive and intent that prompts our praying.

---

2. D. A. Carson, *The Sermon on the Mount: An Evangelical Exposition of Matthew 5–7* (Grand Rapids: Baker, 1978), 60–61.

The lesson of Luke 18 is simple and direct. We should persist in our prayers because God, unlike the judge, is good and gracious. If you are inclined to think that God is like the judge, you will mistakenly conclude that the quality of a prayer is dependent on the quantity of your words. Do you repeat a request because you think God is ignorant and needs to be informed or that he's unconcerned and needs to be aroused? Do you think your prayers will prevail upon God and transform a hard-hearted God into a compassionate and generous one? Do you really think that God cannot see through the veil of our hypocrisy and will be swayed in his decision? The conclusion of Luke 18 is clear: we should persist in our prayers because God, unlike the judge, is good and gracious.

This story from Jesus was designed to be a massive encouragement to us all never to give up, never to quit or conclude that prayer is a waste of time and energy. I trust it will serve to bless and encourage you as well. When you draw near to the throne of grace, never think of God as a grouchy, selfish, uncaring bully who only answers our requests when they serve his interests. God is nothing like that judge. You and I are entirely different from the widow. We do not come to God alone, helpless, with no status in the eyes of the judge. We are the blood-bought children of our heavenly Father whose love for us is so giving and generous that he spared not his own Son but delivered him up for us all.

As you pray, envision in your mind's eye an abundant, effusive, incredibly generous God who smiles as he meets your deepest and most pressing needs. He may not always do so in the way you think is best. But whose wisdom and insight do you trust more? Yours or God's? Come to him, confident that he always answers us with what he knows is in our best, long-term interests. Come with the unshakable assurance that your Father looks on you with compassion and delight. Come again and again and again, persistent, yet humble; relentless, yet submissive; determined, yet resolved to take comfort in knowing that Father knows best!

Learning Persistence in Prayer from the Psalms

I know of no better or more poignant example of unwavering persistence in prayer than what we read throughout the psalms. It's almost embarrassing to read how relentless the psalmists are in their pleading with God for mercy, deliverance, vindication, healing, and all manner of need.

As you read these urgent pleas, ask yourself what words you would employ to describe your approach to prayer? Lethargic, lifeless, boring? When you finally get around to praying, are your requests interspersed with an occasional yawn? Do you struggle just to stay awake? Is your prayer life devoid of energy and low in expectation? Does it feel more like the discharge of a duty than a delight to your soul? It grieves me to say this, but many tell me that they are actually afraid to come boldly to the throne of grace.

Do you confidently lay before the Lord your most desperate petitions, or do you stammer and balk in cowardice? Perhaps I should use other words. Are you tentative, hesitant, apologetic, or timid? Do you tremble, fearful that God will find your requests audacious and beyond all reason? Are you tempted to say to God, "Lord, I'm so sorry for bothering you with this again. I know you're busy with a lot on your plate. If you don't mind, I've got a few minor requests I hope you will consider." Is that your posture in God's presence? If so, I want to challenge you as forcefully but lovingly as possible to come to God with unbridled zeal. It is not presumptuous for you to do so. It is not insolent or irreverent.

At no time anywhere in the psalter do we read of someone apologizing for being overly zealous. At no time do the psalmists circle back around, after expressing their heart's desire, and try to make amends with God, as if he is offended by their urgent cries for help. At no time in the psalms do we find God calling for their repentance for having been so vocally bold and brash. If anything, God encourages their relentless, passionate, urgent appeals for help.

If you doubt what I'm saying, consider how the many psalmists articulated their mindset and heart's attitude when they prayed to God. Here are just a few examples, a small sampling of what we find repeatedly on their lips. And never are they rebuked or challenged or accused of being sinful and arrogant.

The psalmist pleads with God to "answer me" (69:13) and "deliver me" (69:14) and "hide not your face from your servant" and "make haste to answer me" (69:16–17; cf. 70:1; 71:12). Does that sound a bit brash, perhaps even a bit presumptuous? Listen again: "I cry aloud to God, aloud to God, and he will hear me" (77:1). "Restore us, O God" (80:3). "Turn again, O God of hosts! Look down from heaven, and see" (80:14). "O Lord God of hosts, hear my prayer; give ear, O God of Jacob!" (84:8). In Psalm 86 David's cry is almost unbearably repetitious, but not for that reason sinful: "Incline your ear, O Lord, and answer me" (86:1). "Preserve my life" and "save your servant" (86:2). "Be gracious to me, O Lord, for to you do I cry all the day" (86:3). Yes, that's right, "all the day"! "Give ear, O LORD, to my prayer; listen to my plea for grace. In the day of my trouble I call upon you, for you answer me" (86:6–7).

Again, should there be lingering doubt in your mind about how frequently you should pray for God's gracious help, consider Psalm 88:1–2: "O LORD, God of my salvation, I cry out day and night before you. Let my prayer come before you; incline your ear to my cry!" "Every day I call upon you, O LORD; I spread out my hands to you" (88:9).

But will God respond? Is his reaction to the repeated pleas for help, "Enough already! Give me a break. I heard you the first time." No. Here is God's answer to the one who cries incessantly for his grace: "Because he holds fast to me in love, I will deliver him; I will protect him, because he knows my name. When he calls to me, I will answer him; I will be with him in trouble; I will rescue him and honor him. With long life I will satisfy him and show him my salvation" (91:14–16). And again, "Moses and Aaron were among his priests, Samuel also was among those who called upon his name. They called to the LORD, and he answered them" (99:6; cf. v. 8). No fewer than four times in Psalm 107 we read that God's people "cried to the LORD in their trouble, and he delivered them from their distress" (vv. 6, 13, 19, 28). "On the day I called, you answered me" (138:3a).

Consider even more examples of godly, humble, yes, *humble* prayer.

> Hear my prayer, O LORD;
> let my cry come to you!
> Do not hide your face from me
> in the day of my distress!
> Incline your ear to me;
> answer me speedily in the day when I call! (102:1–2; cf. 120:1)

> Out of my distress I called on the LORD;
> the LORD answered me and set me free. (118:5)

> With my whole heart I cry; answer me, O LORD! (119:145a)

> O LORD, I call upon you; hasten to me!
> Give ear to my voice when I call to you!

> Let my prayer be counted as incense before you,
>> and the lifting up of my hands as the evening sacrifice! (141:1–2)

> With my voice I cry out to the LORD;
>> with my voice I plead for mercy to the LORD.
> I pour out my complaint before him;
>> I tell my trouble before him. (142:1–2)

> Hear my prayer, O LORD;
>> give ear to my pleas for mercy!
> In your faithfulness answer me, in your righteousness! (143:1)

The psalmist "cried aloud to the LORD" (3:4). He pleaded with God to "give ear to" his words (5:1). "Give attention to the sound of my cry, my King and my God, for to you do I pray" (5:2). He asked the Lord to "turn" and deliver his life (6:4). "Awake for me" (7:6). "Arise, O LORD; O God, lift up your hand; forget not the afflicted" (10:12). "How long, O LORD? Will you forget me forever? How long will you hide your face from me?" (13:1). "Hear a just cause, O LORD; attend to my cry! Give ear to my prayer from lips free of deceit!" (17:1). "I call upon you, for you will answer me, O God; incline your ear to me; hear my words" (17:6).

Awake! Arise! Turn! Attend! Rouse yourself! Give ear! Deliver! Give attention! Hasten! Don't delay! The psalmist is no bully, demanding of God as if he were entitled to an answer. These are just a few ways a desperate and needy soul expresses his plight and his understanding that if God doesn't help, no one can.

Does that sound like your prayer life? It should. But hold on. I'm just getting started!

"Hear, O LORD, when I cry aloud; be gracious to me and answer me! You have said, 'Seek my face.' My heart says to you, 'Your face, LORD, do I seek'" (27:7–8). "To you, O LORD, I call; my rock, be not deaf to me, lest, if you be silent to me, I become like those who go down to the pit. Hear the voice of my pleas for mercy, when I cry to you for help, when I lift up my hands toward your most holy sanctuary" (28:1–2). "To you, O LORD, I cry, and to the Lord I plead for mercy: . . . Hear, O LORD, and be merciful to me! O LORD, be my helper" (30:8, 10).

But does God ever answer? Does he supply what the psalmists so desperately need? Here are a few texts that provide an unmistakable answer:

> I call upon you, for you will answer me, O God;
>> incline your ear to me; hear my words. (17:6)

> I call upon the LORD, who is worthy to be praised,
>> and I am saved from my enemies. (18:3)

> In my distress I called upon the LORD;
>> to my God I cried for help.
> From his temple he heard my voice,
>> and my cry to him reached his ears. (18:6)

Do these sorts of exclamatory petitions make you feel uncomfortable? Do you recoil, perhaps looking for somewhere to hide lest God's anger be vented on you for using this brash and unashamed language? You shouldn't.

There's more!

"Awake and rouse yourself for my vindication, for my cause, my God and my Lord!" (35:23). "Hear my prayer, O LORD, and give ear to my cry; hold not your peace at my tears!" (39:12). "Be pleased, O LORD, to deliver me! O LORD, make haste to help me!" (40:13). "Give ear to my prayer, O God, and hide not yourself from my plea for mercy! Attend to me, and answer me" (55:1–2a). "Hear my cry, O God, listen to my prayer; from the end of the earth I call to you when my heart is faint. Lead me to the rock that is higher than I, for you have been my refuge, a strong tower against the enemy" (61:1–3).

Does any of that sound familiar? Do you speak to God in these terms? Do you find the emotional energy of the psalmist to be offensive? I can assure you that God takes great delight when his people come to him desperate and needy and intensely dependent on what he alone can give them.

David's requests in Psalm 143 are like rapid-fire bullets from a machine gun: "Hear my prayer," "give ear to my pleas," "answer me," "answer me quickly," "hide not your face from me," "let me hear in the morning of your steadfast love," "make me know the way I should go," "deliver me from my enemies," "teach me to do your will," "let your good Spirit lead me on level ground"!

The Persistence of Jeremiah and Paul

It's one thing to talk about persisting in prayer. It's another (and much better) thing to see it in action in the lives of God's people. So, let's look at two examples, the first from the life of Jeremiah and the second from the apostle Paul.

First, a bit of background. Having conquered and overrun Israel and destroyed Jerusalem, the Babylonians installed Gedaliah as governor over the land. But Ishmael and his cohorts started a coup and killed him (Jer. 41:18). Johannon, the son of Kareah, leads a force against Ishmael, and the latter flees. The people now fear reprisal from the Babylonians because of what Ishmael had done. So they run to Jeremiah for counsel on whether or not God wants them to go to Egypt for safe haven or to remain in the land (Jer. 42:1–6). Jeremiah said to them, "I have heard you. Behold, I will pray to the LORD your God according to your request, and whatever the LORD answers you I will tell you. I will keep nothing back from you" (Jer. 42:4).[3]

Now, here is the stunning result. We read in Jeremiah 42:7 that it was only "at the end of ten days" that "the word of the LORD came to Jeremiah." The text doesn't say that Jeremiah received an immediate answer to his prayer and waited ten days before telling the people. God waited ten days before responding to Jeremiah's request. Jeremiah was sixty years old and had ministered as a prophet of God for over forty years. He had considerable experience, maturity, wisdom, and insight. And yet he prayed and got no answer for ten days! There were times when God explicitly told Jeremiah that he wasn't supposed to pray for the people (see Jer. 7:16; 11:13–14; 14:11–12). But no such prohibition is given in this instance. So, he prays but hears nothing!

I can't help but wonder if Jeremiah was discouraged. Perhaps after the first day, he returned to the people and said, "Gee, folks, I'm sorry. But I got no answer. Maybe God wants you to figure this one out on your own." The same story would be repeated after the second day, and the third, and the fourth, and so on. We assume that if an answer to our prayers isn't immediate in coming, it must be that we are asking something contrary to God's will.

---

3. As it turns out, the people refused to obey what God said through Jeremiah and accused him of lying (Jer. 43:1–7).

But not in this case. The people of Israel may have concluded that God's delay meant God's denial. But they would have been wrong. For we read in Jeremiah 42:7 that "at the end of ten days the word of the LORD came to Jeremiah."

So, how do we account for this obvious but mysterious delay? I'll come to that in a moment. But first, let's look at how the apostle Paul dealt with God's delay in answering his prayers. You may recall that his good friend, Epaphroditus, "was ill, near to death" (Phil. 2:27). Epaphroditus had been sent by the church at Philippi to Paul, bearing a substantial financial gift (4:18). He then decided to stay with Paul to minister to him in whatever way the apostle might need. While serving at Paul's side, Epaphroditus fell deathly ill. But God healed him, and he is now being sent back to Philippi bearing the letter Paul wrote to the church there (2:28–30).

Epaphroditus must have been ill for a lengthy period before God healed him. We know this from the fact that the Philippians had heard of his illness, and he had heard that they had heard (2:26). If Paul wrote this letter from Rome, as most believe he did, considerable time would have elapsed while word of Epaphroditus's illness was taken back to Philippi, not to mention the time it took for a messenger to return to Rome with news of how the Philippians had responded to their brother's condition. Rome was over six hundred miles from Philippi. Several weeks, perhaps even months, would have passed from the time Epaphroditus fell sick to the time he received word that the Philippians were grieving over his condition.

Here's my point. When Epaphroditus first fell sick and was not immediately healed through Paul's prayers, why didn't the apostle conclude from this that this was his friend's "cross to bear" and cease to pray? Why didn't Paul conclude that this illness and impending death was God's "will" for Epaphroditus and then encourage him to bear up under the load? That's not what he did. He persevered in interceding for his friend, most likely for a considerable period. Eventually, "God had mercy on" Epaphroditus (v. 27). Paul could easily have assumed that when Epaphroditus wasn't immediately healed, he should stop praying for him. Paul might have concluded that God's answer is obviously no, or he would have responded by healing Epaphroditus on the spot. But this delay was clearly not a denial. Paul's persistent praying eventually secured a glorious response. Epaphroditus was healed! So, why did God wait to answer Paul's prayer? Why did he wait to answer the prayer of Jeremiah?

But Why Does God Delay His Answers?

After all is said and done, there is yet a lingering question that haunts us all. Why does God suspend his answers and compel us to be persistent? Let me suggest a few possible answers.

In the first place, God wants us to persist when we pray so that we may be compelled to depend wholly upon him. Curtis Mitchell explains:

> If all we had to do was ask the Father for something once and then sit back and wait until the request was granted, our humanness, ever prone to independence, would inevitably lead us in the direction of self-sufficiency. But by God's conditioning our prayer success on importunate asking, it tends to make us aware of our dependence on him.[4]

In light of the apostle Paul's near-death experience and ultimate deliverance, described in 2 Corinthians 1:8–10, James Denney makes this highly relevant point:

> It is natural . . . for us to trust in ourselves. It is so natural, and so confirmed by the habits of a lifetime, that no ordinary difficulties or perplexities avail to break us of it. It takes all God can do to root up our self-confidence. He must reduce us to despair; He must bring us to such an extremity that the one voice we have in our hearts, the one voice that cries to us wherever we look round for help, is Death, death, death. It is out of this despair that the superhuman hope is born. It is out of this abject helplessness that the soul learns to look up with new trust to God.[5]

I can think of no more effective way to cultivate in our hearts this very sense of utter dependence upon God than through persistence in prayer. Frequently, someone objects that Christian faith is an emotional and psychological crutch. Although this is intended to be ridicule, I confess it is gloriously true. In fact, it is not nearly true enough. For when a man uses a crutch,

---

4. Curtis C. Mitchell, "The Case for Persistence in Prayer," *JETS* (June 1984):168.
5. James Denney, *The Second Epistle to the Corinthians*, Fourth Edition (New York: Armstrong, 1907), 24.

even two, he still stands to some degree on his own two legs. Christianity, therefore, is more like a wheelchair!

God is determined that we would be wholly and utterly dependent upon him. I am not the least ashamed to admit that I am emotionally and psychologically dependent upon God, as well as physically and financially and in every other conceivable way. And there is no more explicit evidence of this than in my need to continually and persistently prostrate myself in prayer before the throne of grace (Heb. 4:16).

Persistent prayer also serves to put us in a frame of mind and spirit in which we may properly receive what God desires to give. God may be willing to give, but we may not be ready to receive. Being forced to persist will eventually produce in us the calmness of spirit and clarity of thought necessary to hear what God is saying.

Furthermore, when we pray persistently about some specific matter, we are enabled to differentiate between impetuous, ill-conceived desires and sincere, deep-seated ones. Rarely will someone pursue something which, after a time, is seen to be less than worthwhile, if not downright harmful. Thus, by insisting that we pray with persistence, God will prevent us from praying for things that would ultimately prove unedifying. Such perseverance in prayer helps weed out improper petitions.

Related to this is the fact that persistence serves to purify the content of our requests. By repeating our prayer, by bringing it again and again to God, we force ourselves to think and rethink the nature of our request and the purpose for which we desire it. In doing so, we will begin to discern any error or sin in it that may otherwise have gone unnoticed. In this way, persisting in prayer is somewhat like proofreading a manuscript for a book. While writing this book, I read and reread the material at least a dozen times. And no matter how carefully or how thoroughly I thought I had read it, each time I would find another error, another misspelled word, another grammatical slip, another idea that needed rephrasing. Anyone who has done it will tell you that proofreading is tedious and tiring. But it makes a huge difference as far as the final product is concerned. It is the same way with prayer. Repetition perfects petitions.

When we are compelled to pray persistently, God's grace enables us to overcome impatience. Through importunity in prayer, we learn one of the hardest lessons of life—how to wait on God. And certainly, such patience and diligence, cultivated by the refusal to give up, will spill over into other areas of our lives.

God will often seem deaf or indifferent to our pleas, not because he is unwilling to grant them, but because it is not in his timing to say yes now, that is, when we want them. Perhaps he intends to secure some great and good end, to achieve some goal by means of the answer he will give to our request, and can do so only when the answer comes at the opportune time, in the appropriate circumstances, and possibly only when our hearts are properly prepared. The apparent silence of heaven may be due more to the designs of a loving and compassionate providence than to an unwilling God. But persistence is our duty whether we perceive the reasons for it or not.

If we still cannot understand why we should persist in prayer, we should do it anyway, trusting in Christ's wisdom as the one who requires it in his people. Even more to the point, we should repeatedly and persistently pray for the insight and wisdom we need to understand why repeated and persistent prayer is important!

PART 2

LEARNING ABOUT PRAYER FROM THE APOSTLE PAUL

CHAPTER 6

The Most Shocking Prayer
the Apostle Paul Never Prayed

Additional reasons why some people fail to pray relate to two of God's fundamental attributes: his omniscience and his sovereignty. I'll briefly address the former, but the latter concerns me most in this chapter.

It is not uncommon for people to justify their failure to pray by appealing to God's omniscience, the fact that God is all-knowing. We saw this earlier in Jesus' introduction to the so-called Lord's Prayer. In Matthew 6 he spoke this to his disciples:

> And when you pray, do not heap up empty phrases as the Gentiles do, for they think that they will be heard for their many words. Do not be like them, for your Father knows what you need before you ask him. Pray then like this: . . . (Matt. 6:7–9a)

There are many excuses people give for not praying: God already knows what I need, so why bother telling him or asking him to fulfill those needs; when I pray, I'm not informing him of something he doesn't already know. After all, God is omniscient. He knows everything. So, it seems to be a waste of time and energy to bring to him requests of which he is already and always aware. Jesus, on the other hand, disagrees. He couldn't have been more explicit. It is precisely *because* God "knows what you need before you ask him" that he commands us to pray. The original text of Matthew 6:8 is quite explicit: "Your Father knows what you need before you ask him. Pray then like this . . ." The truth of God's omniscience serves as the foundation and motivation for your prayers.

Jesus doesn't say, "Hey, look, folks. Since your heavenly Father obviously knows everything, including what you need most, devote yourselves to other matters and don't waste your time and energy on telling him things that he already understands." No, Jesus tethers the exhortation to pray on the truth of God's comprehensive knowledge of your life. But why?

The answer to that question has already been addressed, but it bears repeating. God has suspended the bestowal of his blessings to us and others on our asking him for them. Simply because God knows what you need before you ask doesn't mean he will give you what you need even if you don't ask. Again, I will say this with all the force I can muster: Don't ever expect God to give you apart from your prayers what he has promised only to give you through and in response to your prayers.

Our heavenly Father is an endless storehouse of blessings, gifts, privileges, and wonderful experiences. But he has determined that we will receive such things only when we come to him and ask for them. Prayer is the ordained means by which God has determined to fulfill his purposes. I realize that in saying this, yet another question pops into your head: Why? Why has God orchestrated life and our relationship with him in this way? Why is prayer so important to God and essential for us?

God does everything in order to magnify his glory and greatness. And prayer is one of the primary ways God's majesty and beauty are revealed. When we come to him in humility and desperation, he responds to us with the outpouring of his many blessings: we are seen as needy and he is seen as resourceful; we are seen as dependent, and he is made known as the one who is depended upon; we are shown to be the ones who lack and he is shown to be the one who is infinitely and eternally abundant and resourceful. Nothing is out of bounds or inappropriate for you to bring to the throne of grace. Your heavenly father knows in exhaustive detail every need, every struggle, every hurtful experience before you ever articulate them in prayerful petition. So don't hesitate to speak boldly and honestly to the one who knows everything. You can't surprise him nor inform him concerning things of which he is ignorant. He wants to hear your expression of need precisely so that he can magnify his bountiful goodness by providing you with everything needed to enable you to grow in conformity to the Lord Jesus Christ.

But there is yet another truth about God that threatens to undermine our commitment to pray. I have in mind his sovereignty, his omnipotent determination to accomplish everything that he desires. I often hear people say, "If God is sovereign and his will is decisive in the salvation of sinners, why bother praying for them?" I understand where this question comes from. There is probably no deeper mystery or baffling truth than how our prayers factor into God's purpose in saving his elect people. So, let's dig deeply into this issue.

If God Is Sovereign, Why Pray?

Brothers, my heart's desire and prayer to God for them [Israel, Paul's kinsmen according to the flesh] is that they may be saved. (Rom. 10:1)

Many insist this statement by Paul makes no sense. They conclude that if God is sovereign in the salvation of sinners, prayer is useless. Maybe the biblical authors such as Paul suffered from some sort of temporary brain freeze and didn't realize that divine election unto eternal life makes prayer entirely unnecessary. I want to argue, on the other hand, that divine election or predestination and prayer go hand in hand and that one cannot exist without the other.

I say this while acknowledging that everyone, regardless of the denomination to which they belong and the theological tradition in which they were raised, struggles to reconcile how God can be sovereign in the salvation of souls on the one hand, and how we can sincerely pray for the lost and share the gospel with them on the other. No one is exempt from addressing this problem. Their question to Paul is often phrased this way: "Okay, granted that a person's conversion is ultimately determined by God, I still don't see the point of your prayer. If God chose before the foundation of the world who would be converted, what function does your prayer have?"

The answer is that prayer functions much the same as preaching. We see this explained in Romans 10 where Paul asks this question: How shall the lost believe in whom they have not heard, and how shall they hear without a preacher, and how shall they preach unless they are sent (Rom. 10:14f.)? Belief in Christ is a gift of God (John 6:65; 2 Tim. 2:25; Eph. 2:8), but God has ordained that the means by which men believe on Jesus is through the prayers and preaching of his people.

The point is that our intercessory prayers for the lost and our preaching of the gospel are just as predestined as is the believing of the gospel on the part of those for whom we pray and to whom we preach. Just as God will see to it that his Word is proclaimed to save the elect, so he will see to it that all those prayers are prayed which he has promised to respond to. *Thus, prayer is how we obtain those blessings from God that God himself has foreordained to give to those who pray for them.*

In Romans 8:28–9:23, Paul spoke about divine foreknowledge and election and predestination, based not on anything in us but solely based on his sovereign good pleasure. So: Why, then, should we *pray* for or *preach* the gospel to lost souls to be saved? As much as this may be a problem for you and me, it wasn't a problem for Paul. Or, if it was a problem, he never let on. He never minimized God's sovereignty or our responsibility to pray for and preach to lost souls. He never for a moment so much as hinted at the possibility that one of these two truths canceled out the other. He believed in God's absolute and unchallenged sovereignty on the one hand, and in the urgent necessity of prayer and preaching on the other.

How could he do this? The bottom line is that Paul believed that God rarely, if ever, operates apart from means. Whatever ultimate purpose God may pursue, he achieves it through countless steps, causes, or conditions that precede. On the one hand, I want to assert that the gospel's success depends on God's sovereign good pleasure. As Paul said in Romans 9:11, God is determined that his "purpose of election" will stand. On the other hand, I also want to assert that its success depends on the prayers of Christians like Paul in the first century and you and me today. Some are tempted either to inflate the power of prayer, thereby making God contingent, or to exalt divine sovereignty to make prayer superfluous.

Paul's handling of the problem is of a different order. He does not conclude from divine sovereignty in salvation that people need not bother interceding on behalf of lost souls. He refuses to suggest that the certainty of the end precludes the necessity of means. If you had asked him, "Has God's elective purpose guaranteed the salvation of its objects?" he would have happily said, "Yes." Were you to have then suggested that certainty of this sort reduces prayer and evangelism to a religious charade, nice but not necessary, I can almost hear his angry *mē genoito*! "God forbid!" "May it never be!"

The sincerity of Paul's words can be tested by reading Romans 10:1 in light of what he wrote in chapter 9. Paul's passion for the salvation of Israel is not inconsistent with his belief in the doctrine of unconditional election. The eternal purpose of God, outlined in chapter 9, is not incompatible with his prayer in chapter 10. *Our attitude toward people and our prayer for their salvation are not to be governed by God's secret counsel concerning them.* If anyone should argue that the truth of divine election negates the necessity of prayer, he must explain why Paul felt no such tension. Human logic and earthly reasoning say: "Why bother praying for people if they are elect or nonelect by God's sovereign decision? They either will or won't come to salvation because of God's predestination, not your prayers." But Paul will not let us think this way.

The apostle was following the example of the Lord Jesus Christ who, on more than one occasion, juxtaposed the certainty of eternal election with the urgency of gospel proclamation. Consider the words of Jesus in Matthew 11:27–28: "All things have been handed over to me by my Father, and no one knows the Son except the Father, and no one knows the Father except the Son and anyone to whom the Son chooses to reveal him. Come to me, all who labor and are heavy laden, and I will give you rest." Here, Jesus extols divine sovereignty in determining who shall receive a saving knowledge of the Son. At the same time, he urgently exhorts sinners to seek their soul's rest in him. Jesus was not theologically dishonest with his audience, nor was Paul with his. Divine sovereignty and human responsibility are not mutually exclusive propositions.

Be it noted that neither Paul nor any other biblical author suggests that prayer can alter or somehow change God's purpose in election. Our prayers do not increase the number of the elect, nor does our disobedience deprive God's kingdom of those whom he otherwise wished to save. Paul asks us to pray because he is persuaded that *God does not will the saving end apart from the specified means.* Don't ever think that the divine decree makes an event certain irrespective of the causes and conditions (such as prayer) on which it depends. The latter are encompassed in God's sovereign purpose no less than the former.

We must also remember that our responsibility to pray fervently and urgently is not dependent upon our speculations about who is elect or our ability to comprehend the relationship between praying and predestination.

God's command, not our curiosity, is the measure of our duty. Much to our chagrin, it is not a part of God's revealed will in Holy Scripture to indicate who is and is not elect. The names of those written in the Lamb's Book of Life cannot be found by reading between the lines of Scripture. No such information is to be found nestled between Malachi and Matthew, or tucked away in the notes of certain study Bibles, or listed under the heading *Elect* in a concordance.

Let's take one hypothetical example to illustrate the relation of sovereignty to prayer.[1] Let's suppose that, unbeknownst to me, God has decreed that my friend Joe should come to saving faith in Christ on August 18, 2026. Suppose also that, again without my knowledge, God wills to regenerate Joe and bring him to faith on the eighteenth only in response to my prayer for him on the seventeenth. Of course, my prayer for Joe should not be restricted to one day of the year. I am using these two specific days for the sake of illustration. Apart from my prayer on August 18 that Joe be saved, he will remain in unbelief. Does this mean that God's will for Joe's salvation on the eighteenth might *fail* should I forget or refuse to pray on the seventeenth (perhaps because of some misguided notion about divine sovereignty)? No.

We must remember that God has decreed or willed my praying on the seventeenth for Joe's salvation, which he intends to effect on the eighteenth. God does not will the end, that is, Joe's salvation on the eighteenth, apart from the means, that is, my prayer on the seventeenth. God ordains or wills that Joe come to faith on August 18 in response to my prayer for his salvation on August 17. If I do not pray on the seventeenth, he will not be saved on the eighteenth. But I most certainly *shall* pray on the seventeenth because God, determined to save Joe on the eighteenth, has ordained that on the seventeenth I should pray for him.

Thus, from the human perspective, it may rightly be said that God's will for Joe is dependent upon me and my prayers if it is understood that God, by an infallible decree, has secured and guaranteed my prayers as an instrument with no less certainty than he has secured and guaranteed Joe's faith as an end.

---

1. The following has been adapted from my book, *Chosen for Life: The Case for Divine Election* (Wheaton, IL: Crossway, 2007), 176–77, and is used here with permission.

Someone may object at this stage by saying, "But if your prayer on August 17 is ordained or willed by God, why bother?" I bother because I do not know what God has ordained relative to my prayer life. I do not know what he has determined to accomplish through it. And it is inexcusably arrogant, presumptuous, and disobedient to suspend my prayers based on a will that God has declined to disclose. What I do know is that he has commanded me to pray for this lost soul. Whether or not he has willed for Joe to believe in consequence of my prayer is not mine to know until after the fact (and perhaps not even then). But it must not, indeed cannot, be made the reason for praying or for not praying before the fact.

Often, when God wants to pour out his blessings, he begins by awakening in his people an awareness of their great need, thereby provoking them to ask him for what he longs to give. Or, as Jonathan Edwards put it, "God has been pleased to constitute prayer to be antecedent to the bestowment of mercy; and he is pleased to bestow mercy in consequence of prayer, as though he were prevailed upon by prayer. When the people of God are stirred up to prayer, it is the effect of his intention to show mercy."[2] Thus prayer becomes an effective way to obtain those blessings from God that God himself has foreordained to give to those who pray for them. D. A. Carson has expressed the same point in somewhat different terms:

If I pray aright, God is graciously working out his purposes in me and through me, and the praying, though mine, is simultaneously the fruit of God's powerful work in me through his Spirit. By this God-appointed means I become an instrument to bring about a God-appointed end. If I do not pray, it is not as if the God-appointed end fails, leaving God somewhat frustrated. Instead, the entire situation has now changed, and my prayerlessness, for which I am entirely responsible, cannot itself escape the reaches of God's sovereignty, forcing me to conclude that in that case there are other God-appointed ends in view, possibly including judgment on me and on those for whom I should have been interceding![3]

2. Jonathan Edwards, "The Most High a Prayer-Hearing God," in *The Works of Jonathan Edwards*, vol. 2 (Edinburgh: Banner of Truth Trust, 1979), 116.

3. D. A. Carson, *A Call to Spiritual Reformation: Priorities from Paul and His Prayers* (Grand Rapids: Baker, 1992), 165.

What Specifically Are We Asking God to Do?[4]

I assume that you, like Paul, pray fervently for the salvation of close family members or colleagues at work. In Paul's case, they were the many Jewish men and women of his day who had openly and persistently denied that Jesus was the Messiah. He expressed his profound and persistent sorrow and grief over their lost condition in Romans 9:1–3, a passage we'll examine momentarily. In Romans 10:1, he declares unashamedly that his "heart's desire and prayer to God" is "that they may be saved."

Paul doesn't say anything about the nature of this prayer or give any details about the wording that he might use. We don't know beyond his general affirmation how he would ask God to save them, but I suspect he prayed that God might ravish their hearts with his beauty and unshackle their enslaved wills and cause them to come alive!

When you pray for lost souls, what are you asking God to do? Do you ask God to orchestrate circumstances in their life that might open the door for someone to share the gospel with them? Do you ask God to put a Bible in their hand or another book or a gospel tract? Do you ask God to stir their hearts to ask relevant questions, such as: What happens when I die? Does my life have any meaning? Do you ask God to plant in their hearts an uneasiness with their lost condition, such that they begin to ask questions about whether there is a God and what is their relationship with him? Although those are certainly legitimate things to bring to God, I want to suggest that there is far more that we should make the focus of our prayers.

A person in need of conversion is "dead in the trespasses and sins" (Eph. 2:1); he is enslaved to sin (Rom. 6:17; John 8:34). Paul says that Satan, the god of this world, has blinded the minds of lost people that they might not see the light of the gospel of the glory of Christ (2 Cor. 4:4). In one of his more graphic portrayals of the condition of the unsaved, Paul describes them as being "darkened in their understanding, alienated from the life of God because of the ignorance that is in them, due to their hardness of heart. They have become callous and have given themselves up to sensuality, greedy to practice every kind of impurity" (Eph. 4:18–19). We read in Romans 8:7 that

---

4. What follows has been adapted from my book, *Chosen for Life: A Defense of Divine Election* (Wheaton, IL: Crossway, 2007), 201–11.

the unbeliever is "hostile to God." These are reasons why we must ask God to make the lost person alive, release his will from bondage, enlighten her mind, and soften their hearts so that hostility is replaced with affection and rebellion is turned to submission.

As noted, although Paul doesn't give specific information on the content of his prayer for unsaved Jewish people, I believe he would pray that God might do for them what he did for Lydia: he opened her heart (which would have otherwise remained "closed") so that she gave heed to what Paul said (Acts 16:14). I will pray that God, who once said, "Let there be light!" will by that same creative power utterly dispel the darkness of unbelief and shine "in our hearts to give the light of the knowledge of the glory of God in the face of Jesus Christ" (2 Cor. 4:6). I will pray that he will "remove the heart of stone from [their] flesh and give [them] a heart of flesh" (Ezek. 36:26; 11:19). And with all my praying I will try to "be kind and to teach and correct with gentleness and patience, if perhaps God may grant them repentance and freedom from Satan's snare" (see 2 Tim. 2:24–26). I trust that you will pray, "Lord, circumcise their heart so that they love you" (see Deut. 30:6). Pray: "Father, put your Spirit within them and cause them to walk in your statutes" (see Ezek. 36:27). Here is how J. I. Packer put it:

You pray for the conversion of others. In what terms, now, do you intercede for them? Do you limit yourself to asking that God will bring them to a point where they can save themselves, independently of Him? I do not think you do. I think that what you do is to pray in categorical terms that God will, quite simply and decisively, save them: that He will open the eyes of their understanding, soften their hard hearts, renew their natures, and move their wills to receive the Saviour. You ask God to work in them everything necessary for their salvation. You would not dream of making it a point in your prayer that you are not asking God actually to bring them to faith, because you recognize that that is something He cannot do. Nothing of the sort! When you pray for unconverted people, you do so on the assumption that it is in God's power to bring them to faith. You entreat Him to do that very thing, and your confidence in asking rests upon the certainty that He is able to do what you ask. And so indeed He is: this conviction, which animates your intercessions, is God's own truth, written on your heart by the Holy Spirit. In prayer, then (and the Christian is at his sanest and wisest when he prays), you *know* that it is God who saves men; you *know* that what makes men turn to God is God's own gracious work of drawing them to Himself; and the content of your prayers is determined by this knowledge. Thus by your practice of intercession, no less than by giving thanks for your conversion, you acknowledge and confess the sovereignty of God's grace. And so do all Christian people everywhere.[5]

Those who advocate what is known as libertarian free will (or the power of contrary choice) do not believe that God has the right to work so decisively in an unbeliever's heart that he will be irresistibly brought to saving faith in Jesus.[6] I say this because, as John Piper explains, those who affirm the power of contrary choice "do not believe that God has the right to exert himself so powerfully in grace as to overcome all the resistance of a hardened sinner. Instead they believe that man himself has the sole right of final determination in the choices and affections of his heart toward God. Every person, they say, has final self-determination in whether they will overcome the hardness of their hearts and come to Christ."[7]

According to libertarian free will, the most that God can do is restore in fallen people a measure of enabling grace. This being the case, the ultimate reason one person repents and another does not is to be found in them, not God. My question is this: *Does enabling grace actually and effectually save anyone?* The answer is, of course, no. It only makes it possible that each soul might believe. If that is the case, when an advocate of libertarian freedom prays for the lost, he is not really praying for God to act upon their souls or to influence their wills so as to actually and effectually bring them to saving

---

5. J. I. Packer, *Evangelism and the Sovereignty of God* (Downers Grove, IL: InterVarsity Press, 1961), 15–16 (italics in the original).

6. For those not familiar with "libertarian freedom," here is an explanation by two of its advocates. John Sanders contends that "a person does not have to act on her strongest desire. It is within the agent's self-determining ability to change her desires" (*The God Who Risks: A Theology of Providence* [Downers Grove, IL: InterVarsity Press, 1998], 221). Thus a person is free if and only if he or she "could have done otherwise than she did in any given situation" (*The God Who Risks*, 221). Be it noted that libertarians do not argue that there are no causes for human choices, but only that no one cause is sufficient to move the will in one direction over against another. According to the notion of a "self-determining" being, writes Gregory Boyd, "the power to decide between alternatives, to turn possible courses of actions into actual courses of action, must ultimately lie within themselves" (*Satan and the Problem of Evil* [Downers Grove, IL: InterVarsity Press, 2001], 60). Thus, according to libertarianism "the ultimate source and explanation" for one's deeds must reside within oneself (*Satan and the Problem of Evil*, 60).

7. John Piper, *The Pleasures of God: Meditations on God's Delight in Being God* (Colorado Springs: Multnomah, 2000), 217.

faith and repentance, but only to act so as to *make it possible for the soul itself* to act in such a way that salvation will be the result. Clark Pinnock's description of God's influence on the human soul confirms this point. "God," says Pinnock, "puts the question and does everything possible to win our consent but . . . 'the final decision, the final right of refusal, he has vested in us, and we, not God, are answerable for the answer we return.'"[8]

Thus, according to Pinnock, God "does everything possible" to bring someone to faith short of actually bringing someone to faith. God persuades, motivates, inspires by the Spirit, enables, prepares, and graciously empowers. Pinnock rightly envisions the unregenerate soul as "dissenting" from the gospel, as being "unpersuaded" of its truth, lacking motivation to believe and feeling "uninspired" to repent given his "desire" to remain in sin. So, what precisely is it that Pinnock is asking God to do? For him to act on such a will in any degree is to move it contrary to present preference. But how can this be done without depriving the will of "ultimate responsibility" for what it prefers? If the "self" must exercise ultimate "determination" for all present preferences, God can't. And if God can't, it is futile for us to ask him to. Pinnock contends that we are not asking God to "move" the will, but to give the will good reasons for choosing to move itself. But if such be true, we are *not* asking God to exert saving, converting, or regenerating influence on the soul, which is my point.

Libertarian or self-determining freedom would demand that, in the case of any particular act of will, God is *not* ultimately responsible. Only the individual free moral agent is responsible. One wonders, yet again, if this be the case, what is it that we are petitioning God to do in an unbeliever's soul when we intercede for their salvation? If God cannot be "ultimately responsible" for the transition of this soul from unbelief to belief, for what should one pray? One cannot pray that God effectually and efficaciously save this soul, for if God were to do so then "ultimate responsibility" would shift from the individual to God, something that is antithetical to the notion of self-determination.

God may communicate by revelation or illumination reasons why Christianity is true and may orchestrate providentially an encounter that confirms the truth of Christianity. But *how much* communication is permitted? *How clear* can it be? *How impressive* is the evidence? *How powerful*

---

8. Clark Pinnock, *Most Moved Mover: A Theology of God's Openness* (Grand Rapids: Baker Academic, 2001), 163.

is the encounter? According to libertarianism, all such inducements or acts of illumination or providential encounters must be ultimately ineffective and must fall short of actually causing the transition from unbelief to belief. Simply put, according to libertarianism, there is a definitive limit beyond which God cannot go in exerting influence on the way people think, feel, and choose. At no point can God exert such influence on the will of an individual that would invariably result in faith. God must be meticulously careful that his work of illumination is not *too* clear, his arguments *too* convincing, his reasoning *too* logical, his love *too* appealing, his conviction *too* painful, or his providential oversight of external circumstances *too* stunning.

Those who affirm libertarian freedom, as expected, deny irresistible grace. They argue that God graciously makes it *possible* for us to believe. But he does not make it *necessary* for us to believe. But how can God make it even "possible" for us to believe without effectually overcoming our volitional resolve to disbelieve at some point, or whatever volitional resolve accounts for the impossibility that God's grace has now effectually neutralized?

It seems advocates of libertarian freedom have reduced prayer to the following: "Oh God, please do something ineffectual in John's soul in such a way that you don't bring him to act contrary to his current convictions." But couldn't we pray that God would "plant in the lost soul an inner unrest and longing for Christ?" Let me say two things in response to that question.

First, to say that in response to our prayers God might cause the unregenerate soul to experience "unrest" and "longing" implies that the soul, of its own accord, preference, and choice is, in fact, "at rest" without Christ and "longs" to remain in unbelief. Therefore, any action God might take in answering our prayer for that lost soul would violate the soul's self-determination to say no to Christ. In other words, you must ask yourself: "When I ask God to plant unrest and longing in an unregenerate soul, what exactly am I asking God to do?" It would seem that for God to do *anything at all that might to any degree* sway the unbelieving heart to believe or the unwanting heart to want, is to violate or infringe upon the soul's alleged right to determine itself. To influence the will to choose against its present choice is inconsistent with the belief in absolute free will and self-determination.

Second, if one should somehow overcome this first problem and conclude that it is, in fact, legitimate for God to "plant a longing" in an unregenerate person's heart, another question must be answered: "How strong and powerful and persuasive can that longing be which you are praying that God plant in his heart?" As Piper notes, "there are two kinds of longings God could plant in an unbeliever's heart. One kind of longing is so strong that it leads the person to pursue and embrace Christ. The other kind of longing is not strong enough to lead a person to embrace Christ. Which should he pray for? If we pray for the strong longing, then we are praying that the Lord would work effectually and get that person saved. If you pray for the weak longing, then we are praying for an ineffectual longing that leaves the person in sin (but preserves his self-determination)."[9]

This would appear to mean that people who really believe that man must have the ultimate power of self-determination can't consistently pray that God would convert unbelieving sinners. Why? "Because, if they pray for divine influence in a sinner's life, they are either praying for a successful influence (which takes away the sinner's ultimate *self*-determination), or they are praying for an unsuccessful influence (which is not praying for *God* to convert the sinner). So either you give up praying for God to convert sinners or you give up ultimate human self-determination."[10] It would appear that advocates of libertarian freedom must opt for the former.

A Shocking Prayer That Paul Never Prayed

We now come to one of the more stunning statements ever penned by the apostle Paul. Here is how he opens Romans 9:

> I am speaking the truth in Christ—I am not lying; my conscience bears me witness in the Holy Spirit—that I have great sorrow and unceasing anguish in my heart. For I could wish that I myself were accursed and cut off from Christ for the sake of my brothers, my kinsmen according to the flesh. (Rom. 9:1–3)

We've looked repeatedly in this book at the many reasons people give for not praying. But none of them touches the primary reason why we often stink at intercessory prayer. And that reason is simply this: *We have not been sufficiently*

---

9. Piper, *The Pleasures of God*, 219.
10. Piper, *The Pleasures of God*, 219.

gripped by the reality of hell and the fact that people without Jesus Christ are going there. If we sincerely believed in the reality of hell and that people without Christ are going there, our hearts would break. And if our hearts were broken for lost souls, our prayers for their salvation would be passionate and persistent and radically different from what they currently are.

Needless to say, hell isn't politically correct today. It's not even religiously correct in some circles and churches. Some of you believe that it's not polite to talk about hell. It makes people feel uneasy and uncomfortable. But hear me well: If there is *not* a hell and if people are *not* going there, *intercessory prayer is stupid.* Worse still, it is a colossal waste of time, energy, and money. But if there *is* a hell and people *are* going there, we can no longer afford to stink at prayer.

That Paul prayed fervently for lost souls is evident from what we just read in Romans 10:1. Jesus prayed for the lost. In John 17:20 he was praying to the Father and said, "I do not ask for these only ['these' being a reference to his disciples], but also for those who will believe in me through their word." In 1 Timothy 2:1–2 Paul urged "that supplications, prayers, intercessions, and thanksgivings be made for all people, for kings and all who are in high positions . . ." But nowhere in Scripture do we find a prayer and passion for the lost more explicitly stated than in Romans 9:1–3. The statement "for I could wish" (v. 3) is probably a prayer for three reasons: first, it parallels Moses's prayer in Exodus 32:11–14, 31–32; second, of the other six occurrences of the verb in the New Testament, five refer to prayer (Acts 26:29; 2 Cor. 13:7, 9; James 5:16; 3 John 2); and third, Gordon Wiles has shown that such wishes are in most cases prayers transposed for use in a letter. Consequently, a wish such as we find in Romans 9 is "the expression of a desire that God take action regarding the person(s) mentioned in the wish."[11]

Even if one concludes that this isn't a formal prayer, these words reveal the spirit in the apostle that shaped and formed his prayers for the lost. And what Paul says here is more than profound; it is deeply disturbing. The only way for us to see this is by unpacking, phrase by phrase, what Paul says and praying as we do that God would awaken in us a similar zeal for the lost people of the world.

---

11. Gordon Wiles, *Paul's Intercessory Prayers* (London: Cambridge, 1974), 22. For other examples of "wish-prayers," see Rom. 15:5, 13; 16:20; 1 Thess. 3:11–12; 5:23; 1 Cor. 1:8.

A Meaningful Repetition

When we are afraid that someone won't believe us, we often reinforce our words or repeat ourselves or even take an oath and swear that what we are saying is genuinely true. Look at how Paul does that here. He does it five times!

First, "*I am speaking the truth*" (v. 1a). Most of us are inclined to say, "Well, of course you are, Paul. None of us ever doubted that you would always tell us the truth. So why are you making such a big deal of it here?" Paul knew the Christians in Rome had confidence in him. But something weighed so heavily on his heart that he couldn't help but declare, "If you ever doubted me before, don't doubt me now. I am speaking the truth."

There's a good reason why Paul speaks this way. As you will see in a moment, he is about to say something that will stretch credulity to the breaking point. He's going to claim something that he knows most people, even those who trust him implicitly, will think is a lie. They will face the temptation to say: "Paul, come on, you've gone a bit too far this time. Cut out the exaggeration. Be real. Be honest. You obviously can't expect us to take your words at face value." That is why Paul insists: "As much as you may think I'm lying, as much as you may think I've lost my perspective, I assure you that I am speaking the truth."

Second, notice how he grounds the truthfulness of his words on his relationship with Christ: "I am speaking the truth *in Christ*" (v. 1b). He seeks to root his utterance in his personal relationship to Jesus as Lord. He means that his union with Christ, his relationship with Jesus, is the orbit within which his emotions and beliefs move. His union with Christ is the spring from which his statement proceeds. What he will say derives its impulse and authenticity from the Lord Jesus himself. His statement is guaranteed accurate because it emerges from the one who could never lie: Jesus. Jesus is himself the personal guarantor of the truth of Paul's words. Jesus is more than a character witness to Paul's integrity. He has staked his own reputation on the accuracy of Paul's declaration. It is as if Christ has come up alongside the apostle, placed his arm around him and his hand on Paul's heart, and says: "I vouch for this man. I testify that his words are true. They are a perfect representation of what is in his heart." But even that wasn't enough! He continues.

Third, "*I am not lying*" (v. 1c). It sounds a bit redundant. After all, if you are telling the truth, you are obviously not lying. Perhaps Paul includes this as the negative counterpart to the opening assertion, reinforcing the accuracy of what he is about to say. You may be inclined to say to Paul, "Hey, fella. Enough is enough. We believe you. Settle down. You've made your point." But when you finally hear what he says about his love for the Jewish people, you will be sorely tempted to say in response, "Paul, you're lying!" So, he goes on.

Fourth, *"my conscience bears me witness"* (v. 1d). In Scripture the "conscience" is that faculty or dimension by which we judge ourselves and bring our own souls under moral scrutiny. At one time, conscience may *accuse* us. At another time, conscience may *excuse* us. It either approves or disapproves. Here Paul appeals to a clear conscience. It is as if he says, "I've searched my heart; I've laid it open before the Lord; I've beseeched him to alert me to anything wrong in what I'm about to say, and I've only received from conscience and Christ, 'You're spot on, Paul. Your conscience is clean.'"

Paul refers to his conscience and the role it plays in holding him accountable in such texts as Acts 23:1 (where he testifies before Ananias, the high priest) and 2 Corinthians 1:12 (where he appeals to "the testimony" of his conscience). He appeals to his son in the faith, Timothy, to hold "faith and a good conscience" (1 Tim. 1:19). One of the qualifications for a deacon in the local church is that they "must hold the mystery of the faith with a clear conscience" (1 Tim. 3:9). And in 2 Timothy 1:3 Paul declares that he has served God "with a clear conscience."

"Okay, Paul. We believe you. We really do. For heaven's sake, get on with it." That may be easy for you to say now. But wait until he actually makes his statement. That is why he seals it all with the fifth expression.

Fifth, and finally, "my conscience bears me witness *in the Holy Spirit*" (v. 1e). Earlier the guarantee came from his union with and relationship to Christ. Now it comes from the Holy Spirit. The Holy Spirit himself enters into the issue to confirm and certify that Paul's conscience in this matter is clear and upright. It's as if Paul says, "You have to believe what I'm about to say because the Holy Spirit of God indwells me and governs my thoughts and even now gives shape to my words."

Why this prolonged, repetitive, emphatic reassurance to us that his statement is the truth? Why appeal to both Jesus Christ and the Holy Spirit as guarantors of his declaration? It can only be because what he is about to say is utterly contrary to the natural instincts of human beings. Our immediate reaction to what Paul is about to say is: "You're a liar!"

How deeply does Paul feel about what he is going to say? He says in Romans 9:2 that he has "great sorrow and unceasing anguish" in his "heart." Not only is this emotional distress crushing, it is "great," it is "unceasing." There is a burden that Paul carries that is oppressive and ceaseless. What can account for this? Moments earlier in chapter eight we find Paul at the pinnacle of joy, the mountaintop of exhilaration. Now we see him in the valley of sorrow and distress. Why? The answer comes in verse 3. Here, in paraphrase, is what Paul is declaring:

> My love for my fellow Jews is so deep and my concern for the eternal welfare of their souls is so passionate and intense that if by sending me to hell God could grant them entrance into heaven, I'd pray for it. The sorrow and unceasing anguish I feel for them is so real and riveting that if my being accursed and cut off from Christ would accomplish their salvation, I'd say, "Do it God."

Some contend that Paul is saying that he prayed such a prayer at some time in the past, perhaps during a weak moment. But later, on second thought, he realized that this kind of prayer would be inappropriate for a Christian to pray. So, he ceased. Thus, we might translate the verse: "for I used to pray" or "I used to wish that I might be accursed for their sake, but I don't anymore. I know better now." Others argue that what Paul means is that he contemplated praying this way but never actually did. The idea came into his head to pray such a prayer, but he immediately dismissed it.

I think there is a better way of understanding what Paul is saying. The particular form of the verb Paul uses here suggests he is saying that he *would* have prayed for this *had it been permissible*, had it been possible for such a prayer to be effective.[12] Had the end been genuinely attainable, he would have prayed. *If it were possible* for Paul to be cut off from Christ, and *if* by doing so his Jewish countrymen could have been saved, *he would have been willing* to pray for it to happen.

---

12. The Greek imperfect tense fills in for the optative and denotes "a present-time action that is potential or attempted but never carried out" (Douglas Moo, *The Epistle to the Romans* [Grand Rapids: Eerdmans, 1996], 558).

But Paul knew all too well that in theological fact he couldn't be severed from Christ. Even if he could, it wouldn't avail to save Jewish souls. Each person must believe in Jesus for themself. In Romans 5:9–10 and 8:31–39, he clearly taught that the Christian is inseparably united to Christ. The security of the believer precludes any such prayer that has for its end the loss of eternal life.

Also, if it were an obligatory act of Christian love that not only Paul but all of us should pray such a prayer, then those who might be saved as a result would also have to pray such a prayer. The result would be that no one is saved because each person would have prayed to be condemned in order that others might be saved. They in turn would pray the same prayer, and the cycle would go on without end.

So, how do we know that Paul was contemplating the loss of eternal life? The word translated "accursed" in verse 3 is the Greek word *anathema*. This word is used consistently in the New Testament to describe someone delivered over to suffer divine wrath and eternal condemnation. See especially 1 Corinthians 12:3; 16:22; and Galatians 1:8–9. It means to come under the curse of divine wrath and be consigned to condemnation. If there is any doubt that this is what Paul had in mind, the following phrase seals the deal. Here, Paul says that he envisions being "cut off from Christ." Nothing less than utter exclusion from the blessed presence of Jesus himself is in view (see Matt. 7:23; 25:41). The early church father, Chrysostom, put it this way:

> What meanest thou, O Paul? From Christ? From thy Beloved? From him, from whom neither kingdom nor hell could separate thee, nor things seen, nor things conceived, nor other things so great—dost thou now pray to be accursed and separated from Him?

Unfortunately, the artificial chapter divisions in our English Bibles obscure the force of Paul's statement. When the book of Romans was read aloud in the churches of the first century, Romans 9:3 would have echoed throughout the congregation only seconds after the closing words of 8:39—"Nor anything else in all creation, will be able to separate us from the love of God in Christ Jesus our Lord." Paul, then, is saying that so deep and genuine is his love for his Jewish brothers and sisters that he *could wish* to experience what no Christian will ever experience if it were possible. But it isn't.

The full force of this confession must not be missed. Were it possible and permissible, Paul is willing to take the place of the lost in hell. He is not saying that he is willing to give up his home, property, health, family, fame, or fortune. He is saying, were it possible, he would have his name erased from the Lamb's Book of Life if it would result in the salvation of the Jewish people. I love them so much, says Paul, that I would voluntarily forfeit the comfort, consolation, and eternal joy of Christ's presence if only they themselves could experience it.

Remember that Paul never actually made this a part of his prayers to God. He knew that he couldn't be cut off from Christ. He knew that even if he were cut off from Christ, it would not result in the salvation of the Jewish people. But *if* it were possible, he was willing to do it. The response of many would be something like this:

> Ah hah! See, Paul, it's *easy* for you to say that you *would* pray that way because you know you *can't* pray that way!

Paul's response would be as follows:

> And I knew that this is precisely how you'd react when I told you what was in my heart. That's why I said it over and over again: "I'm not lying. I'm telling the truth. Christ bears witness to what I say. The Holy Spirit bears witness to what I say."

Now you can see why Paul went to such seemingly absurd, repetitive lengths to confirm the truth of what he was about to say. Again, Paul goes to such elaborate lengths to confirm the truthfulness of what he says because it is so *utterly contrary to the natural instincts* of human beings that our immediate response is to accuse the apostle of lying to us.

Dear friend, such is Paul's depth of love and concern for his non-Christian friends and countrymen. Is it any wonder why he was so passionate and effective in his intercessory prayers and evangelistic efforts? *Paul didn't stink at either prayer or evangelism because he knew that hell was real, he knew that people were going there, and his heart was broken.* He endured daily, hourly "sorrow and unceasing anguish" (Rom. 9:2) in his heart.

This love for lost souls was not unique to Paul. David Brainerd (1718–47), friend of Jonathan Edwards and missionary to the American Indians, was similarly burdened by the eternal peril that awaited those who died without Christ. In his Diary, edited by Edwards following Brainerd's death from tuberculosis, Brainerd spoke of "wrestling" with God for the souls of the lost. The entry for Monday, April 19, 1742, reads as follows: "God enabled me so to agonize in prayer that I was quite wet with sweat, though in the shade, and the wind cool. My soul was drawn out very much for the world; I grasped for multitudes of souls."[13]

It isn't possible to lay out before you a lengthy or detailed strategy of how you should pray for lost souls, so let me keep it extremely simple and short. Commit yourself today to pray every day like this:

Oh God, illumine my mind to understand the reality and horror of hell. Give me insight into the inescapable certainty of eternal condemnation for those who die without Jesus Christ. And Lord, as you intensify in my heart the truth of an eternity separated from Christ, break my heart for lost souls! Give me the same "great sorrow and unceasing anguish in my heart" that the apostle felt in his. Fill me with such passion for their welfare and your worship that I refuse to stink at prayer any longer.

13. Jonathan Edwards, *The Life of David Brainerd*, ed. Norman Pettit (New Haven, CT: Yale University Press, 1985), 162.

CHAPTER 7

Praying for Pleasure

May the God of hope fill you with all joy and peace in believing,
so that by the power of the Holy Spirit you may abound in hope.
(Rom. 15:13)

I rarely venture out into the shopping malls of Oklahoma City during the
Christmas season, but when I do, once is enough. Although the atmosphere is electric and people seem to be having a good time, I can't help but wonder how these same people will feel the week after Christmas, after all the holiday festivities have died down and they suddenly discover that life hasn't changed much.

You see, for the non-Christian, Christmas is incredibly artificial. It's a little bit like nitrous oxide or laughing gas that some dentists use to calm you down before a tooth extraction. It's pleasant, and no one feels any pain for a while. And then its numbing effect slowly begins to dissipate, and the pain of life returns in full force.

For those who do not know Jesus Christ as Lord and Savior, Christmas only gives them an excuse to pretend they *somewhat like* their family, all is well, and there is hope for the future. But once the lights are turned out, the food is eaten, and family members have returned home, life is still there, waiting for them. The problems they faced before Christmas haven't magically disappeared, the broken relationships haven't healed, and the bills they must pay have only gotten bigger and even more unmanageable.

So how is it any different for the Christian? Well, there are countless ways, but let me mention only three. For those who know and follow Jesus, there is an abiding *joy* that no amount of family discord or financial pressure can undermine. For those who know and follow Jesus, there is *peace*, a tranquility of soul and spirit that has the power to overcome whatever turmoil and tragedy we've yet to face. And there is *hope*; rock-solid, confident assurance that God will absolutely fulfill his promises to us.

Romans 15:13, as you can see, is all about joy, peace, and hope. The holiday season may be over, but for those who know and follow Jesus Christ, there will never be an end to joy, peace, and hope. I know this because of how the apostle Paul prays for the Christians at Rome, that they might continue to abound in joy, peace, and hope. And I assure you that if Paul prayed this for them back then, you and I are justified in praying this prayer for ourselves and one another today.

Why Study the Prayers of Paul?

I'm devoting considerable space in this book to the prayers of the apostle Paul. Let me tell you why I think it's important that we do so.

First, prayers such as this reveal God's heart for his people! This is what God wants for you! He passionately longs for his children to experience an abundance of joy, peace, and hope and, in essence, says, "Just come to me and ask for these gifts, and I will supply them in overwhelming abundance!"

Second, in Paul's prayers, I discover what was of greatest value to him and, therefore, what ought to be of greatest value to me. The apostolic prayers in Scripture challenge our priorities, strip away the veneer of superficial spirituality, and expose our value systems. They reveal what we cherish but shouldn't. They uncover what we shouldn't embrace but do. If you want your spiritual world shaken to the core, compare what Paul prayed for with what you pray for.

In case you hadn't noticed, the church in the Western world is slowly and imperceptibly becoming more secularized. In its attempt to be *relevant* to culture, the church is becoming *indistinguishable* from it. It is becoming increasingly difficult to tell the difference between Christian and non-Christian. The church does not exist to conform to culture but by the grace of God to influence it. So, what does this have to do with Romans 15:13? Simply this: Paul's prayer is just one of many biblical texts that set forth who we, the church, are to be. It describes our values, our priorities, our goals.

This prayer is gospel! It declares to the world: "Here is what may be found in Jesus Christ: joy, peace, and hope!"

Third, in Paul's prayers, I discover what only God can do for me. There are undoubtedly countless blessings and virtues and goals I think are in my power to produce. By looking at the apostolic prayers of the New Testament, I see what I am absolutely dependent on God's grace to produce. After all, *if Paul thought something was ultimately ours to create or generate, he wouldn't bother asking God to do it!* Looking at Paul's prayers typically disabuses me of self-confidence and self-reliance and casts me on the strong arms of my heavenly Father.

A good example of this is seen in Paul's prayer for "joy." In the final analysis, only God can create joy in God. The psalmist prays: "Make us glad for as many days as you have afflicted us" (Ps. 90:15). To be satisfied with the beauty and glory of God (which is the essence of joy!) does not come naturally to sinful souls. By nature, we turn to anything other than God for the joy that he alone can give.

The spiritual goals we long for are ultimately beyond our reach. The changes we desire in our hearts can happen only by a sovereign act of God's grace. That's why it's important to note how Paul refers to God: he is "the God of hope," not so much because he is the object of our hope, although he assuredly is that. Rather, he is the *source* of hope. If there is to be hope, it must come from God.

Fourth, prayer glorifies God by revealing the extent of my need and the depths of God's resources to supply them. Prayers like this reveal how desperately helpless we are and how infinitely rich God is. God is not glorified by my efforts to do things for him, but by my confession that he and he alone can do for me what my soul most desperately needs, and then through me what most blesses others and advances his kingdom.

Praying for Joy, Peace, and Hope

Let's now turn our attention to this prayer. There are several things I want to share with you from Paul's short but powerful prayer.

The first thing that we see is that *God is no miser with his mercy.* Note the words *fill, all,* and *abound.* Paul prays that God will "fill" us with joy and peace, not simply "give" or "impart" or "enable" us to experience these blessings, but that he might "fill" us with them! He emphasizes the effusive, generous, expansive, abundant, overflowing, and measureless way in which God answers prayers (cf. Ps. 16:11). We don't simply "have" or "possess" these blessings: we are "filled" with them, inundated and awash and overflowing with them. Note also that it is not "some" joy or a "fraction" of peace or "a small measure" of hope. Paul prays that we be filled with "all" joy and "all" peace. Not just a little here and there but with the totality of joy and the entirety of peace.

Furthermore, we don't simply "hope." Far less do we hang on by our fingernails. Rather, we "abound" in hope! Again, Paul points to the lavishness of God's grace. God is no miser when it comes to his mercy. This is no tentative, anxious, uncertain, doubt-filled wish. It is a prayer for the overflowing and effusive gift of God's grace.

Paul also prays for joy and peace because he knows that pleasure in God is the power for purity. In another passage, Paul stated clearly that his motive for ministry was the joy of God's people (2 Cor. 1:23–24). Whatever decisions he made, whatever he wrote in his epistles, was always based on what he believed would best serve their *joy*! Paul had some harsh things to say to the Corinthians (deservedly so, I might add). His rebukes often stung. But his aim was always their *joy*! Paul didn't discharge his apostolic calling to expand his personal power, broaden his influence, bolster his reputation, or increase his control but *to intensify their joy in Jesus.*

Paul can almost be heard to say, "Whether I'm rebuking you for sectarianism in the church (1 Cor. 3) or laxity in moral conduct (1 Cor. 5–6) or abuse of spiritual power (1 Cor. 12–14), *my aim is your joy in Jesus.* Whether I appeal to you to be financially generous (2 Cor. 8–9) or warn you of false apostles (2 Cor. 11), *my aim is your joy in Jesus.*"

If Paul had been pressed for an explanation, he would have said: "I'm always aiming for your joy because apart from your souls relishing and resting in the all-sufficiency of Jesus Christ, you don't stand a chance against Satan." I believe Paul would have answered like the good Christian hedonist that he was: "I aim for your joy because God is most glorified in you when you are most pleased and satisfied and at rest in the plenitude of his beauty that can be seen in the face of Jesus Christ."

God's commitment to our joy in Jesus is motivated, at least in part, by the fact that Satan is no less committed to our joy in the passing pleasures of sin (cf. Heb. 11:25). The diabolical strategy of the enemy is to seduce us into believing that the world and the flesh and sinful self-indulgence could do for our weary and broken hearts what God can't. This is the battle that we face each day. We awaken to a world at war for the allegiance of our minds and the affections of our souls. The winner will be whoever can persuade us that he will bring greatest and most soul-satisfying joy. That is why Paul labored and prayed so passionately and sacrificially for joy in Jesus in the hearts of that first-century church.

Paul prays for joy in Rome and labors for joy in Corinth because of what he wrote to the church in Ephesus. In Ephesians 4:22 he referred to "deceitful desires." They are called this because they lie to us and deceive and mislead us about the superiority of what they can do that God supposedly can't. "'Deceitful desires' can trick us into feeling that sinful thoughts and acts will be more satisfying than seeing God. This illusion is so strong it creates moral confusion, so that people find ways to justify sin as good, or, if not good, at least permissible."[1]

So, then, what precisely are "joy" and "peace"? I assure you it has nothing to do with the transient feelings of holiday euphoria experienced by those people in the shopping malls before Christmas. Joy and peace are not some superficial, psychological giddiness that comes from reaping the material comforts of Western society. Countless feelings, passions, and desires arise in our hearts that are not the fruit of light in the soul. Paul wants nothing to do with them. The joy for which he prays is a deep, durable delight in the splendor of God that utterly ruins you for anything else. It is deep, rather than the superficial so-called "joy" that only scratches the surface of your soul. It is durable in that it survives the worst of circumstances in life.

Joy is experiencing a spiritual taste for the glory of Jesus. This joy has an "expulsive" power: it drives out all competing pleasures and leads the soul to rest content with the knowledge of God, the blessings of intimacy with him, and companionship with Jesus. This is the kind of joy that rather than being dependent on material and physical comfort actually frees you from bondage to physical comforts and liberates you from dependence on worldly conveniences and gadgets and gold.

There's something a bit odd and even ironic about this joy. Although

---

1. John Piper, *When I Don't Desire God: How to Fight for Joy* (Wheaton, IL: Crossway, 2004), 102.

true joy is an experience, it is deep, solid, firm, and substantive, not fleeting, flippant, and superficial. We know this because the Bible describes joy as flourishing in the midst of suffering (see Rom. 5:3; 2 Cor. 8:2; 1 Thess. 1:6; 1 Peter 4). My point is that there is a world of difference between joy in God and joy in the comforts God gives. We are grateful for the latter, but our joy is in the former! True spiritual, biblical joy is not the product of the human will in response to pleasant circumstances. It is the product or fruit of the Holy Spirit. That is why Paul asks God to generate it within our hearts.

What about "peace"? The peace for which we are to pray is not the objective peace with God that Paul describes in Romans 5:1, but an inward, subjective, experiential state of mind and spirit. *Peace is confident repose in the truth that what God has promised he will fulfill; it is the restful assurance that nothing can separate us from the love of Christ.* It is that glorious work of the Spirit in my heart that says:

A sudden tornado may sweep away my house and family, but nothing can separate me from the love of God in Christ Jesus!

A terrorist may separate my head from my body, but nothing can separate me from the love of God in Christ Jesus.

An incurable disease may ravage my body, but nothing can separate me from the love of God in Christ Jesus.

An unfaithful spouse may walk out on me, never to return, but God will never leave me nor ever, under any circumstances, forsake me.

This is Christian hedonism: a joy and delight and satisfaction in God so deep, unmovable, and indelible that no amount of suffering can shake it or induce me to take offense at God!

Paul also tells us here that *pleasure in God is the fruit of faith in God*. It is from or through the Scriptures that joy and peace arise. Why do I say this? I say it because Paul prays in Romans 15:13 that God would "fill you with all joy and peace *in believing*, so that by the power of the Holy Spirit you may abound in hope." The phrase "in believing" could as easily be rendered "as" you believe or "because" you believe or "in connection with" believing. In any case, the point is that God will most assuredly *not* fill you abundantly with these if you *don't* believe. Both joy and peace are the fruit of *believing*, which in turn yields hope.

But believe *what*? Belief is confidence placed in the truth of what God has revealed to us in Scripture about who he is and our relationship to him through Jesus. The "believing" Paul has in mind confidence and faith and trust in (1) the person of God revealed in Jesus, (2) the promises of God articulated in Scripture, and (3) the power of God by which he makes it all come to pass. Belief does not plant itself in midair but in the firm foundation of inspired, revelatory words inscripturated for us in the Bible.

And it's not just joy and peace that come from believing God's Word. The Word of God is the spring from which the waters of faith arise. Paul says in Romans 10:17 that "faith comes from hearing" and that hearing comes "through the word of Christ." People are drowning in skepticism and suffocating from doubt. They desperately need faith, but it doesn't just happen serendipitously. Faith doesn't miraculously appear out of thin air; it comes only if and when we hear and treasure the word of Christ.

There's still more. It is from or through the Scriptures that the Spirit imparts endurance and encouragement: "For whatever was written in former days was written for our instruction, that through endurance and through the encouragement of the Scriptures we might have hope" (Rom. 15:4). These virtues don't fall like manna from heaven! They are imparted through the inspired Word of God. This statement in Romans 15:4 thoroughly refutes the notion so prevalent today that the Old Testament is useless to Christians.

How often have you found yourself on the verge of saying, "God, I'm about to quit! Give me strength to endure. God, I'm inconsolable. Give me encouragement." Then we stand, waiting with open hands, looking to heaven. No! If you need encouragement and the endurance to persevere, turn to Scripture and let the Spirit of God awaken your heart and fill your soul with the revelation of God and his work for you in Christ.

The problem is that people want joy and peace *without believing*, or at least without the hard work that true believing requires. They expect it. They pray for it. They are angry with God when it doesn't happen. Jonathan Edwards had this in mind when he spoke of the necessity of "*laying ourselves in the way of allurement,*" that is, taking steps to posture our lives in that place where the Spirit is most likely to energize faith. And that place is not only the sacraments, worship, and prayer but preeminently the Scriptures.

The way the temptations of the world, the flesh, and the devil are defeated is to hear and believe the Word of God when it says that God and his ways are more to be desired than all that sin can offer. When sin confronts you with a strong and attractive and appealing promise of satisfaction, stand firm and let the promises of God do battle on your behalf.

How, then, are we to get "joy" and "peace"? Cry out to God in prayer that the Holy Spirit would stir up within your heart and kindle afresh a flame of fascination, delight, and satisfaction in God. Pray that God would energize your heart and mind to deeply explore God's revelation and all he is for us in Jesus as set forth in Scripture.

Let's pause and summarize what we've seen thus far. God is not a miser with his mercy. Paul prays for joy and peace because pleasure in God is the power for purity. Pleasure in God is the fruit of faith in God. Now, finally, the purpose of pleasure in God is hope in God.

Why do we lack hope? Could it be because we've been "burned" by putting our confidence in something that we really didn't need in the first place? We "hope" for a good-paying job when we graduate. Some are "hoping" for a husband to wake up spiritually and get off the couch. Others "hope" for some way to cover next month's car payment. But in the end, all we need is Christ. He is the object and focus and obsession of our hope:

Paul applauds the Thessalonians for their "steadfastness of hope in our Lord Jesus Christ" (1 Thess. 1:3). What is our "blessed hope"? It is "the appearing of the glory of our great God and Savior Jesus Christ" (Titus 2:13). We are to "hope in Christ" (Eph. 1:12). The mystery of the gospel is "Christ in you, the hope of glory" (Col. 1:27). John Piper put it best when he said, "Sometimes what we need from the Bible is not the fulfillment of our dream[s], but the swallowing up of our failed dream[s] in the all-satisfying glory of Christ."[2] The reason that may not resonate with our souls or sound very encouraging is because we really don't believe Jesus Christ is all-satisfying. We don't savor him. And we don't savor him because we don't see him, and we don't see him because we fail to look upon him as he has revealed himself in holy Scripture!

---

2. Piper, *When I Don't Desire God*, 101.

Hope is ultimately beyond our ability to produce. When we try to create it or crank it up, it either degenerates into presumption or soon gives way to despair. But in this prayer in Romans 15:13 we are protected from presumption by Paul's emphasis on "believing." In other words, the revelation of God which we believe and trust establishes the boundaries, parameters, and the limits of what we may justifiably hope for. Joy and peace come from trusting only in what God has promised.

Finally, Paul clearly says that there is no hope for hope in God apart from the power of the Holy Spirit. If you feel utterly exhausted, both spiritually and physically, and are on the verge of despair because nothing you can do will avail to awaken hope in your heart, you are in precisely the condition where God can perform his most glorious work in you. It isn't your willpower or good intentions or New Year's resolutions that will bring hope. It is the Holy Spirit! It is the power of the third person of the Trinity!

The Spirit of God does far more than merely perform miracles, signs, and wonders. His work goes beyond that of setting people free from demonic oppression. Yes, he imparts spiritual gifts, converts the lost, and causes people to be born again unto faith in Christ. But never lose sight of the fact that it is the Spirit and the Spirit alone who awakens and sustains genuine hope in your heart.

Conclusion

Were you disappointed with the gifts you received last Christmas, or the gifts you had hoped for but never saw? When our daughter Melanie was about eight years old, all she wanted for Christmas was a Swatch watch. When Christmas morning arrived, she was crushed when we discovered that her mother had accidentally thrown it out as trash along with some wrapping paper and other discarded items. My other daughter, Joanna, experienced her own disappointment one year at Christmas. She kept complaining about how cold she was, so her mom got her a space heater. A space heater? Yes, and to say she was crushed and disillusioned hardly captures her emotions.

You may have had a lousy Christmas. You may have failed to give the gifts people expected from you. You may not have received the gifts you had hoped for. But here's the indescribably good news for those who know and follow

Jesus: our God is the source of hope, and he is unstinting and lavish in his desire to fill you up with joy and peace as you trust and treasure the truth of all that is revealed in his Word, and the Holy Spirit will never disappoint you but will graciously and powerfully awaken and sustain genuine hope in your heart, that you might forever enjoy all that God is for you in Jesus.

CHAPTER 8

Partnering with God through Prayer
to Shape the Course of History

O kay. I agree. That title sounds a bit grandiose and over the top. Have I succumbed to hyperbole to elicit a response from you? Is this pastoral sensationalism, claiming more for prayer than is warranted from Scripture? Or could it possibly be true? I think it best to let the apostle Paul answer that question. To do so, let's look at the closing words of Romans 15:

> I appeal to you, brothers, by our Lord Jesus Christ and by the love of the Spirit, to strive together with me in your prayers to God on my behalf, that I may be delivered from the unbelievers in Judea, and that my service for Jerusalem may be acceptable to the saints, so that by God's will I may come to you with joy and be refreshed in your company. May the God of peace be with you all. Amen. (Rom. 15:30–33)

I'll be the first to admit that prayer is one of the more perplexing mysteries in the Christian life. Why does God repeatedly encourage us to pray? If God wants to accomplish some goal for his own glory, why doesn't he just do it? Why does God tell us that if we hope to experience certain blessings, we must first ask for them? Does prayer really make a difference? These are important and challenging questions, and there is hardly a more helpful and instructive passage in Scripture where answers can be found than right here in Romans 15.

Paul's Plans, Prayer, and the Providential Will of God

Paul was not the sort of man who made plans in defiance of God's providential leading. He knew that his schedule was always subject to divine revision. No one knew better than Paul himself that his proposed journey to Jerusalem (Rom. 15:25), then to Rome, and eventually to Spain (Rom. 15:24) depended on God's sovereign will. But he also knew that God has chosen to accomplish his will for us in response to the prayers that we bring to the throne of grace on behalf of one another. This is why he writes what he does in Romans 15:30–33.

Earlier in this letter, Paul assured the Roman Christians that he was praying for them (1:9), so now he asks that they pray fervently for him. Several elements in this text call for comment.

First, we must note the basis for Paul's appeal. He mentions two things: the Lord Jesus Christ and the love of the Holy Spirit. Second, we must give full weight to what Paul says about *striving* in prayer. What does he mean by this? Strive against whom or what? Third, there are clearly three things Paul hopes will come to pass due to their fervent striving on his behalf. Fourth, there is a concluding prayer by Paul for the Romans, or perhaps we should describe it as a blessing he pronounces over them.

The Basis of Paul's Appeal (Rom. 15:30a)

The word translated "appeal" is quite forceful. This is more than a polite request. Paul isn't saying, "Hey, Romans, if you find some free time in the next few days and God brings me to mind, would you consider devoting a few minutes to interceding with him on my behalf?" No. This is an urgent plea, a passionate appeal that reflects the emergency Paul faced. He is in great need, and he is genuinely desperate for the prayerful support of these believers in Rome. I would not go so far as to say that Paul was frightened, but he was undoubtedly greatly concerned about what lay ahead and the possibility that his best efforts might be thwarted, and his life put in danger.

The apostle would undoubtedly have prayed that God would accomplish through him the three things that he mentions in verses 31–32. But why does he ask the Romans to join him in praying for this to occur? Does it really matter how many people are praying for something to occur? Is there a greater likelihood that God will do what Paul wants if the Romans join him in prayer? Does God count heads and give preferential treatment to those joined by others in asking for something? Do numbers matter?

I could as easily ask, "Why do we invite everyone in our local churches to join us in prayer at specific times during the course of a week? Does it really matter how many people show up? Why do we at Convergency Church OKC invite people to join our intercessory team on Sunday morning to pray for our two services? In fact, why do we even have a 'team' of people? Does God say to us, 'Sorry folks, but only one of you asked me to do this. If more of you had joined in, I might then have been inclined to say yes.'"

Paul's appeal here is that they strive together "with me" in praying for these things. Clearly, Paul is himself praying that God would answer these requests. But why does he need the Romans to partner with him in prayer if he is praying? I can think of a couple of answers to this.

First, God encourages multitudes to join in prayer because it builds community and love and unity among Christians. When we all pray as one, we experience a deeper spiritual connection with each other, and that can only serve to increase our effectiveness in ministry.

Second, God wants us to see how powerful prayer can be. When many, instead of just a handful, are praying in unison for the same thing, and what they are asking God to do is done, we are confronted with the power of prayer and how God has chosen to honor it. I'm not opposed to the suggestion that God's will is to respond more readily to the prayers of many when they intercede in unison than he would if only one or two prayed. I can't explain why God seems more likely to say yes to our prayers when many are engaged in unified intercession, but that appears to be the clear implication of this and other New Testament texts.

Third, and perhaps most importantly, when many pray, rather than just a few, God is more greatly glorified. When many, rather than just a few, give him thanks for answering those prayers, he is exalted. This is clearly what Paul said in 2 Corinthians 1:11: "You also must help us by prayer, so that many will give thanks on our behalf for the blessing granted us through the prayers of many." In other words, when many pray, many more expressions of gratitude will rise to God than if only a few pray. And those expressions of gratitude draw attention to God and his greatness and goodness. So, a multitude of prayers serves to bring God more glory than only a small handful. And let us never forget that prayer's ultimate purpose is to magnify God's glory and greatness. Jesus said in John 14:13, "Whatever you ask in my name, this I will do, that the Father may be glorified in the Son." The aim of prayer is that the Father be glorified through Jesus.

In the final analysis, we don't need to know why God is pleased with the prayers of many. Of course, he is eminently pleased with the prayers of each individual alone. But he is extraordinarily pleased when his people come to him in unity and oneness. Even if we can't figure out why, the New Testament is clear that this is something for which we must strive.

So, on what basis does Paul appeal to the Romans to join with him in prayer for these issues? He mentions two things. First, he issues his appeal "by (or through) our Lord Jesus Christ" (Rom. 15:30). This may simply mean, because of what Jesus has done for us, join me in prayer. Based on the fact that his life, death, and resurrection have opened a door for us into heaven and to the throne of grace itself, join me in praying. Or it may be that he means, "for the sake of Jesus Christ" or "for the glory and praise of Jesus." There are numerous things Jesus has done for us that make prayer urgent and important. He commanded us to pray and not to lose heart (Luke 18:1). He told us to pray in his name, which again refers to all he has done to reconcile us to the Father (John 14:13; 15:16). He modeled prayer by spending entire nights seeking his Father's will (Luke 6:12).

But I think something else is in Paul's mind. I think he appeals to Jesus as "Lord" because he knows that the risen Christ exercises absolute sovereignty over the lives and wills of humans. Jesus can respond to the prayers of his people to accomplish otherwise seemingly impossible things. He is the one to whom all authority in heaven and on earth has been given (Matt. 28:18). Thus, Paul knows that Jesus has the right and the power to orchestrate events and turn the will of government leaders and religious zealots to do whatever he pleases. And that is precisely what he asks for in verse 31.

Second, he also bases his appeal on "*the love of the Spirit.*" This is difficult to interpret. Is he saying, because of the love that the Holy Spirit has for you and me? Or is he referring to the love the Spirit has created in our hearts for one another? I can't dismiss the first option, but the second is more likely.

The Struggle of Prayer (Rom. 15:30b)

Paul writes something similar to Romans 15:30 in Colossians 4:12—"Epaphras, who is one of you, a servant of Christ Jesus, greets you, always struggling on your behalf in his prayers, that you may stand mature and fully assured in all the will of God" (see also Col. 2:1). With whom or against what are we striving and struggling in prayer? We aren't striving with God, as if he can be cajoled or bullied into giving us what we want. We aren't striving to overcome his reluctance to help. We aren't striving to persuade him to change his mind and do things our way. Prayer is never a conflict of wills, God's against ours. The purpose of prayer isn't to bend God's will to conform to ours, as if we puny creatures were capable of overpowering the Creator. The obstacles to prayer against which we strive find their origin in us and in our Enemy.

So, at minimum, Paul would be referring to demonic forces that don't want us to pray. In Ephesians 6:12 Paul said we "wrestle" (i.e., strive and struggle) "against the rulers, against the authorities, against the cosmic powers over this present darkness, against the spiritual forces of evil in the heavenly places." Demons are determined to sow seeds of doubt in our minds about whether prayer is important or whether it even works. They constantly try to undermine your prayer life by suggesting that God isn't listening. You're too sinful. You're too insignificant. You've failed too many times, and he's given up on you. Who are you, anyway, to think God will intervene in your life?

But we also strive against *distractions*. Just as you start to pray, the phone rings, your kids need your help, you remember something urgent that needs your immediate attention, or someone shows up at the front door. We also strive against the *laziness* of our souls. Life may have worn you down and you just don't have the energy to pray. Or it may be that you have run out of words. You don't know what more you can say, so why not quit? Perhaps the greatest threat to persistence in prayer is a track record of what appears to be *unanswered* prayers. Many times, we didn't get what we thought we needed, and we wonder why it should be any different this time. So we quit.

There is also a sense in which we must strive against the *sin* in our lives that may hinder prayer. The psalmist declared, "If I had cherished iniquity in my heart, the Lord would not have listened" (Ps. 66:18). We must strive against *unbelief*. Do you remember the story of the demonized young boy whose father cried out to Jesus: "I believe; help my unbelief!" (Mark 9:24). The apostle Peter exhorted us to "be self-controlled and sober-minded for the sake of your prayers" (1 Peter 4:7).

Whatever the distraction, whatever the obstacle, Paul's appeal and exhortation here is clear: Fight against everything that causes you to cease praying! Resist the temptation to throw in the towel! Cling to the promises of God! Press into his heart ever more intensely! Remind yourself often of the truth of Hebrews 4:16—"Let us then with confidence draw near to the throne of grace, that we may receive mercy and find grace to help in time of need."

Do you want to see one excellent example of what it means to "strive" in prayer? Consider Daniel:

> Then I turned my face to the Lord God, seeking him by prayer and pleas for mercy with fasting and sackcloth and ashes.... Now therefore, O our God, listen to the prayer of your servant and to his pleas for mercy, and for your own sake, O Lord, make your face to shine upon your sanctuary, which is desolate. O my God, incline your ear and hear. Open your eyes and see our desolations, and the city that is called by your name. For we do not present our pleas before you because of our righteousness, but because of your great mercy. O Lord, hear; O Lord, forgive. O Lord, pay attention and act. Delay not, for your own sake, O my God, because your city and your people are called by your name. (Dan. 9:3, 17–19)

Whatever the obstacles to perseverance in prayer may be, don't ever think they can be overcome in your own strength. This isn't a matter of human willpower or teeth-clenching determination. It is a matter of looking to, crying out for, and trusting in the strength that Jesus supplies. When Paul described his efforts on behalf of the Christians in Colossae, he made sure that everyone knew the source of his strength:

> For this I toil, struggling with all his energy that he powerfully works within me. (Col. 1:29)

Striving, struggling, and pressing through in prayer is not an issue that draws attention to you and your willpower but to God and "his energy" working powerfully in us. So, when you are tempted to quit, to throw in the towel, to turn your attention to less demanding tasks, thinking that prayer doesn't work, turn to God and cry out for his help. Ask him to impart his power into your weak, failing, faltering mind, soul, and body. God will not say no to your request. He will faithfully supply you with the strength to push out of the way the barriers and obstacles that would otherwise cause you to quit.

The Threefold Request of Paul (Rom. 15:31–32)

There can be no doubt that Paul believed in the power of prayer. He clearly believed that his success in life and ministry depended on the prayers he prayed and that others prayed for him. Earlier, I mentioned two examples:

> Yes, and I will rejoice, for I know that *through your prayers* and the help of the Spirit of Jesus Christ this will turn out for my deliverance. (Phil. 1:18b–19; italics mine)

> At the same time, prepare a guest room for me, for I am hoping that *through your prayers* I will be graciously given to you. (Philem. 22; cf. 2 Cor. 1:8–11; italics mine)

I find it incredibly instructive here that Paul confesses he does not know whether it is God's will that he finally makes his way to Rome. He knows it is God's will to spread the gospel. That has clearly been revealed to him. But God's sovereign and secret will is something Paul does not presume to know in advance. We can all know God's revealed, moral will. It is found in the pages of Scripture. But his secret, sovereign will is hidden from us unless God should choose to reveal it. We see this in several texts:

> But on taking leave of them [Christians in the church at Ephesus] he said, "I will return to you if God wills," and he set sail from Ephesus. (Acts 18:21)

> For God is my witness, whom I serve with my spirit in the gospel of his Son, that without ceasing I mention you always in my prayers, asking that somehow by God's will I may now at last succeed in coming to you. (Rom. 1:9–10)

> But I will come to you soon, if the Lord wills. (1 Cor. 4:19a)

> For I do not want to see you now just in passing. I hope to spend some time with you, if the Lord permits. (1 Cor. 16:7)

> And I trust in the Lord that shortly I myself will come also. (Phil. 2:24)

Do you live each day trusting in the will of God? Do you recall the counsel of James?

> Come now, you who say, "Today or tomorrow we will go into such and such a town and spend a year there and trade and make a profit"—yet you do not know what tomorrow will bring. What is your life? For you are a mist that appears for a little time and then vanishes. Instead you ought to say, "If the Lord wills, we will live and do this or that." (James 4:13–15)

We should all embrace this perspective on life: everything that happens, be it prosperity, pain, opportunity, or obstacles, is subject to God's providential will. I find that incredibly comforting. So, what then does Paul ask them to pray about?

First, "that I may be delivered from the unbelievers in Judea" (Rom. 15:31a). Why did he need them to pray for this, and were their prayers answered? The need arose from Paul's experience of facing opposition everywhere he traveled. And yes, it was answered, but not in the way he and the Roman Christians might have expected. Let me summarize what happened.

When Paul arrived in Jerusalem, we are told that "the Jews from Asia, seeing him in the temple, stirred up the whole crowd and laid hands on him" (Acts 21:27). Later, "all the city was stirred up, and the people ran together. They seized Paul and dragged him out of the temple" (Acts 21:30). So how was Paul saved? Luke tells us that "as they were seeking to kill him, word came to the tribune of the cohort that all Jerusalem was in confusion" (Acts 21:31). The Roman soldiers rushed to the scene and rescued him and put him in jail. The church's prayers in Rome that Paul be "delivered" from unbelievers in Judea were answered when God responded to their request by making certain that "word" came to the tribune of the cohort. *God did that!* We don't know who delivered the word. What we do know is that by God's sovereign providential oversight of the situation, in response to the prayers of the Roman church, Paul was protected! The prayers of the Roman Christians 1,400 miles away were answered as God influenced the will of someone to inform the tribune, whose will God influenced to rush to the scene and rescue Paul!

That was only the first answer to their prayers. While he was in jail, "the Jews [more than forty] made a plot and bound themselves by an oath neither to eat nor drink till they had killed Paul" (Acts 23:12). But "somehow" (!) Paul's nephew heard of the plot and informed the Roman tribune, who immediately dispatched two hundred soldiers with seventy horsemen and two hundred spearmen to escort Paul to Caesarea. All this, mind you, was God's doing in response to the faithful, fervent prayers of the Roman Christians!

Second, he asks them to pray that his "service for Jerusalem may be acceptable to the saints" (Rom. 15:31b). Paul is aware that some Jewish Christians in Jerusalem still didn't fully trust him. They are somewhat suspicious of the gospel he preached and mistakenly assumed he was trying to undermine Jewish traditions. Perhaps they would consider the financial gift as a bribe, an attempt by Paul to win their favor and a good standing. If they refused to receive the gift or interpreted it as an attempt by Paul to purchase their affirmation, it would only widen the rift between gentile and Jewish believers. Remember: the gift to the Jewish believers in Jerusalem came from gentile believers in Corinth and Philippi.

Was this prayer of Paul's and the Roman Christians answered? It appears so. For one thing, we don't see or read anything in Scripture to suggest the monetary gift was rejected. The only biblical statement is in Acts 24:17 where Paul says, "Now after several years I came to bring alms to my nation and to present offerings." If this had been turned down, one would think something would be said to that effect. So, once again, God answers the prayers of Christians in Rome regarding events in Jerusalem!

We might be inclined to conclude that prayer changes people's wills. But the more accurate way of saying it is that God changes people's wills in answer to our prayers that he do so. In this case, the willing of a multitude of angry Jewish enemies of Paul is in the power of God to change. And the willing of suspicious Jewish Christians to disapprove of his monetary gift is in the power of God to change. If Paul didn't believe that God had the authority, power, and disposition to change human choices, he wouldn't have asked the Romans to join him in praying for these things.

Third, and finally, Paul wants them to pray with him "so that by God's will I may come to you with joy and be refreshed in your company" (Rom. 15:32). Paul isn't talking about the sort of refreshment that comes from a week at the beach or in the mountains! He has in mind the joy and mutual encouragement and love that come from Christian fellowship. He described this earlier in Romans 1:11–12: "For I long to see you, that I may impart to you some spiritual gift to strengthen you—that is, that we may be mutually encouraged by each other's faith, both yours and mine."

Clearly, it is God's design and desire that you experience spiritual refreshment and encouragement that come from close relationship and interaction with other believers. You cannot grow up spiritually all on your own. You need the blessings and benefits and encouragement and prayers and love and support that come from mutual fellowship and joint prayers one for another.

Your Prayers, God's Judgments, and the End of the World!

Still not convinced? There is one passage in Scripture that should forever put to rest your doubts about prayer's role in God's purposes on earth and in heaven. If you have lingering questions from what we've just seen in Romans 15, let Revelation 8 supply a resounding answer. Here is what we read:

> When the Lamb opened the seventh seal, there was silence in heaven for about half an hour. Then I saw the seven angels who stand before God, and seven trumpets were given to them. And another angel came and stood at the altar with a golden censer, and he was given much incense to offer with the prayers of all the saints on the golden altar before the throne, and the smoke of the incense, with the prayers of the saints, rose before God from the hand of the angel. Then the angel took the censer and filled it with fire from the altar and threw it on the earth, and there were peals of thunder, rumblings, flashes of lightning, and an earthquake. (Rev. 8:1–5)

We are reading here of the seventh seal judgment poured out on the earth. I don't want us to get bogged down in the significance of the half hour of "silence in heaven." A dozen or more possible interpretations need not distract us from the primary point of the text.[1]

The imagery of the smoke of incense (see Ps. 141:1–2) rising before God (Rev. 8:4) points to a positive answer to the martyrs' request in Revelation 6:9–11 that God execute vengeance against his enemies. Indeed, Revelation 8:5 would constitute the actual historical execution of God's verdict on behalf of his people. It would be a mistake, however, to conclude that "the prayers of all the saints" refers exclusively to the request by the martyrs whose souls John saw beneath the altar (the fifth seal of Rev. 6:9–11). Although surely inclusive of their request, "all the saints" must be a reference to the totality of God's people throughout the present church age. Thus, we see in Revelation 8:3–4 that our prayers are taken seriously by God, are heard by him, and undoubtedly are one of the primary means by which God brings his purposes in history (including his judgments on an unbelieving world) to fulfillment.

Are you beginning to hear what John is saying? If not, note closely what John Piper says about the prayers of the saints:

> The utterly astonishing thing about this text is that it portrays the prayers of the saints as the instrument God uses to usher in the end of the world with great divine judgments. It pictures the prayers of the saints accumulating on the altar before the throne of God until the appointed time when they are taken up like fire from the altar and thrown upon the earth to bring about the consummation of God's kingdom. In other words, what we have in this text is an explanation of what has happened to the millions upon millions of prayers over the last 2,000 years as the saints have cried out again and again, "Thy kingdom come . . . Thy kingdom come." Not one of these prayers, prayed in faith, has been ignored. Not one is lost or forgotten. Not one has been ineffectual or pointless. They have all been gathering on the altar before the throne of God.[2]

---

1. I'm among those who believe that the meaning of "silence" must be found in the OT where it often points to divine judgment. See, for example, Pss. 31:17; 115:17; Isa. 47:5; Lam. 2:10–11; Amos 8:2–3; Hab. 2:20 (cf. Isa. 23:2; 41:1–5). To be even more specific, perhaps the silence is an indication that God has heard the prayers of the martyrs for vengeance (Rev. 6:10) and is now prepared to respond. In this way the seventh seal is linked to 8:3–5 where the silence is related to God's heavenly temple and sacrificial altar, from which judgment comes forth.

2. John Piper, "The Prayers of the Saints and the End of the World," January 9, 1994, https://www.desiringgod.org/messages/the-prayers-of-the-saints-and-the-end-of-the-world.

If you need to slow down, go back, and read that paragraph again, I urge you to do so. I realize that at first hearing it sounds a bit grandiose. But if we are to fully grasp the power that our prayers wield in God's global purposes, this passage in Revelation must be understood. Piper continues:

> And the flame has been growing brighter and brighter and more and more pleasing in the presence of God. And the time will come when God will command his holy angel to take his mighty censer and fill it with fire from the altar where the prayers burn before the Lord, and pour it out on the world to bring all God's great and holy purposes to completion. Which means that the consummation of history will be owing to the supplication of the saints who cry to God day and night. Not one God-exalting prayer has ever been in vain.[3]

If at any time in the reading of this book or during your Christian life, and especially in the midst of your seasons of prayer, you begin to wonder what happens to your prayers, what role do I play in God's providential plans, the answer is found, at least in large part, in this text. Your prayers be they long or short, simple or complex, go to the altar of God before his throne, having been mixed with "the smoke of the incense" (v. 4a). Then something quite stunning occurs. The angel throws the censer onto the earth which provokes "peals of thunder, rumblings, flashes of lightning, and an earthquake" (v. 5b). These phenomena "simply represent the action of God from heaven on the world as the scroll of the end of the age begins to open and the seven trumpets and the seven bowls are poured out. The unmistakable point is that your prayers bring that about."[4] George Ladd sums it up in one breathtaking sentence. Revelation 8:5, he writes,

> dramatically pictures the fact that it is in answer to the prayers of the saints that God's judgments will fall upon the earth.[5]

---

3. Piper, "The Prayers of the Saints and the End of the World."
4. Piper, "The Prayers of the Saints and the End of the World."
5. George Eldon Ladd, *A Commentary on the Revelation of John* (Grand Rapids: Eerdmans, 1972), 125–26.

Read that again if you must, but don't miss the point that our prayers are preserved by God and made the catalyst, in response to which, God's judgments are poured out in bringing human history to its Christ-exalting climax.

Conclusion

I hope that by now you can see the indescribably powerful and critically important influence that you can exert in the church and the world through your faithful and fervent prayers. It is not going too far to say that God has invited us to join him in shaping history through our intercessory prayers. In 1 Timothy 2:1–2 Paul exhorts us to pray "for kings and all who are in high positions." That means state representatives, judges, governors, senators, the president, and, yes, even the Supreme Court.

We are to pray for God to exert a redemptive and Christ-exalting influence on the leaders of our universities, be they professors or provosts or presidents or the board of regents. We are to pray for business leaders and military officers. We should be regularly praying that God would move on the wills of administrators and teachers in our elementary schools, that they resist the pressure to promote secular agendas that would warp the minds and hearts of our kids.

Above all else, we are to intercede passionately for our missionaries. Don't let the distance between here and Slovenia hinder your prayers for missionaries and church planters who are laboring there. Don't let the even greater distance between your home and foreign lands hinder your prayer. God is sovereign over every square inch of this world and every human heart and decision.

I can't think of a better way to close this chapter than with Romans 15:33: "May the God of peace be with you all. Amen."

CHAPTER 9

Praying for Perception and Power

I n one of the more famous chapters in the epistles of Paul, Philippians 3, the apostle shines a bright light on two of his most urgent passions, two aspirations, if you will, that I'm quite sure became the content of his repeated prayers to the Lord. Paul declares that he gladly "counted as loss" (Phil. 3:7) his earthly achievements and status "because of the surpassing worth of knowing Christ Jesus my Lord" (v. 8). He goes even further, and gets substantially more graphic, in saying that he counts all such worldly gain as "rubbish" in order that he might gain Christ and be found in him and be granted, through faith, the very righteousness of God (v. 8–9).

But he doesn't stop there. This monumental decision that proved quite costly to the apostle in terms of his acceptance by and respect from the religious power brokers and educated elite of his day was so that he might "know him [i.e., Christ Jesus] and the power of his resurrection" (v. 10). There is no way to sidestep this point. Paul had an insatiable hunger in his soul to know Jesus and experience the power that raised him from the dead. I have no doubt but that he made these two issues a focal point in his prayers to God. And not surprisingly, these are the very two matters that he prays on behalf of the Christians in ancient Ephesus. When he brought these believers to the throne of grace, Paul asked the Father that he might graciously supply them with *perception* and *power*. I can almost hear him speaking: "Great God and heavenly Father. My prayer to you on behalf of the Ephesians is that by the enlightening work of the Holy Spirit, you would enable them to perceive and grasp deep within their hearts the knowledge of Christ Jesus. Help them know Jesus! I also ask that you empower them with the same omnipotent energy by which you raised Jesus from the dead and seated him at your right hand in authority and majesty."

How's that for praying with passion and boldness!

The good news is that these are the very requests that we are authorized to bring to God on our own behalf. Of course, not solely on our own behalf but also for countless others for whom we intercede. Here is the passage in question:

> For this reason, because I have heard of your faith in the Lord Jesus and your love toward all the saints, I do not cease to give thanks for you, remembering you in my prayers, that the God of our Lord Jesus Christ, the Father of glory, may give you the Spirit of wisdom and of revelation in the knowledge of him, having the eyes of your hearts enlightened, that you may know what is the hope to which he has called you, what are the riches of his glorious inheritance in the saints, and what is the immeasurable greatness of his power toward us who believe, according to the working of his great might that he worked in Christ when he raised him from the dead and seated him at his right hand in the heavenly places, far above all rule and authority and power and dominion, and above every name that is named, not only in this age but also in the one to come. And he put all things under his feet and gave him as head over all things to the church, which is his body, the fullness of him who fills all in all. (Eph. 1:15–23)

I want to zero in on two specific requests that Paul makes, the same two that he undoubtedly prayed for himself in Philippians 3:10. In both places, the apostle prays for *perception* (or knowledge and insight) and *power*:

> I want them to know Jesus. I'm not asking that they be more thoroughly informed of his identity and accomplishments, although that too is a good thing to know. No, Father. I want them to *know* Jesus, to walk in close fellowship with him, to feel his presence and love, to gain insight into his character and his commitment to them. Holy Spirit, shine the light of illumination into their hearts and minds and dispel the darkness of ignorance and pride. Enable them to see Jesus for who he really is: his values, his loves, his hates, his desires, indeed, all that he is committed to do for them.
>
> Oh, Father, there's more in my heart for these brothers and sisters. They are weak, as I am. They are fickle, as I am. They are prone to wander,

doubt, and waver, as I am. Supply them with your infinite strength and the "immeasurable greatness of your power." I'm not asking that you explain your power, like a professor writing propositional statements on the white board. I'm asking that you enable them to experience it in their lives, choices, and struggles with the world, the flesh, and the devil. Infuse your power into their souls so they might overcome the limitations inherent in finite creatures.

Like I said, how's that for bold and audacious praying!

We must also note the "reason" why Paul prays this way. It hasn't changed these many centuries. Paul is especially energized to intercede for them because he had heard of their "faith in the Lord Jesus" and of their "love toward all the saints" (Eph. 1:15; cf. Col. 1:3–4). It grieves me to say this, but all too often when God blesses others, be it spiritually or materially, we begrudge it or are jealous or question their worthiness ("She doesn't deserve that!"). But Paul rejoices with those who rejoice. Nothing pleased him more than other Christians' progress and prosperity (though he remains in prison as he writes this!).

When faith and love are mentioned, one expects to hear of hope as well, but that will come in verse 18. It's important to point out that if "faith" and "love" were ultimately the result of something these believers had done, I can't imagine that Paul would have thanked *God* for them. Certainly they displayed faith and love, but Paul evidently felt that God was the ultimate source of both. John Calvin put it this way:

Now, with all this, he shows that faith and love are the very gifts of God and do not come from ourselves, as men always imagine through a devilish pride. . . . If every man was able to believe and have faith of his own accord, or could get it by some power of his own, the praise for it ought not to be given to God. For it would be but mockery to acknowledge ourselves indebted to him for what we have obtained, not from him, but from elsewhere. But here St. Paul blesses God's name for enlightening the Ephesians in the faith and for framing their hearts to make them loving. It is to be concluded, therefore that everything comes from God.[1]

---

1. John Calvin, *Sermons on the Epistle to the Ephesians* (Edinburgh: The Banner of Truth Trust, 1973), 83.

We also see a feature of Paul's prayer life that will appear repeatedly in his letters: *constancy*. "I do not cease to give thanks for you." This refrain appears in Romans 1:8ff.; 1 Corinthians 1:4; Philippians 1:3ff.; Colossians 1:3; 1 Thessalonians 1:2; 2 Thessalonians 1:3; and Philemon 4. Of course, Paul doesn't mean that he does nothing but give thanks, but that he regularly gives thanks for them each time he prays (most likely, morning, noon, and evening, the customary three hours each day).

His Prayer for Perception

There are several things Paul prays for, things we too should pray for, but I want us to focus on two: perception and power. One more point that will reappear in other prayers of Paul's is the sharp contrast between what he prioritized in his requests and what we typically ask for. Our prayers are frequently peppered with requests for promotion at work, a new car, more money, the respect of our peers, and other such items. Paul's prayer is that God would act so that they might more fully grasp and understand the implications of the many spiritual blessings with which God has already blessed them in Christ. Paul doesn't assume that simply because they have been so richly blessed, they need no further understanding, growth, or application of these truths.

Here in Ephesians 1:17 God is referred to as "the Father of *glory*," which might well be translated, "the *glorious Father*." Or it may be that the Father is the *source* of all glory. In the three preceding paragraphs of Ephesians 1, Paul concluded each with a reference to God's glory as the purpose in his saving and sanctifying work (see vv. 6, 12, 14). It seems only fitting that glory be predicated of him yet again here in verse 17.

Note the word *give* in verse 17b. *The knowledge of God is the gift of God!* We see this in other such texts such as Matthew 11:27; 16:17; 1 John 5:20. Human genius cannot account for the knowledge of God. Neither native abilities, education, nor human willpower can attain insight into the character and heart of God. God is known by what Jonathan Edwards called "a divine and supernatural light." The youngest and lowliest of children can exceed the oldest and most elevated of scientists when it comes to the knowledge of God!

So, what precisely does God "give" us? He gives us "the Spirit of wisdom and of revelation" (v. 17b). Some English translations make use of the lowercase *s* and suggest that it refers either to a principle or to the human spirit. But there are several convincing reasons why this must be a reference to the Holy Spirit himself.

The Holy Spirit is the agent of revelation (cf. John 15:26) and illumination (1 John 2:27). Indeed, *revelation* always finds its source in either the Father, Son, or Spirit (see Matt. 11:25, 27; 16:17; Rom. 2:5; 8:19; 1 Cor. 1:7; 2:10; Gal. 1:12, 16; Eph. 3:5). One telling argument against taking "spirit" as a reference to the human spirit is the word *revelation* itself. As Gordon Fee notes, "Whereas one might be able to understand 'a spirit of wisdom' to mean something like 'a wise disposition' or 'a wise spirit,' to speak that way of 'revelation' is to speak near nonsense. What, one wonders, can 'a spirit of revelation' possibly mean in *any* sense in English?"[2]

Consider also the trinitarian structure of Ephesians 1. It also seems to appear here in verse 17 where we find a reference to Jesus and the Father. How appropriate, then, that the Spirit should also be in view. In this regard, see especially Isaiah 11:2 where we read of "the Spirit of wisdom." The parallel in Colossians 1:9 points to the Holy Spirit, as does the close verbal parallel in Romans 8:15 ("Spirit of adoption").

If the "spirit" refers to the Holy Spirit, as I believe it does, we should understand the verb "give" to mean an increased activity or deepening experience or intensified ministry of the Spirit. After all, believers already have the Spirit, as verses 13–14 make clear. In the words of Fee, "The prayer is not for some further Spirit reception, but for the indwelling Spirit whom they have already received to give them further wisdom and revelation. The emphasis, therefore, is not in receiving the Spirit as such, but on receiving (or perhaps realizing?) the resident Spirit's gifts."[3] Paul's prayer, then, is that God would grant us his Spirit, who in turn will supply the wisdom to understand what he also reveals to us about the character of Jesus and the purposes of God in our salvation.

Note well: here we have an unmistakable reference to *revelation* being given to nonapostolic Christians, *revelation* that is, therefore, noncanonical. Contrary to the cessationist argument, *revelation* is not restricted to the biblical authors or to the biblical canon. God can and does speak and grant

---

2. Gordon D. Fee, *God's Empowering Presence: The Holy Spirit in the Letters of Paul* (Peabody: Hendrickson, 1994), 676.

3. Fee, *God's Empowering Presence*, 676.

knowledge, insight, illumination, and truth to the average believer without such revelatory activity threatening the finality or sufficiency of Scripture! Back in Philippians 3, the text noted earlier, Paul is confident that "if in anything" some may disagree with him, "God will reveal that also" to them (Phil. 3:15).

Our main concern, of course, is how the Spirit's revelatory activity is to increase our *knowledge* of God (see Phil. 1:9; Col. 1:9–10; Philem. 6). But who, precisely, is the "him" about whom the Spirit supplies knowledge? Is it God the Father, Jesus Christ, or perhaps even the Holy Spirit himself? Yes! Our great and majestic triune God, three in person and one in nature, works in us to illumine our minds to know him.

I must pause here and ask all of us a question. Do we "know" our heavenly Father, Jesus, and the Holy Spirit? I know my wife and my children. I'm intimately acquainted with their personality, behavior, talents, desires, shortcomings, and achievements. Do we know God in this way? This "knowledge" surpasses a merely intellectual grasp of theological facts. I marvel at the contestants who win each day on the game show *Jeopardy*. How they can learn and retain so many facts regarding so wide a variety of topics amazes me. But I seriously doubt if their "knowledge" is of a personal, intimate, loving nature. Reciting data on any subject, even if that subject is God himself, is of little value if we don't personally and relationally know the God of whom these many facts are true.

So, let's be clear about what Paul is telling us he prays for the Ephesians and what we should pray for ourselves and others. It's as if he cries out to the Lord, "Father, help them! Overcome their opposition to you and your ways. Holy Spirit, illumine their minds that they might grasp the beauty and majesty of who you are in the depths of their inner being. Show them Jesus! Awaken their hearts to a new level of love and joy that is inexpressible and full of glory" (see 1 Peter 1:8).

Here in Ephesians 18 Paul further defines what it means for the Spirit to give us wisdom and revelation in the knowledge of God: it means *having the eyes of one's heart enlightened*, that is, receiving spiritual insight (contrast this with their former, unenlightened condition of the unregenerate in Ephesians 4:18 and 5:8). All the study in the world will avail little in the true knowledge of God apart from the energizing, enabling, enlightening ministry of the Spirit! Note the relationship between "knowledge" of God and the "heart"

(1:17b–18a). Here, "heart" refers to the core of a person's spiritual and mental life, including our emotions and will.

It goes without saying (although I'm going to say it anyway!) that Paul employs vivid figurative language in verse 18. My "heart" doesn't have "eyes," and neither does yours. He isn't talking about the enlightenment that comes through our physical eyesight. This is an intuitive knowledge imparted by the Spirit directly into the soul or heart of each believer. Paul is talking about that moment when the proverbial light bulb shines above your head, only in this case the light shines within and we exclaim, "Now I see it! Now I get it! That's who Jesus is! Wow!"

I don't want to spend much time on the first two truths for which Paul prays, but only on the third. So let me simply say the "hope" of which God's calling is the source or cause is our anticipation of the inheritance referred to in the following verses. But it also refers back to the summing up of "all things in Christ" which is the ultimate purpose of God's saving activity (Eph. 1:10). The "calling" Paul has in mind is related to divine election in 1:4. In other words, Paul is praying that we will know the significance and implications of God's sovereign, pretemporal choice of us. God's sovereign saving purpose for you is something God wants you to know and appreciate, not ignore or merely argue over.

He also prays that we might know "the riches of his glorious inheritance in the saints" (Eph. 1:18b). Once again, there is ambiguity in the word translated "inheritance." Some contend that the inheritance is ours and that God is the one who *gives* it (cf. 1 Peter 1:4). What might our inheritance entail? Eternal life (Titus 3:7), glory with Christ (Rom. 8:17), immortality (1 Cor. 15:50), the kingdom of Christ (Eph. 5:5), and the heavenly city (Rev. 21:2–7), just to mention a few. But more likely, this is the inheritance God *receives* (namely, us). Note that Paul says it is "*his*" glorious inheritance. We are God's inheritance (see Deut. 4:20; 9:26, 29; 2 Sam. 21:3; 1 Kings 8:51, 53; Pss. 28:9; 33:12; 78:62, 71; 106:5, 40; Isa. 19:25; 47:6; 63:17; Jer. 10:16; 51:19; etc.). Thus, Paul would pray that we might be enabled to understand the glory, honor, and wonder of that privileged status, to understand and reflect upon the spiritual wealth of what it means to belong to God, to be his people. God wants us to fully understand, grasp, and experience *what we are to him!*

As if that weren't enough to leave us breathless, Paul declares that there is *glory* in being God's inheritance. Indeed, there are spiritual *riches* or great *wealth* in this glory. Such is what it means to be chosen by God (1:4) and predestined to adoption as his children (1:5). We are the principal means by and through which God now and forever after will display the indescribable splendor of his resplendent beauty! Paul's prayer is that the Spirit might enable us to appreciate, enjoy, celebrate, and marvel at this unfathomable value that God places on us.

His Prayer for Power

We now come to the second of two primary emphases in Paul's prayer. The first was our *perception* of who God is in Christ Jesus. But he also wants us to know "what is the immeasurable greatness of his *power* toward us who believe" (Eph.1:19a). Observe how Paul piles up words in verse 19 to highlight the magnitude of God's power. It isn't enough for him simply to refer to God's "*power*," so he refers to the "*greatness*" of God's "*power*." Nor is it enough for him to refer to the "greatness" of God's "power," so he refers to the "*immeasurable* [or, *surpassing*] greatness of his power"! The best part is that this power is not an abstract energy or a theoretical assertion of what God *can* do but a declaration of what God *actually does* "toward (or unto) us who believe." This indescribably great and awesome power of the great and awesome God is intended for and on behalf of you and me!

This declaration would have had special significance for the people living in southwest Asia Minor who "lived in a milieu characterized by flourishing magical practices, the renowned Artemis cult, and a variety of other Phrygian mysteries and astrological beliefs."[4] In this religious diversity, there was a common fear of hostile religious (i.e., demonic) powers. Paul's prayer, notes O'Brien, "presupposes and emphasizes the supremacy of God's power, which was shown particularly in Christ's resurrection and exaltation to a position of authority over all things. In the light of this superior power of God, who works all things in accordance with the purpose of his will, there is no longer any reason for the readers to fear tyrannical evil powers."[5]

What application might this have for us today? For one thing, it is a

---

4. Clinton E. Arnold, *Ephesians: Power and Magic: The Concept of Power in Ephesians in Light of Its Historical Setting* (Grand Rapids: Baker, 1992), 167.

5. Peter T. O'Brien, *The Letter to the Ephesians* (Grand Rapids: Eerdmans, 1999), 138.

much-needed reminder that we need not fear the demonic forces that Satan sends against us. We are not to act presumptuously or arrogantly when it comes to our encounters with the demonic. Nor are we to neglect adorning ourselves with the full armor of God (Eph. 6:10–20).[6] What it does mean is what Jesus meant when he spoke to the seventy-two disciples who returned "with joy" declaring that "even the demons are subject" to them in Christ's name (Luke 10:17). To this Jesus responded with these incredibly encouraging and empowering words: "Behold, I have given you authority to tread on serpents and scorpions, and over all the power of the enemy, and nothing shall hurt you" (Luke 10:19).

But Paul doesn't stop with the truth of our access to and experience of divine power. This power was manifested specifically in three ways. First, God's power was manifested in the resurrection of Jesus (Eph.1:19b–20a). Note again in verse 19b the piling up of terms. This power designed for believers is the self-same power by which God raised Jesus from the dead. Again, it wasn't just God's "might" (*ischus* = ability, latent strength), but the "strength" (*kratos* = power in action) of his "might." In addition, it is in accordance with the "working" (*energeia* = the efficiency of the power) of the "strength" of God's "might"! And all this . . . for believers![7]

Second, God's power was manifested in the exaltation of Jesus (vv. 20b-23). Paul alludes here to Psalms 110:1 and 8:6 (for the exaltation and ascension of Jesus, see Acts 2:33–35; 5:31; 7:55–56; Rom. 8:34; Col. 3:1; Heb. 1:3, 13; 8:1; 10:12; 12:2; 1 Peter 3:22; Rev. 3:21). The exaltation of Jesus to the "right hand" of God enthroned him above all power and authority (vv. 20b–21). To be seated at someone's "right hand" was to be afforded the highest honor, privilege, and authority. In the Old Testament, God's "right hand" symbolized many things: victory (Ps. 20:6; 44:3; Isa. 41:10), the position of favor (1 Kings 2:19; Ps. 80:18; Jer. 22:24), and power (Ex. 15:6; Ps. 89:13; Isa. 48:13). O'Brien reminds us that "although Ephesians will later assert that God has seated believers with Christ in the heavenly realms (2:6), significantly

---

6. See my extended treatment of this passage in my book, *Understanding Spiritual Warfare: A Comprehensive Guide* (Grand Rapids: Zondervan, 2021).

7. Some have questioned why Paul doesn't mention the death of Jesus. There seem to be at least two reasons. First, the resurrection and exaltation are more suitable expressions of divine power than the cross, the latter typically portrayed in the NT as an expression of weakness ("For he was crucified in weakness, but lives by the power of God" [2 Cor. 13:4])." Second, it is usually in relation to the *love* of God that Paul mentions the cross.

there is no mention of their being placed at 'his right hand.' Christ's exalted status cannot be shared."[8]

The reference to the "heavenlies" or "heavenly places" (v. 20b) where Christ has been seated indicates that for Paul, "Christ had not simply disappeared nor had he evaporated into a universal spirit, but he had departed to a new sphere, that of heaven, which would be appropriate to his transformed body's mode of existence."[9]

The four words in verse 21a translated "rule," "authority," "power," and "dominion" are among six typical Pauline terms for demonic spirits found in Romans 8:38; Ephesians 1:21; 3:10; 6:12; Colossians 1:16; 2:10, 15. Does this imply there are six classes or categories of angelic (demonic) beings? Probably.

Principalities/rulers (*archē*) must have someone or something over which to exercise dominion (Eph. 1:21; 3:10; 6:12; Col. 1:16; 2:10; Rom. 8:38). Authorities (*exousia*), by definition, demand subordinates (Eph. 1:21; 3:10; Col. 1:16). Powers (*dunamis*; cf. Rom. 8:38) reminds us that demons are not weak but operate in the strength of their master, Satan. In Mark 9:29, Jesus refers to a type of demon that "cannot be driven out by anything but prayer." The point seems to be that some demons are stronger and more powerful than others. Hence, there is implied a hierarchy or differentiation based on spiritual strength.

Dominion (*kuriotētos*) again begs for the answer, over what, whom, and where (Eph. 1:21; Col. 1:16)? Elsewhere in Paul (Col. 1:16), the word *thrones* (*thronoi*) is used of angels, and "world rulers" (*kosmokratoras*) is found only once, in Ephesians 6:12. My point is simply that if all angels and demons are of the same type or rank or carry the same authority, why are they described by such a variety of terms? It would also seem that with difference in rank comes difference in power, task, etc. These four words are not intended to be exhaustive. Paul also includes "every name that is named" (Eph. 1:21), encompassing all other intelligent beings, whether good or evil, human or angelic.

There is an extremely practical point for all of us in how Paul extends his description of what happened when Jesus was raised from the dead and exalted to the right hand of the Father. Don't forget, his prayer is that the Holy

---

8. O'Brien, *Ephesians*, 141.

9. Andrew T. Lincoln, *Ephesians*, Word Biblical Commentary (Dallas: Word, 1990), 62.

Spirit would illumine our hearts so that we might come to grips with the marvelous truth that the divine power by which all this was accomplished dwells within and energizes every believer in Jesus. So, let's continue to look at what this power that is now in us did for Jesus.

Not only has Jesus been exalted over all, but all have been placed in subjection to him. This is a *present reality* and not merely a future hope (see Ps. 8:6; 1 Cor. 15:27; Heb. 2:8). "The brow once crowned with thorns now wears the diadem of universal sovereignty; and that hand, once nailed to the cross, now holds in it the sceptre of unlimited dominion. He who lay in the tomb has ascended the throne of (an) unbounded empire."[10]

Jesus was also made head over all things to the church (Eph. 1:22b–23). Here, Paul declares that Jesus, in his exaltation over the universe, is God the Father's gift *to the church*! Thus, not only is the greatness of God's power "toward us who believe" (v. 19), but so too is Christ's cosmic dominion.

Most often in Paul the Greek word *ekklēsia*, translated "church," refers to actual concrete gatherings of Christians in a local setting (see Rom. 16:5; Gal. 1:2; Col. 4:15; 1 Thess. 1:1; 2 Thess. 1:1, 4; 2:14; Philem. 2). But on occasion, especially in Ephesians, it appears to refer to an entity that is much broader than any one local congregation. Such texts as Galatians 1:13; 1 Corinthians 10:32; 12:28; 15:9; Philippians 3:6; Colossians 1:18, 24; and especially Ephesians 3:10, 21; 5:23, 24, 25, 27, 29, 32, as well as here in 1:22, seem to have in view *the universal church*, the "body" of all believers.

Observe Paul's use of the word *head* (*kephalē*) in this passage to indicate the authority of Jesus over the entire cosmos, including the church. The "head" is the ruling, guiding, and sustaining power over its body. This will become important later in Ephesians 5 and Paul's discussion of the relation between husband and wife.

Whereas it is clear that "fullness" (four times in Ephesians: 1:10, 23; 3:19; 4:13; twice in Colossians: 1:19; 2:9; six times elsewhere: Rom. 11:12, 25; 13:10; 15:29; 1 Cor. 10:26; Gal. 4:4) further defines "body" (see esp. Eph. 3:19), which is the church, the meaning is ambiguous. The term "fullness" probably refers to the glorious revelation of God's presence and power. Or, as others have suggested, fullness has in view God's making his presence

---

10. John Eadie, *Commentary on the Epistle of Paul to the Ephesians* (Minneapolis: James and Klock, 1955), 104.

and power felt. The church now embodies, expresses, and mediates that glorious presence to the world. Having said that, there still remain several possible translations:

> The church is that which fills up or completes Christ, he himself being the one who fills all things.

The first half of this rendering is theologically inconsistent with what Paul says elsewhere of Jesus.

> The church is that which fills up or completes Christ, he himself being the one who is filled by all things.

Both halves of this rendering are heretical!

> The church is the fullness of Christ, that is, the church is filled by him, he himself being the one who is filled by all things.

But Christ is already the fullness of God (Col. 1:19; 2:9) and it would be improper to speak of him as dependent on all things; indeed, he himself is *head* over all things!

> The church is the fullness of Christ, that is, the church is filled by him (his fullness having been imparted to it), he himself being the one who fills all things.

The last option is the most likely one. Be it noted that only the church, not the cosmos, is said to be Christ's body. Although Christ rules over the cosmos, he sustains a relationship of loving and leading intimacy only with his church, filling it with his Spirit, grace, and gifts. As for the idea that Christ "fills all in all," that is, fills all things in all respects, O'Brien explains:

> Christ is the one who completely fills "everything," that is, the whole of creation, the earthly and the heavenly, comprising all of humanity as well as the entire angelic realm, especially the rebellious powers. The nature of this filling is not to be explained in a physical or spatial sense: Christ

pervades all things with his sovereign rule, directing all things to their appointed end (cf. Heb. 1:3), and this entails his functioning as the powerful ruler over against the principalities (1:21) and giving grace and strength to his people, the church (4:13, 15–16).[11]

Conclusion

I know how easy it is to get lost in the weeds of a biblical text, which is why I made the effort to unpack this thick paragraph for us, line upon line. My aim in this wasn't primarily to account for all that Paul wrote but to alert you and me to the content of his prayer and thereby to challenge each of us to devote ourselves to seeking God for the same perception of who Jesus is and the same experience of his incredible power.

Is that how you pray? When the Spirit places on your heart a burden for another believer, and perhaps you don't know why or for what you should ask, let your words and petitions be guided by the prayer of Paul. Ask God for them and yourself that you might all perceive and see Jesus for who he truly is. Seek God for insight into the glorious personality and majesty of your Savior. Plead with the Father to impart to you in even greater measure the self-same power through which he raised Jesus from the dead and placed him in authority and dominion over all demonic spirits.

I pray that you can now see how important it is that we understand why Paul prayed and how he prayed so that we in turn might bring our Christ-exalting requests to the throne of grace.

---

11. O'Brien, *The Letter to the Ephesians*, 151.

CHAPTER 10

Praying for the Increase of Intimacy with Christ

For this reason I bow my knees before the Father, from whom every family in heaven and on earth is named, that according to the riches of his glory he may grant you to be strengthened with power through his Spirit in your inner being, so that Christ may dwell in your hearts through faith—that you, being rooted and grounded in love, may have strength to comprehend with all the saints what is the breadth and length and height and depth, and to know the love of Christ that surpasses knowledge, that you may be filled with all the fullness of God.

Now to him who is able to do far more abundantly than all that we ask or think, according to the power at work within us, to him be glory in the church and in Christ Jesus throughout all generations, forever and ever. Amen. (Eph. 3:14–21)

There is a sense in which this expression of prayer in Ephesians 3 ought to precede and undergird all the others we have examined. For it is out of a relationship of intimacy, love, trust, and enjoyment of God that power, commitment, and faith to pray for others and the gospel, as well as for healing, revival, and victory over the enemy, ultimately flows.

Let me begin by giving you an overview of Paul's direction in this prayer. Then, we'll return to examine it in more detail.

Paul prays for several things here, all of which pertain to our *sensible experience* of the person of Christ. He prays that we might be internally strengthened by the Spirit so that Christ might dwell in our hearts. But how can that be, if we have *already* received Christ into our hearts when we were born again? The only viable explanation is that Paul refers to an *experiential enlargement* of what is already theologically true. He wants us to be strengthened by the Spirit so that Jesus might exert a progressively greater and more intense personal influence in our souls.

This expansion of the divine power and presence in our hearts results in the ability to grasp "what is the breadth and length and height and depth" of Christ's love for us. Again, this is Paul's way of saying that God intends for us to feel, experience, and be emotionally moved by his passionate affection for us, his children. In other words, the pinnacle of Paul's intercession is that the Ephesians might experience intimacy with Christ! The ultimate goal in view of which he pleads with God is that Christians might sense or feel or be overwhelmed with God's inexpressible and eternal affection for them! D. A. Carson, in my view, is right on target when he says that,

> this cannot be merely an intellectual exercise. Paul is not asking that his readers might become more able to articulate the greatness of God's love in Christ Jesus or to grasp with the intellect alone how significant God's love is in the plan of redemption. He is asking God that they might have the power to grasp the dimensions of that love in their experience. Doubtless that includes intellectual reflection, but it cannot be reduced to that alone.[1]

But how are we to compute such love? What are its dimensions? Does it come in meters or miles? Do we measure it in yards or pounds? Does Paul intend for you to think in terms of mathematical proportions, as if to suggest that God loves you one hundred times more than he loves the angels or fifty times less than he loves a purportedly more godly Christian?

Quite to the contrary, says Paul. There is a width, length, height, and depth to Christ's love for you that goes beyond human measurement. The immensity and magnitude of that love are incalculable. Its dimensions defy containment. It is beyond knowing. Yet, Paul prays that we might *know* it! This deliberate oxymoron serves to deepen what is already too deep to fathom. Andrew Lincoln summed it up best by saying, "It is simply that the supreme object of Christian knowledge, Christ's love, is so profound that

---

1. D. A. Carson, *A Call to Spiritual Reformation: Priorities from Paul and His Prayers* (Grand Rapids: Baker, 1992), 191.

its depths will never be sounded and so vast that its extent will never be encompassed by the human mind."[2]

But what precisely does "intimacy with Christ" mean? What does it look like? What does it feel like? Allow me to answer that by appealing to our *five senses*. Think of intimacy, first, in terms of *sight*. Much of the affection in my heart for my wife and hers for me is awakened and stimulated by sight. So too in our relationship with God. David spoke of this in Psalm 27:4: "One thing have I asked of the Lord, that will I seek after: that I may dwell in the house of the Lord all the days of my life, *to gaze upon the beauty of the Lord* and to inquire in his temple" (emphasis mine). We "see" his glory and beauty in the face of Jesus Christ as revealed in Scripture.

Then there is the experience of *taste*. "Oh, taste and see that the Lord is good" (Ps. 34:8). David here speaks of savoring the sweetness of Christ; enjoying God as we enjoy the most exquisite of gourmet food.

We can't overlook the joy that comes from our sense of *smell*. The apostle Paul spoke of "the fragrance of the knowledge of him" (2 Cor. 2:14). Enjoying God smells good! There is a spiritually soothing and deeply satisfying reality in being awakened to love for God and his love for us.

And then we also *hear* of God's everlasting love for us. So deep, so profound, so intensely moving is God's affection for his children that he quite literally sings over us (Zeph. 3:17). There is a virtual symphony of song from the Father to his children and from them to him.

Finally, there is our sense of *touch*. Although we do not physically contact the risen Christ, we can often feel his delight in us. His affection has physiological effects, such as weeping, laughter, peace, and even trembling. The biblical authors have in view not simply knowing this love of God but experiencing it in such a way that the whole of our being is engaged: affections are awakened, the mind is stimulated, the will is empowered, and the body is overwhelmed.

Paul's Prayer

After the parenthesis of Ephesians 3:2–13, the apostle resumes the prayer he broke off in verse 1. We see this in the phrase "for this reason" with which verse 1 begins, which is then repeated in verse 14. The specific "reason" in Paul's mind likely points back to all of chapter 2, but especially the concluding

---

2. Andrew T. Lincoln, *Ephesians*, Word Biblical Commentary (Dallas: Word, 1990), 213.

words which focus on his readers being part of the new temple in which God's Spirit dwells (Eph. 2:18–22).

The prayer contains four parts or petitions, each of which is related to the one that precedes it as an effect is related to its cause. These four elements, or stair-steps, as it were, are found in verses 14–19: Paul prays that (1) they may be strengthened by the Spirit, (2) so that Christ may dwell in their hearts, (3) so that they may be able not only to understand but feel Christ's love for them, and (4) so that they may be filled to the fullness of God. Paul then closes his prayer with a doxology in verses 20–21. Note also the Trinitarian structure of the prayer: Paul asks that his readers be strengthened through the *Spirit*, indwelt by *Christ Jesus*, and filled to the fullness of God the *Father*.

Before we examine the content of his prayer, we need to look at its introduction in verses 14–15. Paul's posture is significant: *he bows his knees*, whereas standing (Mark 11:25; Luke 18:11) was normal among the Jews (although, see 1 Kings 8:24; Ezra 9:5; Luke 22:41; Acts 7:60; 9:40; 20:36; 21:5). Kneeling is the instinctive physical expression of worship, humility, and petition. Kneeling may also be an expression of Paul's intensity. For him, intercession was a struggle, a battle, a fight (see Rom. 15:30; Col. 4:2, 12). Lincoln suggests that "kneeling would have had more emotive force and conveyed a greater fervency of entreaty on the writer's part than the earlier reference to his praying in 1:16."[3]

I don't simply assume that everyone knows what Paul means when he speaks of God as "Father" (v. 14). The options available to us include: (1) *Intertrinitarian* (Father of our Lord Jesus Christ); (2) *Creative* (of all mankind; see Acts 17:28–29; Heb. 12:9; James 1:17–18); (3) *Theocratic* (Father of the nation Israel; see Ex. 4:22–23; Deut. 14:1–2); (4) *Adoptive/Spiritual* (of Christians only). It seems likely that the latter is what he has in mind in this text. This can only highlight and intensify the element of intimacy and love: in other words, it is ABBA to whom we come in prayer for this experience!

Power!

The essence of Paul's prayer is for *power*. He earlier prayed that believers might "know" God's incomparably great power toward them (Eph. 1:18–19). Now, he prays that they might inwardly and personally experience it as well.

---

3. Lincoln, *Ephesians*, 202.

We can readily see that Paul prays for four things in particular. He first prays that God might strengthen them (v. 16), or more literally, "that he may give to you to be strengthened with power." What makes this strengthening significant is that it is "according to the riches of his glory" (v. 16). The word translated "according to" points beyond the idea of source or origin. In other words, it is not merely "out of" his riches that he strengthens us but *in proportion to* his riches in glory. There is an emphasis on *correspondence*; that is, God gives on a scale *commensurate with* his riches; God gives as lavishly as only God can (cf. Phil. 4:19).

He prays that we may be strengthened "with power" (v. 16b). To be strengthened with power according to glory may simply mean to be strengthened by God's radiant power! "Believers," notes Best, "are not left to whistle up strength from within themselves in order to be able to do God's will."[4] This strengthening happens only "through his Spirit" (v. 16c). Divine power is, in one sense, synonymous with the Spirit and, in another sense, mediated by the Spirit. This passage, notes Gordon Fee, also "shows that for Paul the 'power of the Spirit' is not only for more visible and extraordinary manifestations of God's presence, but also (especially) for the empowering necessary to be his people in the world, so as to be true reflections of his own glory."[5]

This empowering presence of the Spirit occurs "in your inner being" (v. 16d; see Rom. 7:22; 2 Cor. 4:16). This is the center and locus of our conscious life; the deepest place within our souls where we commune with God. Paul could easily have used the word *heart* or "that part of them which is not accessible to sight but which is open to his energizing influence."[6]

This tells us that if we are ever to experience intimacy with the Lord Jesus, if we are ever to sense and relish and rejoice in his affection, it is something he must do within us by the power of the Holy Spirit. We can't will ourselves into this experience. We can't make it happen. No amount of self-exertion or clenched-fist determination can create this awareness and enjoyment of God's power. We *can* ask God in relentless and prevailing prayer that he do it! Only God himself can impart this knowledge. Divine enabling is absolutely

---

4. Ernest Best, *A Critical and Exegetical Commentary on Ephesians* (Edinburgh: T&T Clark, 1998), 340.

5. Gordon D. Fee, *God's Empowering Presence: The Holy Spirit in the Letters of Paul* (Peabody: Hendrikson, 1994), 695.

6. Lincoln, *Ephesians*, 206.

essential. Human willpower alone, together with good intentions and fervent passion, cannot produce the experiential knowledge Paul has in mind.

The purpose of this divine enabling strength is "so that Christ may dwell in your hearts" (v. 17). Some commentators argue that the dwelling of Christ in our hearts is simply an expansion upon or further definition of what it means to be strengthened by the Spirit in the inner man. But it seems better to understand Paul as praying for inner empowerment of the Spirit so that we might more deeply experience the presence of Christ himself. In the final analysis, the difference is minimal.

Two words are typically used for the concept of indwelling. The first, *paroikeō*, means to abide or to inhabit, but not necessarily permanently. The second, the one used here, is *katoikeō*, which refers to "a settling in or colonizing tenancy."[7] The risen Christ, through his Spirit, lives permanently within us (cf. Col. 2:9). Christ doesn't sojourn in our hearts. He is no divine nomad! He is, reverently speaking, a squatter. He is a permanent, abiding resident.

But this raises an important question. Isn't "indwelling" a ministry of the *Spirit* (see Rom. 8:9–10)? According to the New Testament, Christ dwells in his people through his Spirit (see 1 Cor. 15:45; 2 Cor. 3:17; Gal. 4:6). Also, if Christ, through the Spirit, indwells the believer from the point of the new birth, how can Paul pray as he does in this text? It would seem, once again, that he is praying for the emotional increase or experiential expansion of what is already a theological fact. His desire is that the Lord Jesus, through the Spirit, might exert an ever-increasing and progressively more powerful influence on our lives and in our hearts. It is what I like to call the incessant spiritual reinforcement in the human heart of the strength of Jesus and his love.

Several additional things should be noted. This indwelling influence occurs in the human "heart" (i.e., in the depths of our personality, the core of our souls). And this indwelling influence occurs only through human "faith." It isn't automatic; it is only as we, through the Spirit, continue to trust Christ as our only hope, our only source of salvation, the lover of our souls. The point is that doubt and skepticism concerning who Jesus is and what he has done is the enemy of feeling his affection. Lincoln has this helpful reminder:

---

7. Best, *Ephesians*, 341.

Faith involves a relationship of trust between two parties, and so there can be no implication that the notion of Christ living in the center of a believer's personality means the absorption of that individual personality or the dissolving of its responsibility.[8]

This indwelling influence is in some way related to being "rooted and grounded in love" (v. 17). Here, Paul employs a double metaphor: one from agriculture and one from architecture. Love, says Paul, "is the soil in which believers are to be rooted and grow, the foundation on which they are to be built."[9] Is this yet another, perhaps subsidiary, prayer, or does it describe the attendant circumstances, so to speak, in which this experience might come to pass? If the latter, then a precondition for experiencing the fullness of Christ's indwelling presence is having been rooted and grounded in love.

But whose love? Is it God's love for us in Christ? That would mean you are rooted and grounded in God's love for you so you can know God's love for you. But that sounds oddly redundant. Is it our love for God? I don't think so, for how can that enable us to know his love for us? I believe Paul speaks of *our love for one another* (see 1 John 4:7–12). But there may be another option. O'Brien suggests that these two metaphors express "the contemplated result" of the two previous prayers, providing the condition for the next request. Thus, "through the strengthening of the inner person by God's Spirit and Christ's indwelling in their hearts, the readers are to be established in love so that they will comprehend the greatness of the love of Christ."[10]

Yet, for all its glory and the great heights from which it came, such love can only be experienced together "with all the saints" (cf. 1:1, 15; 3:8; 6:18)! Our experience of Christ's love is personal, but not private. It is meant to be felt and proclaimed and enjoyed in the context of the body of Christ. It is a personal, yet shared, experience. "The comprehension the writer desires for his readers is not some esoteric knowledge on the part of individual initiates, not some isolated contemplation, but the shared insight gained from belonging to the community of believers."[11]

---

8. Lincoln, *Ephesians*, 207 (cf. Gal. 2:20). One more interesting observation: although the concept of Jesus being "in our hearts" is a popular way of expressing what it is to be a Christian, this is the only place in the NT where that precise terminology is found!

9. Lincoln, *Ephesians*, 207.

10. Peter T. O'Brien, *The Letter to the Ephesians* (Grand Rapids: Eerdmans, 1999), 260.

11. Lincoln, *Ephesians*, 213.

Love!

Paul then prays that we might grasp the incalculable dimensions of Christ's love for us (vv. 18–19a). But the breadth and length and height and depth of what? As you might imagine, the options are numerous, and they are all worthy of our consideration.

Perhaps he has in mind the perfections of God (i.e., his infinite attributes; cf. Job 11:7–9). Others point to the mystery of salvation itself (Eph. 1:3–14 and esp. 3:9). It has been suggested (purportedly by Augustine) that Paul is referring to the actual physical structure of the cross (pointing up, down, left, right) which supposedly symbolizes love in its breadth, hope in its height, patience in its length, and humility in its depth. But it is highly unlikely that such developed symbolism would have developed by this early stage in the church's life. Or could it be the dimensions of the Christian temple, that is, the church (cf. 2:19–22 and Rev. 21:16)? Some see here the multiple expressions of divine power as an antidote for reliance on magical practices so common in southwest Asia Minor. The manifold wisdom of God in all its unfathomable dimensions has been put forth as a theory (Eph. 3:10; Rom. 11:33–34).

Likely, this is simply a metaphor of the immeasurable, incalculable, and unfathomable dimensions of Christ's love for his own (as defined in the subsequent clause in Eph. 3:19a). Says Stott: "The love of Christ is 'broad' enough to encompass all mankind (especially Jews and gentiles, the theme of these chapters), 'long' enough to last for eternity, 'deep' enough to reach the most degraded sinner, and 'high' enough to exalt him to heaven."[12]

In verse 19a Paul restates verse 18b. To grasp the incalculable love of Christ for his own is to "know what can't be known"! It is a form of knowledge "that surpasses knowledge" (v. 19). This oxymoron (statement of apparent inconsistency) is designed to emphasize that what we might know in part is ultimately incomprehensible. We may know Christ's love in some measure, but we will never exhaustively comprehend it. No matter how much we learn, no matter how much we think we know and see and feel and grasp, there is always an infinity left over!

John Eadie put it best. His language is somewhat antiquated, but resist the temptation to skip over his insights. They are profound!

---

12. John R. W. Stott, *The Message of Ephesians* (Downers Grove, IL: InterVarsity Press, 1979), 137.

It may be known in some features and to some extent, but at the same time it stretches away into infinitude, far beyond the ken of human discovery and analysis. As a fact manifested in time and embodied in the incarnation, life, teaching, and death of the Son of God, it may be understood, for it assumed a nature of clay, bled on the cross, and lay prostrate in the tomb; but in its unbeginning existence as an eternal passion, antedating alike the Creation and the Fall, it "passeth knowledge." In the blessings which it confers—the pardon, grace, and glory which it provides—it may be seen in palpable exhibition, and experienced in happy consciousness; but in its limitless power and endless resources it baffles thought and description. In the terrible sufferings and death to which it led, and in the self-denial and sacrifices which it involved, it may be known so far by the application of human instincts and analogies; but the fathomless fervour of a Divine affection surpasses the measurements of created intellect. As the attachment of a man, it may be gauged; but as the love of God, who can by searching find it out? Uncaused itself, it originated salvation; unresponded to amidst the "contradiction of sinners," it neither pined nor collapsed. It led from Divine immortality to human agonies and dissolution, for the victim was bound to the cross not by the nails of the military executioner, but the "cords of love." It loved repulsive unloveliness, and, unnourished by reciprocated attachment, its ardour was unquenched, nay, is unquenchable, for it is changeless as the bosom in which it dwells. Thus it may be known, while yet it "passeth knowledge"; thus it may be experimentally known, while still in its origin and glory it surpasses comprehension, and presents new and newer phases to the loving and inquiring spirit. For one may drink of the spring and be refreshed, and his eye may take in at one view its extent and circuit, while he may be able neither to fathom the depth nor mete out the volume of the ocean whence it has its origin.[13]

The ultimate goal in view of all that Paul prays is that we "may be filled with all the fullness of God" (v. 19b; see 4:13). That is the standard or level to which we are to be filled. What does *that* do to our low expectations of what is available to us in this life?

But *with what* are we to be filled? To what does the word *fullness* refer? Is it

---

13. John Eadie, *Commentary on the Epistle of Paul to the Ephesians* (Minneapolis: James and Klock, 1955).

the "power" of God, his moral perfections, or perhaps his majestic excellencies? Or is Paul speaking again of the "love" of Christ? Maybe it is the Holy Spirit? Certainly, all of these are possible, but there is more in Paul's mind. Note well: they are to be filled *by God*, "and presumably if they are to be filled up to the fullness of God, it is *with this fullness* [emphasis mine] that they are to be filled."[14] In some sense, then, it is with the *radiant power and presence of God himself* that we are to be filled, the measure of which is *God himself!* Whereas the church as Christ's body already shares in, embodies, and expresses his fullness (Eph. 1:23), we have not yet experienced the plenitude of God in the way that is available for us. That is why Paul now prays as he does. "What the Church already is in principle, it is increasingly to realize in its experience."[15]

Paul's Doxological Response (3:20–21)

Have you ever felt that perhaps you crossed a line in what you asked of God in prayer? Have you recoiled in fear that what you brought to the throne of grace was far beyond God's ability to provide? If so, stop it! Bring to God your most audacious and seemingly outlandish petitions. Why shouldn't you, if what Paul is about to say of God is true? O'Brien is correct when he says, "It is impossible to ask for too much since the Father's giving exceeds their capacity for asking or even imagining."[16]

Paul's effusive praise of God reflects the unbounded bounty of his ability to bless his people in response to their prayers. This doxological outburst should forever put to rest your concerns about God's power to do for you what needs to be done. God, says Paul, can *do* or work, for he is neither idle nor inactive, nor dead (contrast the dumb idols in Ps. 115:1–8).

He is able to do what we *ask*, for he hears and answers the very prayers that he commands we pray! As we've seen before, when it is God's will to bestow a blessing, he graciously incites the human heart to ask for it.

He is also able to do what we ask or *think*, for he reads our thoughts, and sometimes we imagine things which we are afraid to articulate and therefore do not ask. In other words, his ability to provide for us must never be measured by the limits of our spoken requests.

---

14. Lincoln, *Ephesians*, 214.
15. Lincoln, *Ephesians*, 214.
16. O'Brien, *Ephesians*, 266.

He is able to do *all* that we ask or think, for he knows it all and can perform it all. There is nothing that is proper for us to have that transcends or outstrips his power to perform.

He is able to do *more . . . than* (*hyper*, "beyond") all that we ask or think, for his expectations are higher than ours.

He is able to do much more, or *more abundantly*, than all that we ask or think, for he does not give his grace by calculated measure.

He is able to do very much more, *far more abundantly*, than all that we ask or think, for he is a God of superabundance. The single Greek word that stands behind this idea, *huperekperissou* (see 1 Thess. 3:10; 5:13), has the idea of an extraordinary degree, considerable excess beyond expectations, etc.

And all that he does he does by virtue of his power that even now energetically works within us. We must never envision God's gracious power as some free-floating energy outside of our own experience. The place where God's power resides and operates is "within us"! God does not ask us merely to marvel at how his power achieves great tasks elsewhere, out there, somewhere. His omnipotent strength has been infused into our innermost being. This is what Paul alluded to earlier in Ephesians 1 where he spoke of "the immeasurable greatness of his power toward us who believe" (Eph. 1:19), the "great might" of God "that he worked in Christ when he raised him from the dead and seated him at his right hand in the heavenly places" (Eph. 1:20). This, and nothing less, is the power even now at work in you and me to hear and answer our most outlandish requests.

That God can do this for weak, broken people through his power that dwells within us is cause for the highest praise. "To him be glory," shouts Paul! That this "glory" should be revealed "in Christ Jesus throughout all generations, forever and ever" makes perfectly good sense (3:21). But of all the places one might think God would choose to reveal and embody and express his manifest glory, "in the church" hardly seems to qualify. Yet, notwithstanding all its weaknesses, divisions, pettiness, and failures, the gathered body of Christ Jesus is the vehicle in and through which God's power is displayed (see Eph. 1:22–23; 2:7, 22; 3:10).

CHAPTER 11

Warfare Prayer

D o those two words really go together? Are they not mutually exclusive? After all, I thought prayer was a calm, serene, devotional experience that is incompatible with the violent nature of war? Prayer is about contemplation, not conflict. Right? Well, not always. In most instances I would agree, but not when it comes to our war with Satan. In fact, I would argue that the victory we achieve over the Enemy will only come about by means of perseverance in prayer. In other words, it is only as we turn to God in prayer, over and over again, that we overcome Satan's seductions. Here is a much-needed reminder from John Piper:

> Prayer is primarily a wartime walkie-talkie for the mission of the church as it advances against the powers of darkness and unbelief. It is not surprising that prayer malfunctions when we try to make it a domestic intercom to call upstairs for more comforts in the den. God has given us prayer as a wartime walkie-talkie so that we can call headquarters for everything we need as the kingdom of Christ advances in the world.[1]

Why does God command us to pray when we are under attack by our spiritual enemy?[2] Why utilize prayer as the means for our victory in spiritual warfare? Couldn't God shut down the devil without our asking him to give

---

1. John Piper, *Let the Nations Be Glad! The Supremacy of God in Missions*, 2nd ed. (Grand Rapids: Baker Academic, 2007), 45.
2. Some of what follows below is adapted from my book, *Understanding Spiritual Warfare: A Comprehensive Guide* (Grand Rapids: Zondervan, 2021).

us strength, power, wisdom, and incentive to stand firm in our faith? Yes. *But prayer magnifies him more.* Prayer puts God on display as the only one worthy of our devotion and trust. When you are laid up, sick, and helpless, and you need someone to clean your house and mow the grass and bring food to your kitchen so you can eat, and someone who cares about you answers your phone call for help and says, "Of course, I'd be delighted to help," who gets the glory? Not you. You're weak and helpless and all you did was call for the assistance of another. The glory and praise go to the one who rushes to your side and, in generosity and kindness, provides you with all you need. That is why God wants us to pray during seasons of spiritual attack. It magnifies him as the one who comes to our aid. It honors him as the only one powerful enough to pull it off. It shines a light on his mercy and all-sufficiency to do what only he can do for us.

I think God ordains prayer during spiritual warfare for another reason: he wants us to *partner with him* in securing the victory. When, by God's grace, we stand firm by always praying, we gain far more joy and satisfaction than if we did nothing. God doesn't say to us, "Stand over there and do nothing." He says, "Come to me and ask for all the resources and spiritual strength needed to defeat your Enemy." The principle here is that except on rare occasions, God will not intervene to give you daily victory unless you ask him to. If Paul believed that God would give him strength, clarity, and courage to preach apart from the intercessory prayers of the Ephesian church, he would never have written this in Ephesians 6:18–20:

> [Pray] at all times in the Spirit, with all prayer and supplication. To that end, keep alert with all perseverance, making supplication for all the saints, and also for me, that words may be given to me in opening my mouth boldly to proclaim the mystery of the gospel, for which I am an ambassador in chains, that I may declare it boldly, as I ought to speak.

So, let's unpack this passage to see what insights we can glean from Paul's urgent exhortation.

The Four "Alls" of Prayer

Before we dive into this text, we first need to understand how it relates to what has preceded in Ephesians 6:10–17. Contrary to what some have said, prayer is not the seventh piece of spiritual armor. Nor is it how we wield the sword of the Spirit (the Word of God). Grammatically, both "praying" and "keeping alert" (v. 18) are connected with the verb "stand" all the way back in verse 14. In other words, prayer is what characterizes and permeates the whole of the Christian soldier's activity: "Take your stand, praying. . . . Put on the belt of truth, praying. . . . Put on the breastplate of righteousness, as you pray," and so on. Prayer is the power behind the armor. Prayer is what makes the armor effective in battle. You will probably have little success in putting it on and standing firm if you fail to pray as Paul exhorts us to pray in verses 18–20.

Our approach to what Paul says here will be to highlight the four times he uses the word *all*.

He first tells us that we are to pray "with all prayer and supplication" (v. 18a). In other words, prayer is not monolithic. It is not all the same. There is a wide variety of prayers that God calls upon us to employ. The different kinds or types of prayer include silent prayer, audible prayer, public prayer, private prayer, short and long prayers, prayer with fasting, prayer with feasting, prayer with praise, petition, intercession, rebuke, doctrinal praying, emotional praying, prayer in tongues, resisting-the-enemy praying, prayers of thanksgiving, prayers of confession, prayer for healing, prayers for help, and prayers for courage. As prayer pertains specifically to spiritual warfare, consider six forms it may assume.

First of all, there is prayer for ourselves and for others to be given insight and understanding into who we are in Christ and what is ours through faith (Eph. 1:15ff.). Knowing who you are in Jesus, knowing what he has accomplished for you by his life, death, and resurrection, is a powerful weapon to use in your battle with the enemy. Satan will always lie to you about who you are. If he can undermine and sow doubt in your mind about what Christ has done in making you into a child of God, he can win.

There are prayers of resistance and rebuke of the enemy. Tom White provides this example:

> Satan, I rebuke you in the authority of Jesus Christ. I declare your works in my life destroyed. Jesus triumphed over you in the wilderness, on the cross, and in the grave. His resurrection has sealed your fate. I triumph over you now in the strength of his name. I resist and rebuke your efforts to oppress,

afflict, or deceive me. I remove from you the right to rob me of the joy and fruit of my salvation. Through the power of the blood of Calvary, I command all powers of darkness assigned to me, sent to me, or surrounding me now, to leave. Go where Jesus Christ orders you to go, never to return.[3]

There are prayers of protection in which we ask God to shield and support us. One such prayer may sound like this:

Lord, I commend and entrust _____ into your watchful care. May your glory surround and protect him/her. May you drive away the enemy and deliver him/her from all evil and temptation and every attack of the evil one.

I also recommend that you pray for the places where you go, stay, or live (especially when traveling or in a strange location). I will never forget when I first met Jack Taylor. I picked him up at the Kansas City airport and dropped him off at his hotel. He insisted that I come with him to his room. He said he never stays in a hotel room without praying. He asked me to get down on my knees with him and he prayed:

Father in heaven, would you by your Spirit cleanse and purify this room. Whatever sins have been committed here, I ask that I be shielded from any and all defilement. Whatever evil spirits were invoked or may have taken up residence in this room, by the authority of Jesus Christ I command that they leave. If pornography was viewed in this room, or if adultery was committed in this room, I ask that you drive away all lingering spiritual influence that may have come as a result. In the name of Jesus, I pray. Amen!

Tom White gives us yet another prayer to use in your home or any other place where you may spend extended periods of time:

Lord, I claim this place for your purposes. I stand on the truth of your Word: "The scepter of wickedness shall not rest on the land allotted to the righteous" (Ps. 125:3). I believe you have given me this place. I dedicate it to you, and ask you to fill it with your holy presence. I separate myself

---

3. Thomas B. White, *The Believer's Guide to Spiritual Warfare* (Ventura, CA: Regal, 1990), 116.

from any iniquity that has occurred here in past times. I apply the power of Jesus' blood to remove any desecration of God's name in this place. I ask you, in Jesus' authority, to set watching angels around this property for your purposes, protecting your servant from the work of the evil one.[4]

There is prayer for those afflicted and oppressed when you are ministering to them. A few things that you might wish to pray are:

1. that the demon(s) afflicting this person would be prevented from communicating with other demons or with Satan himself;
2. that the Holy Spirit would confuse and weaken the grip that any and all demons might have on this person;
3. that the person would be strengthened in their faith to understand their position and identity in Christ and to trust and obey the Word, even if their feelings or experience might be different from what Scripture says about them;
4. that the person may be able to distinguish between their thoughts and feelings and the thoughts and feelings of demons; in other words, pray that the individual might have discernment to know the difference between their own ideas and those ideas suggested to them by the Enemy;
5. that God would protect and guide his child and set angelic forces at work to break up every scheme of the enemy.[5]

We should also pray for angelic support, ministry, and protection. If that sounds weird to you, may I remind you that after Jesus had been tempted by the devil himself, we are told that "angels came and were ministering to him" (Matt. 4:11). We are told in Daniel 10:10–21 that an angel was "sent" (Dan. 10:11) to Daniel to give him understanding in God's purposes. The angel "touched" Daniel and "strengthened" him (Dan. 10:18). He told him, "fear not, peace be with you; be strong and of good courage" (Dan. 10:19). And Daniel responded by saying, "as he spoke to me, I was strengthened" (Dan. 10:19; see Acts 12:5–8).

Don't be obsessed with "how" you pray. This betrays the assumption that

---

4. White, *The Believer's Guide to Spiritual Warfare*, 18–19.
5. These five suggestions are adapted from Fred Dickason, *Demon Possession and the Christian* (Chicago: Moody Press, 1987), 255–56.

prayer is a kind of religious formula or magical incantation that requires just the right words to prevail. People often think that the wrong words will anger God, frustrate him, and provoke him to say no to their requests.

Paul's second use of the word *all* in relation to prayer is found in his exhortation that we always pray "in the Spirit" (Eph. 6:18b). Let's begin by reminding ourselves that prayer is not the only thing that Christians are called upon to do "in the Spirit" or "by the Spirit." We are to "walk" in the Spirit (Gal. 5:16), put to death the deeds of the body in the Spirit (Rom. 8:13), worship in the Spirit (Phil. 3:3), and give thanks to God in the Spirit (1 Cor. 14:16). Even our responsibility to restore a wayward brother is to be carried out in the Spirit (Gal. 6:1).

A few other texts use the same phrase, "in the Spirit." We are told in Luke 10:21 that Jesus "rejoiced in the Holy Spirit." Mark refers to King David as declaring "in the Holy Spirit" the truth of Psalm 110 (Mark 12:36). And Paul reminds the Corinthians that "no one speaking in the Spirit of God ever says 'Jesus is accursed!'" (1 Cor. 12:3). And again, in the same verse, "No one can say 'Jesus is Lord' except in the Holy Spirit."

In each case, to do something in or by the Spirit clearly means to do so under the Spirit's influence, by the Spirit's empowering presence, or in response to the Spirit's guidance and prompting. It should be taken in contrast with any exercise done in the power of one's own human flesh or willpower alone. There are two occasions where prayer is specifically said to be "in the Spirit":

> Praying at all times *in the Spirit*, with all prayer and supplication. To that end, keep alert with all perseverance, making supplication for all the saints. (Eph. 6:18, emphasis mine)

> But you, beloved, building yourselves up in your most holy faith and praying *in the Holy Spirit*, keep yourselves in the love of God, waiting for the mercy of our Lord Jesus Christ that leads to eternal life. (Jude 20–21)

It is also the case that to pray in tongues is to do so "in/by" the Spirit.

> For one who speaks in a tongue speaks not to men but to God; for no one understands him, but he utters mysteries *in the Spirit*. (1 Cor. 14:2)

In 1 Corinthians 14:14–16 Paul speaks repeatedly about praying in, with, and by "the Spirit." If you have received the gift of tongues, when you pray in your new language, you are praying "in the Spirit." If you do not have the gift of tongues, you can still pray "in the Spirit" every time you come to the throne of grace. In other words, praying "in the Spirit" includes praying in tongues but is not restricted to it.

Romans 8:26–27 is yet another way in which we are to pray "in the Spirit." Given that we do not know what or how to pray, to pray in the Spirit is to pray confidently that the Spirit is communicating accurately to the Father. In some cases, our burdens are so great that we can't find the right words, but we groan toward God.

So, considering all this, here is what praying in the Spirit means.

We pray "in the Spirit" when we *trust the Spirit to bring to mind* the things for which we should make supplication. Thus, you must pray with an ear turned to heaven. Be silent, listen, and wait for the Spirit's prompting.

To "pray in the Spirit" is to bring requests and supplications to God *in the strength* the Holy Spirit provides. Prayer is hard. To attempt it for a prolonged period in your own power is disastrous. So, start by asking the Spirit to empower you, to fill you with his divine energy, so that you may "strive together" (Rom. 15:30–33) with other believers in prayer.

Or the Spirit is the one at whose *prompting or urging* one is to pray. You suddenly find yourself awakened to some need or urgent crisis, and you pray. Or the Spirit is the one whom we *trust to accurately represent* us at the throne of grace. Or the Spirit is the one who supplies the endurance and energy to *persevere* in prayer rather than so quickly giving up, as we are prone to do. The Spirit energizes our hearts to continually come to God as one who always keeps his promises. And he awakens us to our desperate need for what God alone can provide.

Praying "in the Spirit" means that the Holy Spirit moves and guides our prayers. We are being *prompted* to pray by the Spirit; he's awakening it and moving it. And the things that we pray for *are being shaped and determined by the Spirit*. So, it's his power that carries the prayer, and it's his leading that guides it. And then I think of Romans 8:15–16, where Paul says, "You have received the Spirit of adoption as sons, by whom we cry [that is, we pray], 'Abba! Father!' The Spirit himself bears witness with our spirit that we are children of God." In other words, the Spirit works in our heart to awaken the authentic cry and prayer: "Father! Father!" Then everything that we say in that Spirit, in faith that he's our Father, follows as a work of the Spirit. I wouldn't be crying as a dependent, helpless child toward God as my Father if the Spirit weren't working in my life.

One of the great functions of the Spirit in prayer is to *guard us from praying with bad motives and for wrong things*. Jesus taught us to put "hallowed be your name" at the front, as the priority, of our prayers (Matt. 6:9). That's what the Holy Spirit repeatedly does. He shapes our prayers with the right motives and priorities, with a passion for God's supremacy.

The Final Two "Alls"

The third time Paul uses the word *all* is in his exhortation that we are to pray alertly "with all perseverance" (Eph 6:18c). Simply put, never give up! Never quit! Pray without ceasing (1 Thess. 5:17)! Don't let physical exhaustion get the better of you. Don't be discouraged. Don't grow weary. Resist the temptation to think that God isn't listening or, even worse, that he doesn't care.

Paul concludes by exhorting us to pray for "all the saints" (v. 18d). Yes, that means everywhere, for everyone. Out of sight, but never out of mind or heart. I'm often encouraged by the fact that, although Paul had never visited the church in Colossae and probably couldn't recognize a single face, he prayed passionately for them (Col. 2:1–5). Paul generally closes his letters with a request for prayer for himself (see Rom. 15:30–32; Col. 4:3; 1 Thess. 5:25; 2 Thess. 3:1–2; see also 2 Cor. 1:11; Phil. 1:19). "Like every nervous preacher, he desires 'the liberty of the Spirit to express it (i.e., the gospel) freely, clearly, and boldly."[6]

Asking God for an Infusion of Divine Strength

As prayer pertains specifically to spiritual warfare, Paul makes a powerfully important point in Ephesians 6:10. There, he urges us to be filled and sustained by the strength of God. The phrase "be strong" in the Lord is best taken as a passive: "be strengthened" or "be made strong" (with the implication,

---

6. O'Brien, *Ephesians*, 487.

"by God"; cf. 3:16). The simple exhortation "be strong!" is both dangerous and useless. Self-reliance in spiritual warfare is suicidal. Believers do not strengthen themselves. Our strength must come from an external source, namely, the Lord. The strength of an earthly general is in his troops. But in the Christian life, the strength of the troops is in their general (see Josh. 1:6–9, esp. v. 9b). The exhortation to Joshua to "be strong and courageous" is grounded in the reassuring promise that "the LORD your God is with you wherever you go" (v. 9b). There are numerous texts where we find this same emphasis on being strengthened by God:

> And David was greatly distressed, for the people spoke of stoning him, because all the people were bitter in soul, each for his sons and daughters. But David strengthened himself in the LORD his God. (1 Sam. 30:6)

> And he said, "Listen, all Judah and inhabitants of Jerusalem and King Jehoshaphat: Thus says the LORD to you, 'Do not be afraid and do not be dismayed at this great horde, for the battle is not yours but God's.'" (2 Chron. 20:15)

> I love you, O LORD, my strength. (Ps. 18:1)

> For who is God, but the LORD?
>   And who is a rock, except our God?—
> the God who equipped me with strength
>   and made my way blameless. (Ps. 18:31–32)

> For you equipped me with strength for the battle;
>   you made those who rise against me sink under me. (Ps. 18:39)

> The LORD is my strength and my shield;
>   in him my heart trusts, and I am helped;
> my heart exults,
>   and with my song I give thanks to him. (Ps. 28:7)

> The LORD is the strength of his people;
>   he is the saving refuge of his anointed. (Ps. 28:8)

But I will sing of your strength;
>
> I will sing aloud of your steadfast love in the morning.
>
> For you have been to me a fortress
>
> and a refuge in the day of my distress.
>
> O my Strength, I will sing praises to you,
>
> for you, O God, are my fortress,
>
> the God who shows me steadfast love. (Ps. 59:16–17)

Awesome is God from his sanctuary;
>
> the God of Israel—he is the one who gives power and strength
>
> to his people.
>
> Blessed be God! (Ps. 68:35)

Turn to me and be gracious to me;
>
> give your strength to your servant,
>
> and save the son of your maidservant. (Ps. 86:16)

The LORD is my strength and my song;
>
> he has become my salvation. (Ps. 118:14)

Blessed be the LORD, my rock,
>
> who trains my hands for war,
>
> and my fingers for battle;
>
> he is my steadfast love and my fortress,
>
> my stronghold and my deliverer,
>
> my shield and he in whom I take refuge,
>
> who subdues peoples under me. (Ps. 144:1–2)

With that quality and commitment of strength from the Lord, always available to those who ask, why in the world would we ever strive in our own power? This "strength" to which Paul refers is none other than the "strength" he described in Ephesians 1:19ff. which raised Jesus from the dead and exalted him above all authority! The same trio of Greek terms is used in both passages: *dunamis*, *kratos*, and *ischus* (cf. Eph. 3:16; Col. 1:11, 29). So, how strong is God? Is he weaker now than he was in the first century? Have his spiritual muscles atrophied? Is God out of shape?

Praying against Satan and His Schemes[7]

There are certain things about prayer that we all know to be true. We know, for example, that we are to pray to God the Father, in the name of God the Son, and through the sustaining power of God the Holy Spirit. We know that we are to come to the throne of grace "with confidence" so "that we may receive mercy and find grace to help in time of need" (Heb. 4:16). And Jesus himself reminded us that he delights in answering our prayers because in this way "the Father may be glorified in the Son" (John 14:13). What we need to address is how prayer factors into our obedience to the command that if we "resist" Satan "he will flee" from us (James 4:7).

We may be certain of this: at no time are we to pray *for*, or on behalf of, Satan. As noted above, Scripture repeatedly assures us that his eternal destiny in the lake of fire is sealed and irreversible. Neither Satan nor his demons are capable of repentance. Salvation has not been provided for them. Indeed, "it is not angels that [Christ] helps, but he helps the offspring of Abraham" (Heb. 2:16). The cross is the instrument of Satan's defeat, not his redemption (Heb. 2:14–15; Col. 2:13–15).

Scripture is equally clear that we are not to pray *to* Satan. There is nothing he would do for us but evil, and it is to God alone that we bring our many requests. To petition Satan or to pray to him for his presence and power is what only those who honor him as "lord" would dare to do. So, how does prayer relate to Satan and the demonic hosts? In what ways should we pray against him?

We know that Satan has a plan. Although sinful, he is not stupid. He does not act haphazardly or without purpose. Paul states clearly in 2 Corinthians 2:10–11 that Satan has "designs"—a strategy, an agenda, to undermine unity in the church in that city (and no doubt in every city, yours included). This is similar to what the apostle says in Ephesians 6:11 concerning the "schemes" (literally, *methodia* = methods) of the devil. In other words, he is cunning and wily and employs carefully orchestrated stratagems in his assault against Christian men and women and the local church. Satan energizes and shapes worldly value systems, institutions, organizations, philosophical movements,

---

7. The following is an adaptation of what was originally published on January 28, 2020, at https://www.desiringgod.org/articles/how-to-pray-against-satan, and later in my book, *Understanding Spiritual Warfare: A Comprehensive Guide* (Grand Rapids: Zondervan, 2021), and is used here with permission.

and political, social, and economic systems. Satan sets his goals and then utilizes and exploits the most effective means while avoiding all obstacles to reach his diabolical ends.

We know that Satan works in active opposition to the gospel. Paul says that he blinds the minds of the unbelieving lest they should see the glory of the gospel and be saved (2 Cor. 4:4). He does so by distracting them when the gospel is presented and by stirring up hostility and suspicion in the minds of those to whom we preach. Thus, when we pray, we should beseech God to shine in their hearts "the light of the knowledge of the glory of God in the face of Jesus Christ" (2 Cor. 4:6) and to overcome all resistance to the truth of what Christ has done for sinners.

Satan "hindered" the apostle Paul from visiting the church in Thessalonica (1 Thess. 2:18). We don't know by what means he did this, but surely our prayers should be regular for global missionaries who are making every effort to penetrate areas and people groups who do not yet have the gospel message.

There are other ways in which Satan seeks to undermine our ministries and to lead us to question the goodness of God. He is, on occasion, the source of sickness (Matt. 8:16; Mark 9:17–18; Luke 13:10–17; Acts 10:38) and uses the fear of death to hold us in bondage (Heb. 2:14–15). There are times when he might insert sinful plans or purposes into our hearts to thwart God's designs (Matt. 16:21–23; John 13:2; Acts 5:3).

Once again, knowing the strategy of the enemy will give focus to our requests that God work in us to resist all of Satan's nefarious efforts to wreak havoc in our souls. If Satan produces in us the fear of death, we should seek God's help to remind us of the certainty of our hope of eternal life. If Satan can be the cause of certain physical afflictions, we must relentlessly ask God for "gifts of healing" (1 Cor. 12:9) to bring restoration.

When Satan sought permission to "sift" Peter like wheat (Luke 22:31), Jesus prayed for his apostle that his faith might not fail (Luke 22:32). Should we not pray for ourselves and others in the same manner? Other texts indicate that Satan may well incite persecution of God's people (1 Peter 5:8–9; Rev. 2:10), as well as provoke their imprisonment and cause their martyrdom. Far from crushing our hopes, this reality should drive us with increasing intensity and regularity to the throne of God's grace to ask for his sustaining power and the ability to endure with joy (Col. 1:11).

Jesus himself prayed for our unity (John 17:15, 20–21), knowing full well that Satan often seeks to incite disunity and division in the body of Christ (2 Cor. 2:10–11). This latter text suggests that Satan was determined to exploit the reluctance of certain believers in Corinth to forgive and restore the wayward, but now repentant, brother in their midst. Satan's design was to humiliate the repentant sinner and perhaps drive him to despair. Since Paul alerts us to this sort of Satanic design, our prayers should be for the Holy Spirit to unite our hearts when it comes to restoring a believer and unity of heart and mind in the body of Christ.

Paul was also concerned that Satan would take advantage of the decision by a husband and wife to temporarily refrain from sexual relations to devote themselves to prayer (1 Cor. 7:5). It is consistent with Satan's wickedness that he would take an otherwise godly intention and exploit it for his own evil purposes. Should not the prayers of God's people then be for the strength and commitment of married couples to remain faithful and pure in their sexual relationship? For unity in the church, the home, and the marriage bed?

One of the more instructive texts on the activity of Satan is also found in Paul's letter to the Ephesians. He exhorts us to "be angry and do not sin; do not let the sun go down on your anger, and give no opportunity to the devil" (Eph. 4:26–27). Satan will seek every opportunity to take advantage of our sinful inclinations, in this case, the destructive power of anger in our relationships with one another (and especially in marriage) to divide us.

Satan is not blamed for creating our anger, but he intensifies and expands its presence in our hearts when we delay reconciliation or withhold forgiveness. We must, therefore, be quick to pray and seek God's help, in the name of unity, by humbling ourselves when relational friction occurs.

It seems quite clear, therefore, that to pray effectively against Satan's activity, we must be cognizant of the many ways he seeks to destroy our faith. As Paul wrote to the Corinthians, we do not want to "be outwitted by Satan" which will only happen if we remain "ignorant of his designs" (2 Cor. 2:11). Some may mistakenly think that to pray against Satan's many schemes or designs is a "fear-based" approach to Christian living. Quite to the contrary, it is borne of an attitude of unwavering confidence in God's goodness and power to supply his children with every spiritual resource necessary to grow in conformity to Christ Jesus. May we never forget, in all our prayers, that "he who is in you is greater than he who is in the world" (1 John 4:4).

CHAPTER 12

How an Apostle Prays Is How We Should Pray

I'm often asked why studying how the apostle Paul (or Peter, John, etc.) prayed for people in the early church is important. The answer, at least to me, is obvious. I need to know what matters most to God. What matters most to me is often misguided and needs serious redirection. My prayers are often filled with requests for material prosperity, increased notoriety, and other selfish concerns. But when I see what burdened the heart of the apostles, I also see what I most need. Studying such prayers is an exercise in rebuke and instruction. I'm simultaneously challenged to repent of my self-centered demands and taught what is most needful in my life and the lives of others.

With that in mind, let's look closely at how Paul prayed for the Christians in the church at Philippi.

> I thank my God in all my remembrance of you, always in every prayer of mine for you all making my prayer with joy, because of your partnership in the gospel from the first day until now. And I am sure of this, that he who began a good work in you will bring it to completion at the day of Jesus Christ. It is right for me to feel this way about you all, because I hold you in my heart, for you are all partakers with me of grace, both in my imprisonment and in the defense and confirmation of the gospel. For God is my witness, how I yearn for you all with the affection of Christ Jesus. And it is my prayer that your love may abound more and more, with knowledge and all discernment, so that you may approve what is

excellent, and so be pure and blameless for the day of Christ, filled with the fruit of righteousness that comes through Jesus Christ, to the glory and praise of God. (Phil. 1:3–11)

The first thing that I notice is that he prayed for them constantly. I can't even begin to think of Paul as the sort of man who would pull the hypocritical stunt that you and I are so often guilty of perpetrating on one another. How many times have you said to another Christian, perhaps in passing in the café or down the hall, "It was good to see you; I'll pray for you," all the while knowing you have absolutely no intention of doing any such thing?

May I be so bold as to challenge you, even as I challenge my own soul, that if you promise to pray for another believer, you actually carry through with your pledge. And may you not do it as a perfunctory performance, because you feel morally obligated, or because you made a promise and think *by golly, I'm going to keep my word whether I feel like it or not.* Do it as Paul did, "with joy" (Phil. 1:4).

So you say, "But Sam, life's hard, and time is short, and my schedule is crammed full of things I can no longer afford to ignore. I might be able to devote a few minutes each day to praying for the needs of people, but how am I expected to do it with joy?"

Let me remind you of something. Paul isn't writing this letter from an air-conditioned three-bedroom, two-bath, two-car-garage home in a safe neighborhood in your hometown. He's writing this from a dark, damp, cramped prison cell, most likely in either Rome or Caesarea. His freedom has been taken from him. His food is barely adequate to keep him alive. He doesn't know if he will live or die. Yet he prays for them and does so joyfully. How?

The answer is *the gospel!* When the human heart is gripped with the transcendent truth and unshakable reality of what God has done for us in Jesus Christ, no amount of pain or discomfort or opposition can undermine the deep and abiding joy that it brings. All that Paul had to do to press through the pain and the disappointment of imprisonment was to think about what God had done to secure forgiveness and eternal salvation, not only for himself but for the Philippians. I know this because of what follows in verse 5. This brings us to the second point of emphasis.

Paul is filled with gratitude and prays fervently and joyfully for the

Philippians because they share a common faith in the gospel, a unified commitment to suffer, sacrifice, and support its spread with their finances. This is his point in verse 5 where he speaks of their "partnership in the gospel from the first day until now." He's delighted that they are a part of his life and that he is part of theirs. So, when he prays for them, he is overcome with "joy" as he reflects on how they have joined with him in living for the gospel, giving for the gospel, defending the gospel, and, in Paul's case, eventually dying for the gospel.

Notice again that Paul doesn't have in mind here some superficial friendship based on sharing a common hobby or because of the patriotic fervor they share that comes from knowing they are all Roman citizens. It is because they are united in their belief in the gospel! The grace of God in Jesus Christ is the ground and glue of their love one for another.

Moreover, his joyful gratitude to God is also based on his confidence that "he who began a good work in you will bring it to completion at the day of Jesus Christ" (v. 6). Paul had seen his fair share of people who loudly proclaimed their faith in Jesus only later to betray the fact that they never truly knew him as Lord and Savior. But he is confident beyond all doubt that what God had started in the lives of the Philippians, he would, in fact, finish and bring to consummation. That isn't to say they wouldn't face obstacles to Christian growth. It isn't to say that Satan had given up trying to deceive them and derail their faith. It isn't to say that the Philippians had graduated into some super-spiritual condition that put them beyond the reach of temptation and sin.

Neither is it to say that they need not strive and maintain their spiritual diligence and pursue holiness. Rather, it is to say that God is faithful to his work. It is to say that God will do whatever it takes to uphold the Philippians in their faith and your faith in Jesus. It is to say that God will persevere in his commitment to supply them (and you) with whatever it takes so that our confidence in Christ would not fail or falter and the work of grace he began would ultimately be brought to its proper goal when Jesus returns.

The assurance that fills Paul's heart and accounts in part for the joy that floods his prayers on their behalf is that God will do whatever it takes to guarantee that no born-again child of God will ever lapse into unbelief and apostasy. That isn't to say God's people won't at times wander away, spiritually drift, and even fall into a backslidden and bitter state of soul. It is to say that their loving, heavenly Father will never let them fall completely out of his loving arms.

Take this text right now and impress its truth on your heart. I'm thinking particularly of you who are struggling with doubts about where you stand with God. You're plagued by fear and anxiety that God has given up on you. He's quite simply had enough; he's had his fill of you and your pathetic efforts to remain true to him. Listen to me. No, listen to *God* speaking to you through Paul. *Whatever God starts, he finishes. Whatever God starts, he finishes. Whatever God starts, he finishes.* I pray this truth will echo repeatedly in your mind and spirit, and you will be energized to get back in the race and resume the battle with the world, the flesh, and the devil, renewed with the confident assurance that they can't win!

This is why I say over and over again *that the reason why Christians persevere in their faith is because God preserves them in it.* God will not give up on the elect, he will not abandon them with the job only half done, and he will not permit any obstacle or opposition to stand in the way of bringing all his children into the full inheritance of what he has promised in Jesus.

We also see here that because the Philippians share a common faith in the gospel with Paul, he loves them with a heartfelt and unyielding passion (vv. 7–8). Let's note how this affection is felt and described.

Paul says, "I hold you in my heart" (v. 7). I carry you around not simply in my thoughts but in the depths of my soul, in the center of my being. You are always and ever dear to me! The basis for this abiding affection is again that these Philippian believers had partaken with Paul of God's saving and sustaining grace. And how did he know this? On what basis does his confidence rest? Paul knew this to be true because when he was thrown into prison, it would have been so easy for them to run and hide and protect their own backsides. Instead, they stood with him in defense of the gospel even when it threatened their own lives and freedom.

The depth of passion and affection of genuine Christian fellowship is again stated in more intensely personal terms in verse 8: "God is my witness, how I yearn for you all with the affection of Christ Jesus." It's not clear why Paul felt compelled to call God as his witness. Perhaps he felt inadequate to express his true feelings and thus calls on God to help him. Or maybe the enormity of his love deserved more than his own testimony. Others think that some in the church at Philippi doubted his motives toward them, and thus Paul is saying, "If my expression of affection for you isn't true, may God judge me now!"

In any case, he wants them to know how he "yearns" for them, a strong and emotionally charged term used to describe how desperate he is to see them again. But the important thing here isn't the intensity of his love but its quality—he loves them and yearns for them "with the affection of Christ Jesus" (v. 8b). I think what he means by this is that his love for them originates in Christ's love both for him and them. In other words, he is implicitly referring to the gospel yet again! We love only because Christ first loved us. But more than that, his love for them is of the same quality or kind as the love Jesus has for us. Think about how much Jesus loves you. Reflect on the depths of a love that would lead him to the cross on your behalf. Meditate on how patient and kind and compassionate and forgiving he is toward us all. That, says Paul, is the same love I have for you.

The Content of Paul's Petitions

In verses 9–11, we see the substance of Paul's supplication on behalf of the Philippian believers. The first thing he highlights is their love for one another.

Tertullian (AD 200) was one of the greatest of the early church fathers and was the first man to use the word *Trinity* to describe the nature of God as Father, Son, and Holy Spirit. He lived and wrote at a time when opposition to Christianity and the church was intensifying. Although Tertullian was an apologist, devoting himself to defining and defending the Christian faith against its critics, he was quick to point out that it wasn't any particular theological or philosophical argument that would ultimately persuade pagans of the truth about Jesus. Rather it was the seemingly inexplicable love that Christians had for one another that initially baffled and finally captivated non-Christians. In one memorable statement, Tertullian said this:

It is mainly the deeds of a love so noble that lead many to put a brand upon us. *"See,"* they say, *"[see] how they love one another, . . . how they are ready even to die for one another!"* No tragedy causes trouble in our brotherhood, [and] the family possessions, which generally destroy brotherhood among you, create fraternal bonds among us. *One in mind and soul, we do not hesitate to share our earthly goods with one another.* All things are common among us [except] our wives. (*Apology* 39)

This really shouldn't come as any surprise to us, given that it was Jesus who said, "By this all people will know that you are my disciples, if you have love for one another" (John 13:35). Neither should we be surprised that when Paul finally gets around to defining the content of his prayers for the Philippians, he puts their love for one another at the center of it. Here in Philippians 1:9 Paul unpacks precisely what he had in mind when he said in verses 3–6 that he prayed for the Philippians. Here is the content of his intercession!

One of the more convicting things about reading prayers like that is what we discover about his priorities and hopefully ours as well. While nothing is off-limits in prayer, certain things should be front and center. Later in Philippians 4:6, Paul will tell us that "in everything by prayer and supplication with thanksgiving let your requests be made known to God." In other words, we are to bring all our needs, fears, and desires to God in prayer.

However, when we actually read the prayers Paul himself prayed, they are decidedly different from what we typically pray about. You hear nothing of prayers for money, increased respect, advancement in one's career, or the desire for one's favorite sports team to emerge victorious. Rather, you hear things like we just read here in Philippians 1, where Paul prays for an increase in love, knowledge, discernment, purity, righteousness, and the glory of God.

I trust the Holy Spirit can bring whatever conviction we need to feel about how we pray both for ourselves and others. Several things should be noted about Paul's prayer for the Philippians.

Love for One Another (and God)

Paul does not tell us whether this love is to be for God or one another, probably because he intends both. One thing is certain: any professed love for God that does not find expression in a love for others is hypocrisy! In fact, it is simply impossible. In 1 John 5:1, we are told that "everyone who loves the Father loves whoever has been born of him." So, if you don't love other Christians, you don't love God, no matter how loudly you may insist that you do. You are deceived.

The author of Hebrews makes the same point. He says, "God is not unjust so as to overlook your work and the love that you have shown for his name in serving the saints, as you still do" (Heb. 6:10). How does your love for the name of God display itself? By "serving the saints."

Having said that, I'm persuaded that the primary expression of love that Paul has in mind and for which he prays is that which exists among Christians in the local church. Paul's petition here is like the one we find in 1 Thessalonians 3:12: "May the Lord make you increase and abound in love for one another and for all, as we do for you."

Love in Philippi, Love in Your City

Love already exists and flourishes at Philippi. Paul does not question the sincerity of their affection for him or one another. There is no implied rebuke in this prayer, as if he's subtly suggesting that they had failed to love in the first place. After all, he told us in verse 4 that this prayer was offered in "joy."

Let's not forget that love was in evidence immediately upon the arrival of the gospel in Philippi. As soon as God opened Lydia's heart to receive the gospel, she opened her home to Paul and his companions. And no sooner had the Philippian jailer become a Christian than he attended to Paul's wounds and brought him into his house. And no sooner had Paul and Silas departed from Philippi than the church there began to support them financially.

But he wants to see it increase, deepen, and intensify. We never love perfectly in this life. There are always flaws in our feelings for others and ways in which our generosity, sacrifice, and service for them fall short. As much as we might otherwise prefer, we can never reach a point in our relationship with one another where we feel satisfied and content and think that we've done enough. We can never rest on our laurels of love and say, "Well, I've just about exhausted what is possible in loving this person. They ought to be thankful for what I've done for them." No. Love is never a static achievement but always a dynamic process of growth, expansion, and improvement.

I've had people tell me they came to our church because of the worship, the children's ministry, the missional focus, and even because of the preaching. But I assure you, when non-Christians look upon us from the outside, the one thing that will impress them is how we love one another. They couldn't care less about the excellence of our Sunday services or the precision of our theological understanding. What will captivate their hearts and bring them back for more is how we put aside petty personal preferences, selfish ambition, envy, and competitiveness, and love one another as God in Christ has loved us.

God Has to Make It Happen

Listen again to how Paul said it in 1 Thessalonians 3:12: "May the Lord make you increase and abound in love for one another and for all, as we do for you." If their love is to increase—indeed if our love for one another is to increase—*God has to make it happen.* Yes, we are responsible to love others, to do whatever is needed to clear away obstacles, to extend forgiveness, and to overcome bitterness, jealousy, envy, rivalry, and all the sinful impulses that hinder us from loving others. Yet Paul clearly believed God must be present and prior, working in our hearts to make this possible. After all, *if love were entirely within our power to produce, why would Paul have bothered praying for it?* He goes to the throne of grace and asks God to work in the hearts of these people to alert them to ways in which their love is weak and self-serving, asks him to enlighten their minds to see the depths of how God has loved them in Christ, and pleads with God that his Spirit might convict them, stir them, empower them, and enable them to overcome the defensiveness and selfishness that so often hinders our love for others.

Increase and Abound!

Love can increase far beyond what we think is possible. We may believe that we have loved to the full extent possible for us, that our hearts are stretched to the breaking point, and that we have reached the limit of what is reasonable to ask of a human being. Paul believed love could grow and expand and become increasingly more passionate and authentic and express itself in far more concrete and tangible ways than we imagine. Here, he prays not simply for the maintenance of love in their midst, not simply that they hold fast to the status quo, but that they experience excess, fullness, an overflowing, a love that ignores boundaries, a love that knows no limits!

Knowledge and Discernment

The kind of love Paul has in mind isn't gullible, gushy, or gooey—lacking wisdom and encouraging people to continue in their sin. Love must be governed by "knowledge" and "discernment." Let's take each of these in turn.

True, lasting, Christlike love must be characterized by *knowledge*. Whereas we tend to pit love and knowledge against each other, Paul insists they are essential to each other. In other places, he argues that if all we have is knowledge and lack love, it is useless. In 1 Corinthians 8, he says that "'knowledge' puffs up, but love builds up" (8:1). There is a kind of knowledge, or better still, a way in which we approach it and pride ourselves in it, that shuts out and quenches love. But here in Philippians 1, Paul says that you can't love well if your love isn't guided by knowledge. What can he possibly mean by this? Well, for one thing, it isn't just any sort of knowledge that he has in view. He's not talking about knowledge of the stock market or the rules of golf. It's knowledge of God and his ways and, in particular, the manner in which he loves sinners like you and me.

So what does Paul have in mind that we need to "know" to love well? Our love must be grounded in and flow out of a knowledge of why we should love. In other words, to love well, we must understand how we ourselves are loved by God in Christ. For example, in Ephesians 4:32, Paul exhorts us to "be kind to one another, tenderhearted, forgiving one another, as God in Christ forgave you." If we are to forgive one another properly and sincerely, we must first be fully aware of and in touch with the depths of the forgiveness that God has given us in Christ. And then in the immediately following verses I think Paul says the same thing that he says here in Philippians 1. In Ephesians 5:2 he again exhorts us: "And walk in love, as Christ loved us and gave himself up for us, a fragrant offering and sacrifice to God."

It isn't enough simply to exhort a Christian to love. We need to go deeply into what it means when he says that "Christ loved us and gave himself up for us, a fragrant offering and sacrifice to God." Here we are given the ground or reason why we love others and the pattern or paradigm we are to imitate as we love others.

People love others for all sorts of illegitimate reasons: they feel it is their moral obligation, but their heart isn't engaged; some are trying to repay a debt they think they owe; others are trying to put someone else in their debt, hoping that by "loving" them the other person will do something in return; and then, of course, sometimes what passes for "love" is mere flattery. This is loving *without knowledge*.

To love with knowledge is to realize that we were utterly undeserving of Christ's love; worse still, we were *ill-deserving*. Even though others deserve no good from us—and possibly even deserve bad—we are to love. Christ loved us without regard to the cost that was entailed, subjecting himself to humiliation, shame, suffering, and the unimaginable anguish of being separated from his Father. Do we love others only when it is convenient, only when there's time in the day, only when others are looking, only when we feel like it, only when we are persuaded they deserve it, only when we anticipate being loved in return, only when it makes us look good in the eyes of others ("Oh, my, isn't he a loving person," "Wow, she is really something that she would do that for such a jerk!")?

The point is that we only love well and to the glory of God when our love is energized and governed by knowing the kind of love that God has for us in Christ. That's why you will never be able to love someone in "knowledge" if you live in ignorance of the gospel.

Also, true love, the sort of love that will accomplish good in the life of the beloved, must be characterized by *discernment*. What Paul has in mind with this word is the spiritual ability to make difficult moral decisions amid a vast array of competing and confusing choices. Gullible and naïve love is worse than bad. It is destructive. So, what kind of discernment does Paul have in mind?

Love must discern when it is appropriate and not appropriate to be generous and supportive. Consider the challenge we all face when confronted with the panhandlers that proliferate in virtually every large city in America. When is compassion justified? When does giving money to those who beg for it actually hurt them and reinforce their lack of responsibility? When does an act of what feels like kindness compound a person's problem rather than alleviate it?

A love that accomplishes much should be keenly aware of the circumstances, people, and timing and largely consist of discretion in speech. We need to be wise and discerning regarding the objects of our love. Although we are to love our enemies, we don't love them like we love our friends and brothers and sisters in Christ.

We must remember that no matter how passionate we feel or how extensive our sacrifice may be, we have not loved someone well if we fail to awaken them to the perilous condition in which their sin has placed them. If you think loving someone well means you keep silent about both the temporal and the eternal consequences of their beliefs and behavior, you are sadly mistaken. You are loving in the absence of discernment. If you love someone without speaking the truth to them for fear that it might hurt their feelings, damage your relationship with them, or get them in trouble with someone else, you have failed to love them well.

Loving with discernment means that you never communicate your affection or support for them in such a way that they feel free to continue in a lifestyle of unrepentant sin. If you in any way endorse their behavior, minimize its immorality, or write it off as if everyone is entitled to live as they please, or if you love in such a way that you are fearful of passing judgment on them, you have failed them; you have not loved them well. You have thrown discernment out the window.

To shower someone with love, affirmation, and affection without fulfilling the painful and costly task of pointing out to them the eternal consequences of their sin is not only not loving them, it is loving yourself more than you love them. Your refusal to identify their sin and call them to repentance is probably done to protect yourself and guard your heart from the distress that will likely come from creating discord in the relationship. You're afraid of their anger, their rejection of you; you're afraid they will label you as prejudiced, arrogant, and judgmental. Your so-called love of the other is in fact selfish love of self. You are more concerned with how the truth will boomerang and affect you than you are with the impact their sin will have on them.

Consider one example that is most often in the news these days. How often do we see a famous pastor or spiritual leader interviewed on TV who cowardly refuses to articulate the biblical stance on homosexual behavior? The person is so afraid of being labeled a bigot or a fundamentalist that they weasel out of saying what God said: "Do not be deceived: neither the sexually immoral, nor idolaters, nor adulterers, nor men who practice homosexuality . . . will inherit the kingdom of God" (1 Cor. 6:9–10).

Such a clear statement will invariably bring down angry denunciation of those who will label you as unloving and arrogant. It may end up costing you friendships, money, and advancement in your career. But if it is in fact true that certain unrepentant lifestyle choices threaten your eternal destiny (and I assure you that homosexuality is by no means the only one, so don't think I'm singling it out as unique or as more sinful than other acts of moral rebellion), if it is in fact true that heaven and hell hang suspended on the choices people make in this regard, it is the worst imaginable expression of calloused indifference, indeed hatred, of the other for you not to say so!

If your oncologist lives in fear that telling you the truth about a malignant tumor will ruin your day, make you unhappy, cause you to fall into depression, or appear to rob you of hope for the future, and refuses to disclose your condition and schedule immediate surgery, he is not loving you! If he says, "Hey, all is well! Take a few aspirin, watch how you eat, and you should be fine," thinking that to say otherwise will disrupt your vacation schedule and distress your family, he is not loving you! How much more so when the consequences are not merely temporal physical death but eternal spiritual death!

Let's look at a perfect illustration of what it means to exercise "discernment" in our loving of others. It is found in something Jesus said in the Sermon on the Mount. He tells us in Matthew 7:6: "Do not give dogs what is holy, and do not throw your pearls before pigs, lest they trample them underfoot and turn to attack you."

I can hear someone object: "But wait a minute, Jesus. If we really love these people, we won't call them 'dogs' or 'pigs,' and we certainly won't refuse to share the gospel with them no matter what they do to us in return." Well, Jesus disagrees with you! Jesus has in mind *the danger of being overindulgent and undiscerning.* In loving our enemies, going the extra mile, and not judging unjustly, there is the peril of becoming wishy-washy and failing to make essential distinctions between right and wrong and truth and falsehood. Whereas the saints are not to be judges, neither are they to be simpletons!

The terms "dogs" and "pigs" (perhaps a wild boar) in this text are not what we normally think of when we hear the words. The "dogs" to which Jesus refers are not the cuddly household pets of the twenty-first century, but rather wild and savage street hounds that carried disease and filth. In 2 Peter 2:22, Peter refers to false teachers and portrays them as dogs that return to their vomit. He also describes them as pigs that are washed only to return to wallowing in the mud. Carson explains:

> Jesus sketches a picture of a man holding a bag of precious pearls, confronting a pack of hulking hounds and some wild pigs. As the animals glare hungrily, he takes out his pearls and sprinkles them on the street. Thinking they are about to gulp some bits of food, the animals pounce on the pearls. Swift disillusionment sets in—the pearls are too hard to chew, quite tasteless, and utterly unappetizing. Enraged, the wild animals spit out the pearls, turn on the man and tear him to pieces.[1]

Jesus is not saying that we should withhold the gospel from certain people we regard as unworthy of it, but he does insist that after recurring rejection and disdain, we should move on to share the gospel with others. Some are persistently vicious and calloused, who delight not in the truth of Scripture but only in mocking it.

Therefore, the "dogs" and "pigs" are not simply unbelievers, but defiant, persistently hateful, vindictive unbelievers. "It ought to be understood," wrote Calvin, "that *dogs* and *swine* are names given not to every kind of debauched men, or to those who are destitute of the fear of God and of true godliness, but to those who, by clear evidences, have manifested a hardened contempt of God, so that their disease appears to be incurable."[2] We read in Proverbs 9:7–8, "Whoever corrects a scoffer gets himself abuse, and he who reproves a wicked man incurs injury. Do not reprove a scoffer, or he will hate you; reprove a wise man, and he will love you."

Remember that this instruction from Jesus is set in the context of loving our enemies. So, whereas we are not to cast our pearls before swine, neither are we to be nasty and vicious and uncaring.

All too often, in the name of love, people will give a false assurance of salvation to someone who is living in unrepentant unbelief and immorality. Thinking that it would be "unloving" of them to challenge the legitimacy of

---

1. D. A. Carson, *The Sermon on the Mount: An Evangelical Exposition of Matthew 5–7* (Grand Rapids: Baker, 1978), 105.

2. John Calvin, *A Commentary on a Harmony of the Evangelists, Matthew, Mark, and Luke* (Grand Rapids: Baker, 2005), 349 (emphasis in original).

someone's profession of faith, they pat them on the back and assure them that although we may not agree with each other right now at least we can all be assured we'll spend eternity in heaven together. That is not loving! That is the utter absence of discernment and can contribute to that person's damnation!

Approving What Is Excellent

Learning how to love with knowledge and discernment is essential if we are to "approve what is excellent, and so be pure and blameless for the day of Christ" (Phil. 1:10). Paul refuses to let Christians settle for mediocrity. He prays that our love would grow in knowledge and discernment so we can identify what is above average, what is superior, what is of moral and spiritual excellence, what really counts, and pursue it (see Phil. 4:8).

I find it fascinating that when Paul finally gets around to how we should prepare ourselves for the end of the world, for the coming of Christ, he says nothing about stockpiling of food or guns or digging an underground shelter or quitting our jobs or rushing off to the mountaintops. He says we need to be diligent to cultivate a more discerning and knowledgeable love! He tells us that we need to develop greater moral purity and blamelessness.

Filled with the Fruit of Righteousness

Learning how to love with knowledge and discernment is essential if we are to be "filled with the fruit of righteousness that comes through Jesus Christ" (Phil. 1:11a). It's unclear from Paul's language whether this is the fruit that *consists of righteousness* or the fruit that *comes out of righteousness*. It may be both. What's important to note is that this fruit comes not through our efforts unaided but *through Jesus Christ*, which is to say through the Spirit's empowerment. Of this, we may be sure: it has nothing to do with "religion" or self-made efforts to impress others with our spirituality.

Many in the professing Christian church give mere lip service to the importance of cultivating a spiritual culture and family affection in which love that is characterized by knowledge and discernment can flourish. They say to themselves, "You know, that's just not who I am. I'm not into that right now. Our church has a different calling. We first need to get our theological ducks in a row. We have to be diligent to dot all our doctrinal 'i's and cross our theological 't's. Then, if we can find time and energy, we'll be more conscientious about loving others."

If you want to know the value and importance Paul placed on the ever-increasing and abundant growth of our love for one another, look at verses 9–11. *This* is what brings glory and praise to God!

"By this," said Jesus, "all people will know that you are my disciples, if you have love for one another" (John 13:35).

CHAPTER 13

Anxiety, Prayer, and the Peace of God

Rejoice in the Lord always; again I will say, rejoice. Let your reasonableness be known to everyone. The Lord is at hand; do not be anxious about anything, but in everything by prayer and supplication with thanksgiving let your requests be made known to God. And the peace of God, which surpasses all understanding, will guard your hearts and your minds in Christ Jesus. (Phil. 4:4–7)

Rejoice in the Lord? On first hearing this, it may seem as if Paul is being flippant and indifferent toward human suffering. Does he have any idea what he's saying? Is he so out of touch with the harsh realities of life that he can be this casual and happy-go-lucky? I can vividly recall when a devastating EF-4 tornado hit Moore, Oklahoma, and wiped out a large portion of that city. And yet you expect Christian men and women whose lives were turned inside out by that disaster to "rejoice in the Lord"? Seriously?

Or, how am I supposed to rejoice in the Lord when the memory of past sins weighs so heavily on my heart? How can I obey this command when people I love are being persecuted and are suffering unjustly? "I just lost my job." "My mother died last week." "My children won't even talk to me." "The car won't start, and I don't have the money to fix it." "I'm supposed to see the doctor next week but I'm too scared of what he'll say." Rejoice in the Lord? Yeah, right.

I understand this reaction. Truly, I do. But before you dismiss Paul as some first-century Pollyanna, remember this: He wrote those words while in prison. He wrote those words not knowing if he might be beheaded for nothing more than declaring his allegiance to Jesus Christ. The man who wrote those words knew more about suffering and deprivation than all of us combined. So, if you still want to dismiss his counsel as unhelpful, go ahead. But don't do so on the assumption that he was naïve or unacquainted with grief or was insulated from the kind of pain and heartache that you're facing right now.

Paul is clearly calling us to an experience that is unrelated to our external circumstances and in some way transcends them. Charlie Brown once said, "Happiness is a warm puppy." But what happens when the puppy runs away? What happens when the puppy dies? No, the kind of "happiness" that Paul has in view, the joy and delight that he calls for in this passage, is not tied to a warm puppy or money in the bank or a clean bill of health or peaceful family relationships. It's tied to Jesus Christ.

So, let's begin there, with Jesus Christ. After all, it is there, in him, in relation to our Lord, in the context of all we know that he has so graciously done for us, that we are to rejoice: "Rejoice *in the Lord*!"

Joy is expressed in a variety of styles and circumstances. Paul couldn't care less whether it is with hands raised or one's face pressed against the ground. It matters not whether it is to the rhythm of a fast-paced worship song or in solemn silence with tears streaming down one's face. What concerns Paul, and must concern us, is the ground or reason for our joy. There is a sense in which Paul is declaring: "Jesus is our joy." He is ours and we are his regardless of whether the sky is clear and sunny or threatens us with an approaching funnel cloud. That is why we can rejoice "always," in every circumstance, no matter the pain or pleasure. Our joy is constant not because our circumstances are but because Jesus is.

That is the first of three exhortations: "Rejoice in the Lord always; again I will say, rejoice" (Phil. 4:4). The second exhortation comes in verse 5: "Let your reasonableness be known to everyone. The Lord is at hand." This word, translated as "reasonableness," is hard to interpret. The KJV translates it "let your *moderation* be known unto all." But this is not a call for temperance or abstinence. Others suggest the idea of generosity or the willingness to make allowances; the quality that keeps one from always insisting on one's full rights. It's the opposite of entitlement; the opposite of always demanding one's due. It is the patient willingness to yield wherever yielding does not compromise moral principle.

Paul does not mean we are to be quick to compromise on our doctrinal beliefs. Neither is he suggesting we accommodate or adapt to the world's standards of conduct (see 2:15; Rom. 12:2). He's not telling us to be wimps, but he is telling us to be willing to bend a bit; to not be so brittle or inflexible that people bounce off us like a golf ball on concrete.

And please note that this quality of character is not to be confined within your heart. You must strive for everyone to see it: "Let your reasonableness *be known* to everyone." So, what do you most want to be "known" for? Is it your physical appearance, your bubbly and infectious personality, your wealth, your wit, your wisdom, your ancestry, your work ethic? Perhaps we should focus on something far less sensational but more spiritual: reasonableness.

What reason does Paul give for this advice? "The Lord is at hand" (Phil. 4:5b). This phrase "at hand" could be taken temporally or personally. That is to say, he may be referring to the nearness of Christ in terms of time or space. If it's time, he may be alluding to what he said at the close of chapter three. There we were encouraged to keep our eyes fixed on heaven from which "we await a Savior, the Lord Jesus Christ" (3:20b).

But I think he is speaking in spatial, relational, or personal terms. His point, then, is that the Lord is close to you, present with you, aware of your conduct, concerned about your relationships with others, available and willing to come to your aid and assist you. This may well be why Paul immediately follows this declaration with an urgent command that we pray. If the Lord is near to help, encourage, and strengthen us, we need to be quick to pray to him about everything! We hear an echo of this in Psalm 145:18: "The LORD is near to all who call on him, to all who call on him in truth."

The third of Paul's exhortations is a familiar one and the focus of this chapter. We read of it in Philippians 4:6: "Do not be anxious about anything, but in everything by prayer and supplication with thanksgiving let your requests be made known to God." A Christian might live in two experiential realities: anxiety or peace / worry or rest / consternation or contentment. Here, Paul contrasts these two and tells us that the way to move from one to the other is by prayer.

Clearly Paul is drawing on the teaching of Jesus in the Sermon on the Mount (Matt. 6:25–34). The word translated "anxious" is the same as what we find in Philippians 2:20, where it had the positive and even virtuous sense of being sincerely concerned for the welfare of another person. So, what is the difference between sinful anxiety and sincere, spiritual concern for someone else or for some circumstance in life?

In Philippians 4:6, unlike in 2:20, Paul speaks of godless concern for things over which we have no control and even for things over which we do have control but should still entrust to the Lord. This gnawing, corrosive worry is a form of unconscious blasphemy. Paul is not speaking of imaginary or phantom anxieties. He is not making light of the troubles they face. He is convinced that God is able and willing to help.

But Paul does not simplistically command them to stop worrying without offering an alternative cure. But the cure Paul suggests is not what many have come to expect:

It is not inaction or passivity.

It is not apathy. Paul does not tell us to ignore or deny the problem.

It is not withdrawal. In moments of anxiety, the easiest thing to do is retreat into a corner of safety and complain and grow bitter.

Paul says the alternative to anxiety or worry is the pouring out of one's heart to God in prayer. Release from anxiety comes through laying yourself bare before God. As D. A. Carson has said, "The way to be anxious about nothing is to be prayerful about everything."[1] But how does this work? What is it about anxiety and prayer that puts them in conflict with one another? More specifically, what is it about prayer that makes it an effective antidote to anxiety? I think there are several ways to answer that question:

- Anxiety is rooted in self, while prayer is rooted in God.
- Anxiety is the fruit of a narrow, constricted view of life, focused on problems and perplexities. Prayer is the fruit of a broad, expansive view of life, in which God is so big that even our worst problems shrink into insignificance.
- Anxiety is horizontal in focus. Prayer is vertical in focus. When you worry, you look to the left and right, forward and backward. When you pray, you can't help but look up.

---

1. D. A. Carson, *Basics for Believers: An Exposition of Philippians* (Grand Rapids: Baker, 1996), 112.

- Anxiety never raises your eyes above your problems, situation, and circumstances. Prayer raises your eyes above and beyond yourself to God and his power.
- Anxiety looks to self to solve problems. Prayer looks to God to endure problems.
- When you are anxious, your circumstances and problems control you; they have sovereignty over you; you invest in them life-shaping power and authority. When you are prayerful, your circumstances shrink, and your problems lose such power.
- Anxiety is a concern over circumstances you can't control. Prayer is confidence in the God who controls your circumstances.
- Anxiety is an expression of fear. Prayer is an expression of faith.

That, quite simply, is why the antidote to anxiety is prayer.

There are two elements in Paul's theology of prayer. First are the *characteristics* of prayer, six of which Paul delineates for us.

"*In everything*" we are to make our requests known to God—in every circumstance, no matter how serious or casual, no matter how tragic or trivial, and at all times. The contrast is striking: in *nothing* be anxious, but in *everything* be prayerful.

It is "*by prayer*" that we are to bring these petitions to God. This is a broad term that encompasses all kinds of prayer: adoration, praise, petition, thanksgiving, confession, intercession, etc. In addition to "prayer" there is also "*supplication*." This word is more narrow and specific in its focus. Here, Paul has in mind the reality of need and want. This word thus points to our dependence on God for everything. Could this possibly be why most prayer meetings are attended by women? Men believe the way to success and respect in today's world is by cultivating an image of self-sufficiency and radical independence. Men typically do not open up and confess their inadequacy or give indication of their great need. This is to admit weakness, a fatal mistake in today's world. Male pride is not conducive to the kind of prayer Paul has in mind here.

Our prayers and supplications are to be attended "with thanksgiving." Before you ask God for something new, thank him for something old. Thanksgiving is not another kind of prayer, along with petition and supplication. Here, it is the mood, mindset, or attitude that characterizes all prayer.

So why does Paul want all our prayers to be bathed in thanksgiving? There are several reasons.

First, it is hard to be bitter in the presence of God when our minds and mouths are filled with what God has done for us in the past. When you are thankful, you realize that everything you have is because of grace and you deserve nothing but death. Furthermore, it is difficult to doubt God's promise to answer us when you thank him for the blessings he has already bestowed! If you think I'm making this up, try it. For example: "But God, I'm not sure you can . . . Oh, yeah, okay, yes, I remember when you did something similar before. Okay, thanks." Or again, "But God, I have no reason to think you are either able or willing to step into this situation and make things right. Oh, yeah, okay, yes, I remember now how you did this on several occasions earlier. How stupid of me to think you wouldn't be able or willing to do it again."

Thanksgiving is also the fuel for future requests. In other words, if your mind is first filled with remembrance of what God has graciously done in the past, it will empower and expand your requests for what you need now and tomorrow. Having seen firsthand what God can do in response to prayer, your prayers grow and intensify. If you've received a little in the past, why not ask for a lot in the future?

When you recall God's goodness and mercy in the past, it's hard to remain burdened in the present. Thanksgiving has a way of alleviating the pressure of the present by reminding us of God's power at work on our behalf in the past. By constantly keeping fresh in our minds all that we have to be thankful for, we will be less inclined to disregard others who are less well off.

Finally, as strange as this may sound, we also need to thank God for saying no. Why in the world would we do that? Here's why: on some occasions, if God were to grant us the requests we make of him, it would bring us harm that we cannot foresee in the present. Contrary to what you may believe, you and I do not always know what is best for ourselves. We must pray with confidence that God knows us better than we know ourselves. Just as an earthly father has to deny his five-year-old son's request for a hunting knife, so our heavenly Father has to deny certain requests we make of him.

Sometimes, God will say no to a request in the present because he has something far better in store for us in the future. Thus, what strikes us as a definitive no is, in fact, a loving wait.

There are some prayers to which God says no because, unbeknownst to us, we are praying at cross-purposes with another believer. What happens when a job is open and two or more Christians apply for it? When God answers the prayers of one, he must say no to the other. Or again, when you pray for holiness and happiness, purity may come only through persecution. Sometimes the only way God can answer your prayer for holiness is by leading you through heartache, persecution, and loss.

So, Paul wants us to thank God in every prayer, whether or not what we ask comes to pass as we hoped it might. If it does, thank him. If it doesn't, thank him for having the wisdom to not give us what we couldn't handle. Furthermore, thank him for how he will address your needs in a way far superior to what you envisioned.

By *"requests"* (v. 6) Paul has in view the actual content of our prayers; the precise details. It's Paul's way of reminding us not to hide behind generalities and vague religious platitudes. Be specific. Be concrete. It's amazing when you think of it. On the surface, prayer seems so impertinent: that fallen, hell-deserving, finite creatures should ask the infinitely glorious Creator for anything! What makes it seem even more impertinent is our expectation that God might actually do or provide what we ask!

It is *"to God,"* or more literally, in the presence of God, face-to-face with him, as it were, that we are to direct our petitions. Consider how this works in our relationships with other people. Often, we must know a person really well before the conversation flows freely and we open up and let them in on the struggles and needs of life. We can talk about the weather, pro football, the demise of our favorite team, and the threat of tornadoes, but until we know them and are confident of their love for us, it rarely goes deeper than that. I share certain things with my close friends that I might not share with all of you. I talk about things with Ann that my close friends will never hear. But there are many things that God and I talk about to which no one else on earth may have access.

If your prayer life is dull and sporadic at best, it may be that you're talking to a stranger!

Having unpacked the *characteristics* of prayer, Paul now describes its *consequences*. Paul describes it in one gloriously beautiful and reassuring phrase: the peace of God guarding our hearts and minds in a way that no human mind can fully comprehend.

Did you know that the phrase "the peace of God" occurs only here in the

New Testament? He's not talking about peace "with" God. That is presupposed. If you aren't at peace "with" God, you can't experience the peace "of" God. If the enmity between you and God has not been removed by faith in the blood of Christ's cross, you can't experience the peace Paul has in mind. That feeling in your heart of ease and contentment and all's well in the world is a lie. If you haven't invested your trust in Christ as your treasure and your only hope for forgiveness of sins, what's going on in your mind and heart is a psychological delusion, a deceptive trick that ultimately leads you straight into eternal death.

But for those who've been reconciled to God through faith in the blood of Christ shed for them on the cross, God's very peace now enters their hearts and rules, reigns, and triumphs over all anxiety.

Paul isn't talking so much about the peace God gives as he is about the peace that exists in God himself. It is "God's" peace, not because he gives it, but because he experiences it. This is the tranquility, joy, calm, and serenity that characterizes the being of God himself. And yes, he does give it, impart it; he does infuse it in us when we pray to him. Think of what Paul is saying: When we fervently, honestly, and passionately pour out our requests to God, something of the very nature of God himself takes up residence and governs our hearts, overcoming and replacing our anxious thoughts and enabling us to experience spiritual serenity that God himself feels and enjoys. This is what Isaiah spoke of when he said: "You keep him in perfect peace whose mind is stayed on you, because he trusts in you. Trust in the LORD forever, for the LORD God is an everlasting rock" (Isa. 26:3–4).

Something else is said about this "peace" of God that becomes ours when we pray: it far surpasses and transcends all human comprehension. The human mind can't fully grasp it. The human hand can't reproduce it in a factory. The human eye can't begin to envision what it looks like. As much as we pride ourselves in our scientific and technological achievements, this peace will never be reduced to merely human terms or explained by even the greatest and most brilliant minds.

This peace isn't some cheap psychological trick to get you past a few problems in life. No diagnostic manual or self-help book can reproduce it. It is God-shaped and God-given.

And look at what this peace "does," yes, "does," for it is not impotent or quiet or weak or inactive: it guards your hearts and minds. This would have been an especially vivid image for Paul as he wrote these words, for he did so as he sat in chains in a Roman prison. The city of Philippi was home to a Roman garrison. The sight of soldiers carefully watching the area would have been a common phenomenon for these Christians. Hence, God's peace, like a garrison of soldiers, will stand guard over your hearts and minds. In the midst of God's peace you are as secure from worry and fear as any well-armed fortress.

What precisely does this peace guard as a garrison of soldiers? Not our bodies, because we can still fall sick or suffer damage from a tornado or be cast into prison for our faith and even martyred. Not our possessions, because the enemies of the church can still steal and confiscate our property. Not our bank accounts, because the economy can still collapse. Not our reputation, because we are still objects of slander, gossip, and abuse.

Rather, this peace guards our "hearts" and "minds," which is Paul's way of referring to the core of our spiritual life, our values, our passions, our thoughts, that place of deep intimacy with Christ himself. Spiritually speaking, God will never permit an assault on his children to be successful.

But this is not a universal promise that just anyone can lay hold of. This protection comes from the peace of God that is found *only in Christ Jesus*. If you don't know Christ, if he isn't your treasure, if your faith isn't grounded and fixed in him alone, this passage promises you nothing.

Finally, observe what Paul *doesn't say* about prayer. He doesn't say that all our requests will be answered precisely how we articulated them. He doesn't say that the problems, perplexities, and pain that may have caused the anxiety in the first place will suddenly and forever disappear. What he *does say* is that a loving, heavenly Father will guard your heart and mind in Christ Jesus as you face, endure, and patiently persevere in the midst of whatever this world throws in your direction.

Conclusion

As we conclude this, permit me to remind us all once again of the simply stunning, utterly breathtaking reality that undergirds everything Paul says here. Without the slightest tinge of insincerity or rush of sensationalism, he is telling us that God has designed and ordained this universe so that he will act and intervene on our behalf when we ask him to. That is simply breathtaking!

That truth, apart from which nothing here makes any sense at all, is that God has promised to do for his children, for those who are in Christ Jesus, marvelous things that we simply cannot do for ourselves. And no less true is the fact that if we do *not* pray as we are here instructed to pray, he quite likely will *not* do for us what we need done.

Does it not blow your mind when you hear Jesus say something like, "Ask, and it will be given to you; seek, and you will find; knock, and it will be opened to you" (Matt. 7:7)? Do you and I really take James seriously when he tells us, "You do not have, because you do not ask" (James 4:2)? The all-powerful, all-wise, all-loving God who called this universe into existence out of nothing wills for your prayers to be the occasion of his acting on your behalf.

CHAPTER 14

Prayer as a Profoundly Supernatural Experience

What? Prayer, supernatural, you ask? Like Star Wars special effects and warp speed and alien invaders and stuff like that? Well, no, not stuff like that. Well, then, what? How can something that so often feels mundane and routine be supernatural? How can prayer be supernatural when I can choose when to pray, whether to pray, and how to pray?

When I say that prayer, and, by extension, the entire Christian life is supernatural, I mean that *nothing of eternal value can be accomplished by God's people apart from God's power.* Thus, by "supernatural," I mean a power or energy that comes from outside of us that is somehow imparted or infused into us to enable us to live lives that, in our own human strength, we could never accomplish.

That "power" or transcendent energy that enables us to live as God would have us live is granted to us through prayer. I realize how odd that sounds, given the fact that most of you, if put under pressure, would confess that hardly anything about praying feels supernatural. Most of you are bored with prayer. You find it profoundly unexciting and dull. That's why churches can get a good turnout for most gatherings, as long as it's not a prayer meeting!

Well, Paul is going to do his best, and so am I, to convince you that *prayer is a profoundly supernatural experience,* apart from which we have no hope of living as God would have us live or of seeing God do wonderful and miraculous things in our lives and the lives of those we love.

Paul's Intercessory Prayer for the Colossians

And so, from the day we heard, we have not ceased to pray for you, asking that you may be filled with the knowledge of his will in all spiritual wisdom and understanding, so as to walk in a manner worthy of the Lord, fully pleasing to him: bearing fruit in every good work and increasing in the knowledge of God; being strengthened with all power, according to his glorious might, for all endurance and patience with joy. (Col. 1:9–11)

Let's be sure we understand the nature of intercessory prayer. I've heard any number of definitions, but none better than that of Lloyd John Ogilvie, who said that intercession is not so much my placing my burdens on God's heart, but "God putting his burdens on our hearts."[1] I can't prove it, but I suspect God takes greater delight in blessing me in response to your prayers for me than he does when I ask him myself. That isn't to say we shouldn't pray for ourselves. It's simply to say that with intercession, unlike other forms or expressions of prayer, there is a mutual love, fellowship, and spiritual bond that develops in a way that can't occur if we were only to pray for ourselves and not others.

First, why does Paul intercede in prayer for the Colossians? The ESV makes a mistake here, in my humble opinion. It reads: "And so, from the day we heard ..." But verse 9 opens with the words "*for this reason*" or "*on account of this*." He's obviously referring back to the news concerning their faith, love, and hope described in verses 3–8. I can just imagine Paul's reaction when Epaphras informed him of events in Colossae. He probably called in Timothy, Aristarchus, Mark, Justus, and Luke (cf. Col. 4:10–14), eager to share with them the good news of what God was doing in the lives of these saints.

I wish this were always the case, but it isn't. Often, when Christians hear of other Christians flourishing and prospering, they begrudge those benefits, feel envy rising in their souls, or even question whether such folk deserve God's blessings (as if any of us do!). Not Paul. Although he languished in prison, he rejoiced over the success and spiritual prosperity of those in Colossae. Unable to restrain his exuberance, he lifts these saints before the

---

1. Lloyd John Ogilvie, *Praying with Power* (Ventura: Regal, 1983), 63.

throne of grace with gratitude and intercedes on their behalf for yet more and even greater spiritual benefits. We don't read so much as a word of: "Hey, God, what about me? If it weren't for me, those Colossians wouldn't even be believers. How come you bless them so abundantly and leave me in this stinking Roman jail?" It's a painful question to ask, but how often do we respond with resentment rather than joy when we hear of the success or growth or impact of other churches in our city?

Second, *for whom* does Paul intercede? It's not enough simply to say, "the Colossians." Never forget that Paul had never met these people! As best we can tell, Epaphras brought the gospel to Colossae. Paul wouldn't have known a single name or recognized a single face in that church. Yet he prays for them passionately and persistently, which brings us to our third and final question.

How often did he pray for them? Unceasingly, Paul happily declares in Colossians 1:9, "We have not ceased to pray for you." This doesn't mean that Paul never did anything else but pray, as if every waking moment was spent in intercession. It simply means that every time Paul prayed, which was probably quite often, intense, and prolonged, he came to the throne of grace with the Colossian believers in his heart and on his lips. Although Paul's prayer list must have grown daily as news of the success of the gospel reached him (cf. v. 6), he never failed to include the Colossians.

So, let's ask ourselves again: Why do we pray for others? Is it only because we think they are praying for us? Is it only if we have prior assurance that they will continue to love us and provide for our needs? Is it only because we think that by doing so, God will surely bless us in the way he has blessed them?

For whom do we pray? Is it only those we know and can recall by name and with whom we have shared much in life? Yes, you can pray fervently and successfully for that distant congregation in Sri Lanka you only read about in the newspaper. Yes, you can intercede passionately, for their good and God's glory, for the persecuted church in Iran.

Finally, how often does this occur during your daily routines? You may not have prolonged seasons free from the distractions of life, but you can find a minute here, or perhaps ten there, to bring to heaven those whom God has placed on your heart. And remember, God only places them on your heart because they are first on his.

So, what did Paul pray for? What did he want most for those in Colossae? I wonder what they might have said to him had he asked, "How may I pray for you?" We'll never know, but what we do know is that Paul asked, apparently repeatedly, that God would fill them "with the knowledge of his will in all spiritual wisdom and understanding" (Col. 1:9). That doesn't sound very exciting, does it?

Let's be clear about one thing. Simply because Paul prayed for them to know God's will does not mean we are forbidden to ask for other things. There are countless blessings, both spiritual and material, for which we ought to intercede. But there is significance in the fact that this weighed heavily in Paul's value system. I doubt if knowing God's will is at the top of many of our "want" lists. New cars, better-paying jobs, respect, notoriety, physical comfort, and all the latest technological conveniences are probably of more pressing importance to us than knowing the will of God. It's tragic but all too true.

This prayer is like what we find in Ephesians 1:17, where he prays that God would give them "the Spirit of wisdom and of revelation in the knowledge of him." Likewise, in Philippians 1:9, his prayer is that their "love may abound more and more, with knowledge and all discernment" (see also Philem. 6).

Clearly, knowledge was important to Paul. But not any sort of knowledge will do. He asks for knowledge of "God's will." At minimum, this would involve understanding all Paul teaches in the remainder of this epistle and other inspired writings. In one sense, then, this prayer is for illumination, or to use the words of Ephesians 1:18, it is for the enlightenment of the "eyes of your heart." This is why I regularly include the prayer of Psalm 119:18 before I preach the Scriptures: "Open my eyes, that I may behold wondrous things out of your law (word)."

More specifically, he asks God to fill them with the knowledge of his will "in all spiritual wisdom and understanding" (Col. 1:9b). There are several ways to understand the relationship between "spiritual wisdom and understanding" and the "knowledge of God's will," but I'll share what I think is most likely.

The best rendering is that the knowledge for which he prays *consists of* all spiritual wisdom and understanding. In other words, knowing God's will is not only a matter of understanding what pleases him but also of experiential wisdom in knowing how to apply God's desires to the concrete realities, crises, and decisions of everyday life.

Can a person "know" God in the way Paul describes in Colossians 1:9 and *not* bear the fruit of holiness? Not too long ago, George Barna described 77 million churchgoing Americans as born again. I'm not by nature a cynic, but I think that's a terrible exaggeration. The Scriptures tell me in no uncertain terms that genuine, saving knowledge of the Lord Jesus is transforming, life-changing, sin-killing, and Christ-exalting in its effects. I fear countless people live a religious charade, having been assured by well-meaning ministers that their "decision" for Jesus produced eternal life, in spite of the fact that there is little, if any, spiritual fruit in their experience.

Consider Paul's words in Colossians 1:9–10. He prayed that we might be filled with the knowledge of God's will, which consists of spiritual wisdom and understanding (v. 9). But why? To what end? For what reason? The answer, according to verse 10, is so that we might "walk in a manner worthy of the Lord, fully pleasing to him: bearing fruit in every good work and increasing in the knowledge of God."

The language of verse 10 is clear and inescapable. We know God and his will for this reason: to equip, enable, and encourage us to walk in holiness (see Titus 2:11–14). Knowledge for knowledge's sake is fatal. To learn simply for the sake of learning expands the mind but cannot transform the heart.

All this to say that the knowledge of God and his will is eminently practical in nature and purpose. Paul's aim in praying for the Colossians to be filled with spiritual wisdom and insight is so they will be energized in the daily mortification of sin and cultivation of spiritual fruit and good works. Had Epaphras informed Paul that the Colossians were loudly proclaiming their love for God and knowledge of his ways all the while they lived in unrepentant sin and disobedience, I suspect Paul would have replied: "I beg your pardon!" Well, he probably would have said a lot more than that, but I trust you get my point.

It's interesting to note that what Paul said in verse 6 about the gospel he now says in verse 10 about the Colossians themselves: "it (the gospel) is bearing fruit and increasing" (v. 6), and you are "bearing fruit . . . and increasing." The point seems to be that the way in which the gospel is bearing fruit and increasing (v. 6) is by producing Christlike and holy lives, through the Spirit, in those who have received it in faith (v. 10).

Paul's closing words in verse 10 ("increasing in the knowledge of God") deserve close scrutiny. Two views have emerged.

Some argue that we should render this phrase in an instrumental fashion, hence, "by means of" or "through" the knowledge of God. If this is true, Paul's point is to reinforce what he said in verse 9, namely, that the knowledge of God (of his will, his grace, his character, etc.) forms the basis from which or the means by which the bearing of fruit and the growth in good works comes about. If this view is correct, it reminds us again that all efforts at Christian behavior without a solid foundation of orthodox, theologically robust, and wide-ranging Christian belief will eventually prove to be a mere vapor.

Others contend that Paul's point is that genuine transformation always *includes* growth in understanding of God. Heat without light degenerates into fanaticism, just as light without heat breeds arrogance. The saving presence of the Spirit in our souls yields the rich harvest of both good deeds and deep insights, both orthopraxy (right behavior) and orthodoxy (right belief).

There are two more phrases in verse 10 that call for our careful attention. Observe that Paul speaks of the need for us to walk "worthy of the Lord" (see also Eph. 4:1; Phil. 1:27; 1 Thess. 2:12; 3 John 6). Someone might get the wrong idea from this, especially given the strong emphasis throughout Colossians 1 on the necessity of good works and bearing fruit. Paul is most assuredly not saying our efforts can prove us to be worthy of God or worthy of his salvation, as if it were by our merits that we gain eternal life. Paul is not suggesting that we should strive to earn a place in God's favor or by our good deeds put him in our debt such that he is obligated to acknowledge our efforts and reward us accordingly. This is the opposite of the gospel of grace that we find throughout Scripture.

The idea isn't that we are worthy by virtue of how we walk but that we should walk in a way that *reflects* or *displays* how much *he* is worthy of such obedience. Our great triune God and the marvelous and undeserved kindness that is ours in the gospel are of such infinite value, so exalted and beautiful and full of glory, that we should always live in such a way that it be known. Our lives, by his grace, should reflect positively on God. People should walk away from having observed us saying, "My goodness, what an incredible God they believe in!" Our aim isn't to evoke from them praise and admiration of who we are, but praise and admiration of who *he* is! Jesus, the cross, the gospel of salvation by grace alone through faith alone, are worthy of lives that reflect on *their* value, not ours.

The second thing to note here is that a life worthy of the Lord is one that is "fully pleasing to him" (Col. 1:10) in all things. This is the only place in the New Testament where the noun "pleasing" occurs, but the verb occurs in such texts as Romans 8:8 ("those who are in the flesh cannot please God"); 1 Corinthians 7:32 ("how to please the Lord"); and 1 Thessalonians 2:4 ("to please God who tests our hearts"; see also Rom. 15:1–2; Gal. 1:10; 1 Thess. 2:15; 4:1).

My reason for highlighting the word here in Colossians 1:10 is twofold. First, it reminds us again that good works are pleasing to God! They make God happy. They evoke his pleasure. They incite joy in his heart. God is not devoid of emotions. He feels great delight in good deeds (and displeasure in bad ones).

Of course, we must never forget the incredible words of Hebrews 13:20–21 where the author of that epistle prays, "Now may the God of peace who brought again from the dead our Lord Jesus, the great shepherd of the sheep, by the blood of the eternal covenant, *equip you with everything good that you may do his will, working in us that which is pleasing in his sight*, through Jesus Christ, to whom be glory forever and ever. Amen" (italics mine; see also Phil. 2:12–13). Thus, when God takes pleasure in our good deeds, he is rejoicing in the work of his own grace and power! He is the one who works in us what pleases him. Thus, in rewarding our works, God is crowning his own grace!

The second thing to keep in mind is that if our good works please him, our bad ones displease him. On more than one occasion, the book of Proverbs speaks of certain deeds as being an "abomination" to the Lord. I can't think of anything more horrendous than a life that God regards as an abomination. The great difference, of course, is that all good works that please him are the result (ultimately) of his gracious energy in us, whereas all bad works that displease him are our responsibility, for which we shall give an account.

Power!

Paul's prayer in Colossians 1 actually frightens some people. Some are afraid they won't have the power to live worthy of the Lord and to bear fruit in every good work, while others fear that once they start out in their efforts to do so, they'll end up quitting; they simply won't have the endurance to persevere in what they began. So, either the sense of personal weakness and spiritual impotence, on the one hand, or the lack of steadfastness, on the other, often paralyzes people from even trying to live as they know the Lord wants them to.

Thank God for Colossians 1:11! Here Paul continues his prayer by asking God to strengthen them with power and to sustain them in their endeavors. Let's note seven things about how he prays.

First, Paul does not say "strengthen yourselves," as if the power were inherently ours, resident within us, and we only needed to flip a switch to release it in our pursuit of holiness. You may recall similar words in Ephesians 6:10 where Paul said, "Finally, be strong in the Lord and in the strength of his might." The key words are "in the Lord" and "in the strength of his might." When he prays, "may you be strengthened," he obviously means "by God"! He could as easily have said it more directly, "Oh, God, I ask that you strengthen these otherwise weak and impotent people to do your will."

Second, there is something of a redundancy in Paul saying to be "strengthened with all power." It's as if he says to be "empowered with power." Well, yes, but with what else might one be empowered if not with power? Surely, Paul chose his words carefully. He knew what he was saying. His point is simply to reinforce the magnitude of what is available to us from God when we ask him.

Third, as if that weren't enough, he prays that we be strengthened with "all" power. This could mean power "of every kind" or the "fullness" of power or perhaps power in the "highest degree." Nothing second-rate here! Paul prays (as we should, too) for the best and most potent and most effective and wide-ranging power possible. God, being omnipotent, is more than up to the task of saying yes.

Fourth, when God empowers us with maximum power to do his will, he does it "according to his glorious might" (literally, "according to the might of his glory"). Since the word *might* is effectively a synonym for "power," it may even be rendered "according to his majestic power"! In that case, we would have something like, "May you be empowered with all power according to his majestic power." Wow! God doesn't do anything second-class.

Fifth, the goal of this empowerment is "endurance" and "patience," the former referring to persevering in the face of difficult circumstances and the latter to steadfastness that does not retaliate against those who resist us. Events, trials, and hardships tempt us to quit, but God grants endurance. People, criticism, and injustice tempt us to seek revenge, but God grants patience.

Sixth, Paul was even more explicit in Romans 15:5 where he describes God as "the God of endurance," that is, the God from whom endurance ultimately comes. Also, in that text in Romans, Paul makes clear that the means God typically employs when he imparts endurance is the Scriptures (see Rom. 15:4)!

Seventh, I don't want to press this point, but we should take note of the present tense in Paul's prayer that you are "being strengthened." We might render it, "may you be continually strengthened" or "strengthened repeatedly." The point is that the strength and power we need are available as we confront the circumstances and challenges of life, one after another, day after day.

In sum, there is no addiction God's power cannot break, no sin God's power cannot defeat, no task to which we are called that God's power cannot fulfill, no fruit we are called to bear that God's power cannot produce, no rebellious child God's power cannot restore, no broken marriage God's power cannot reconcile, no physical disease God's power cannot heal. That's why Paul calls it "majestic power"!

Paul's Intercessory Prayer for the Thessalonians

We ought always to give thanks to God for you, brothers, as is right, because your faith is growing abundantly, and the love of every one of you for one another is increasing. Therefore we ourselves boast about you in the churches of God for your steadfastness and faith in all your persecutions and in the afflictions that you are enduring. (2 Thess. 1:3–4)

An oft neglected part of intercessory prayer is the giving of thanks for what God has done and is doing in the lives of other believers. Look at how this is done by Paul in his second letter to the Thessalonians. He states unequivocally that he "ought" (2 Thess. 1:3) to give thanks to God for them. There is a heavy weight on Paul's heart that he can't shake. Evidently, the lives of these Christians were so exemplary and so full of the Holy Spirit that it just didn't feel right for him to hold back praise to God for what he had done through them. There are several things for which he gives thanks.

The first thing that catches Paul's attention is that their "faith is growing abundantly" (v. 3b). There is nothing wrong with thanking God for protecting someone who has just survived a horrible car accident. Yes, thank the Lord for the provision of food and a home and money to pay the mortgage. But I fear that our gratitude is too often tied to our material prosperity.

This is one reason why we are so often shocked and caught off guard when we read what the apostle Paul prayed for and thanked God for. Here he thanks the Lord for the enlargement of the faith in the lives of the Thessalonians. We often think of "faith" as something static, immovable, unchanging. Yet here, their "faith" is obviously a reference to their ever-increasing reliance on the goodness of God, their ever-growing trust and dependent confidence in God's promises to them (and to us!). This is a dimension of Christian "faith" that can grow or, sadly, shrink and shrivel. Our faith can either increase or decrease depending on how we understand and respond to God. The "faith" of the Thessalonians was fat! Better still, it was experiencing expansive growth. It appears that they were not resting satisfied with yesterday's achievements or today's status quo but were continuously on the stretch for God. But how, you ask? How does faith deepen and expand in this way?

One way is when our trust in God's goodness intensifies in the face of heartache and disappointment. Faith grows "abundantly" (v. 3) when our belief in God's power to do what no one could do exceeds normal expectations. When we become ever-more confident that God truly is working all things together for our good, even the bad things (Rom. 8:28), we see faith get bigger, deeper, broader, and higher.

So, how often do you intercede for other believers, praising God for this in their lives and asking him to accelerate it even more? There are undoubtedly many sitting close to you on a Sunday morning who are immersed in doubt, drowning in skepticism, experiencing crippling and spiritually debilitating shame because they can't bring themselves to believe that God would ever view them as anything other than failures and disappointments. Turn to them and pray that God would increase their faith and cause it, in his goodness, to become ever more vibrant and energetic. And give him thanks for even the small measure of faith that is already present in their hearts, even if it is so slight that they can't feel it.

Paul also thanks God that their love for one another "is increasing" (v. 3b). This is truly remarkable when you remember how different people are, even those who share a common trust in Jesus for salvation. There are rich and poor, black and white, educated and uneducated, socially sophisticated and undignified, intense and carefree, extroverted and introverted, people who to all outward appearances seem to share nothing in common. But they share what matters most: faith in Jesus and love for one another.

How often do you pray for others in your local church or your circle of friendship and influence that their faith would continue to grow and their love for one another would increase? Do we plead with God for him to work these virtues in their lives? If not, we "ought" to. It is only "right" that we should.

But Paul doesn't stop there. He actually brags ("boast," v. 4) about the Thessalonians everywhere he goes. He tells everyone of their "steadfastness and faith" amid all their "persecutions" and "the afflictions" they are "enduring" (v. 4). It's important to see that Paul's gratitude to God is not merely private in nature. He makes it quite public! It's as if wherever he goes, you hear him speak of the Thessalonians, saying,

> Hey folks, have you noticed the believers in Thessalonica? Have you seen what God's grace has done in them? Let me tell you about the way they have stood up under persecution without complaining, without blaming God for their adversity. What an example to us all! What an incentive to us that we should behave likewise!

I've said it before, but it merits being stated again. The reason why we are looking so closely at how the apostles prayed is twofold. First, it strips away the façade from our lives and exposes to us what we value and cherish most. It reveals how we have placed too much importance on trivial and transient things, excluding the virtues and values that will last for eternity. In other words, these prayers are a healthy and much-needed rebuke to my own heart. They are a wake-up call to my soul to reconsider the way I have constructed my life and the way I spend my time, energy, and money. Second, these prayers guide how I should be interceding for other believers. They provide a standard for how I should be thanking and praising God for what he has done in their lives and what I hope and pray he will be pleased to accomplish in mine.

Paul's prayers for them don't end with verse 4. We read this in verse 11—"To this end we always pray for you, that our God may make you worthy of his calling and may fulfill every resolve for good and every work of faith by his power." Be careful here! Don't think for a moment that Paul is suggesting that they (or anyone else) are "deserving" of their calling. He is not praying that they might merit God's acceptance through their own efforts. The Thessalonians are already Christians! Paul is simply praying that they might live up to that calling, that their lives might accurately reflect the glorious presence and power of the one who has already saved them by grace. In other words, he's saying, "My prayer for you is that God would so work in your lives that your conduct would continue to shine a light on the greatness and grace of the calling that he has placed on you."

Paul also asks that the Lord enable them to "fulfill every resolve" in their hearts to do "good" and that those works that proceed from saving faith and are the product of God's power would be seen by all (v. 11b). All of us make resolutions, be they formed on January 1 for the upcoming year or during the course of everyday life. We resolve to share the gospel with our neighbors. We resolve to serve the poor in our community. We aim to invite the newcomers we encounter at church to lunch. We hope in our hearts to remember next week to sign up to serve in children's ministry. But we so often come up short. When we do succeed in carrying through on our plans and purposes, we must never forget that such is due entirely to "his power" (v. 11).

Why does God orchestrate our lives in this way? Why not make it so that a tiny bit of the power to achieve these good intentions comes from us? The answer is in verse 12. It is all "so that the name of our Lord Jesus may be glorified" in us. Whatever Paul prays for in their lives and whatever you and I pray for in our lives and in the lives of others always has a more ultimate goal. It isn't simply for the sake of seeing transformation occur, but so that whatever change for good we experience redounds to the glory, honor, and praise of Jesus!

But we must not overlook one additional comment by Paul. God's power works in us to fulfill our determination to live in accordance with his revealed will so that we might be glorified "in him" (v. 12). How does that work? It happens when we are made more like Jesus. It works when we are enabled by God's grace (v. 12b) to display the glorious characteristics of Christ himself. Since God makes this possible, and since he is the one to whose moral character we are being conformed, he naturally receives all the glory and praise.

That, in yet another nutshell, is why intercessory prayer and thanksgiving are so vitally important to our lives and the praise of God's wondrous grace.

Conclusion

Before we close this chapter, I want to circle back around to where we began, with a focus on the supernatural nature of Christian living. I say this again because the "power" with which you and I are "empowered" is nothing less than the person, presence, and power of the Holy Spirit himself. So how do we avail ourselves of this power? Let me suggest these five essential steps.

First, honestly and sincerely acknowledge in your heart and before God in prayer that you are spiritually impotent to do anything apart from him. "Precious Savior, I am helpless without you. I make no pretense to be capable of doing anything apart from your powerful presence in my life."

Second, rest in Jesus, who he is and all he has done for you. In other words, turn from self-reliance and self-confidence to a conscious and deliberate trust in Christ. It's not enough to say, "Jesus, I can't do it." We must also say, "Jesus, only you can." "Whoever abides in me and I in him, he it is that bears much fruit, for apart from me you can do nothing" (John 15:5). To "abide" in Jesus means to consistently immerse yourself in his word. Bathe your heart, mind, and soul in its truths. It means to obey his commands. It means to be always prayerful, embedded in Christian community, worshiping Jesus in all of life. It means to live on mission with him every day. It means that your sense of personal identity is inseparable from Jesus: you are in him and he is in you and this truth consistently governs your life.

Third, always make repentance a mainstay in your life. I'm not telling you to obsess over your sin. No. I'm telling you to obsess over the glorious forgiveness that comes through faith in the blood of the cross. Sin grieves the Holy Spirit (Eph. 4:30–31), and a repentant heart thrills him. Unconfessed and unrepented sin is like a kink in a water hose. It stifles and prevents the water from flowing freely. When you repent and come clean with God and rejoice in his forgiving grace, the kink in the connection between you and the Holy Spirit is loosed and his presence and power will flow freely into your life.

Fourth, pray for it: persistently, relentlessly, confidently. "If you then, who are evil, know how to give good gifts to your children, how much more will the heavenly Father give the Holy Spirit to those who ask him!" (Luke 11:13).

Fifth, avail yourself of all the means of grace: study of God's Word, memorization of God's Word, meditation on God's Word, prayer, worship, fellowship with others of like mind, fasting, meditation on God's mighty works in your life and in nature and in the experience of others, and the Lord's Table (communion).

CHAPTER 15

Cultivating a Culture of Prayer
and Evangelism in Your Local Church

> Continue steadfastly in prayer, being watchful in it with thanks-
> giving. At the same time, pray also for us, that God may open to us
> a door for the word, to declare the mystery of Christ, on account
> of which I am in prison—that I may make it clear, which is how I
> ought to speak. (Col. 4:2–4)

In 2019 John Piper released a book with the title, *Why I Love the Apostle Paul: 30 Reasons*.[1] John says several things in the book about the suffering Paul endured and how, through it all, he remained steadfast and unwavering in his proclamation of the gospel and his loyalty to Jesus. I agree with John. I love the apostle Paul for precisely this same reason. To see him grow ever bolder in his preaching of the gospel at the same time his suffering intensified is incredibly encouraging.

It is encouraging because I've never suffered like Paul, and I doubt if many of you have either. As you may recall, Paul didn't like drawing attention to himself unless the spiritual welfare of his people was at stake, and that is precisely the case in 2 Corinthians. The church in Corinth had bought into the lies of certain false teachers who were insisting that Paul wasn't a genuine apostle: he was an impostor. When Paul finally overcame his reluctance to talk about himself, he listed his qualifications to be an apostle of Jesus. In 2 Corinthians 11:23–28, he said:

---

1. John Piper, *Why I Love the Apostle Paul: 30 Reasons* (Wheaton, IL: Crossway, 2019).

Are they [the false teachers in Corinth] servants of Christ? I am a better one—I am talking like a madman—with far greater labors, far more imprisonments, with countless beatings, and often near death. Five times I received at the hands of the Jews the forty lashes less one. Three times I was beaten with rods. Once I was stoned. Three times I was shipwrecked; a night and a day I was adrift at sea; on frequent journeys, in danger from rivers, danger from robbers, danger from my own people, danger from Gentiles, danger in the city, danger in the wilderness, danger at sea, danger from false brothers; in toil and hardship, through many a sleepless night, in hunger and thirst, often without food, in cold and exposure. And, apart from other things, there is the daily pressure on me of my anxiety for all the churches.

When I read that description of his suffering, I can appreciate and understand far better his brief reference here in Colossians 4 to his condition as he wrote this letter to the church in that city. It is, he says, "on account" of his consistent and faithful declaration of "the mystery of Christ" that he is "in prison" (v. 3). At the close of Colossians 4, his final request of the believers in Colossae is that they "remember [his] chains" (Col. 4:18).

Now, it's time for a little confession. I don't know that I could remain steadfast and faithful in those conditions. I hope I could, but without the sustaining power of the Holy Spirit, it would be utterly impossible. I tried on several occasions over the past few years to put myself in the place of Andrew Brunson, whom I mentioned in an earlier chapter. For 18 months, he was "in chains" in Turkey for the simple and sole reason that he proclaimed "the mystery of Christ." In fact, Andrew's condition was in some respects worse than Paul's. Every time I prayed for Andrew's release, I would ask myself: "Sam, how would you fare if you were in prison with him? Would you remain faithful to Jesus, or would you compromise just enough to secure your release?" I'm often tormented by the possible answer to that question.

In any case, here is Paul, in chains, in prison, most likely in Rome. We hear no complaints. We hear none of the things that you and I regularly say when circumstances in our lives turn for the worse, things like: "Why is God doing this to me? Doesn't he care? If he really loved me, would I be suffering like this? I don't know if God can be trusted with my life." Instead, Paul asks that the Colossians pray for him that he might have more opportunities to do the very thing that landed him in prison in the first place!

Do you find that as surprising as I do? Do you find yourself wanting to push back against Paul and say, "Hey, fella, ease off a bit. You are chafing under those chains and suffering massively precisely because you preached the mystery of Christ. Don't you think that it would be prudent and far safer if you just shut up for a while, do your time, and secure your release?" I hate to say it, but I think that might have been my advice to the apostle. But that's not what Paul says. He says, "Pray for me that God would give me even more opportunities while I am yet in prison, in chains, to talk to people about Jesus. In fact, pray that when I do talk to them that I would do so with such clarity and power that they would have no option but to openly reject Jesus or bow their knees in obedience and faith."

So, as we dig into this short paragraph, I want you to hear not only what Paul says about the priority of prayer and preaching but also where he is when he says it. Trust me, if you do that, it will change everything you know and do when it comes to both praying and sharing the gospel of Jesus.

Perseverance in Prayer (Col. 4:2a)

If anyone knew how easy it would be to quit praying, it was Paul. If anyone had seemingly justifiable cause to quit praying, it was Paul. But the first thing he says to the Colossians and to us is, don't quit! "Continue steadfastly in prayer" (v. 2a).

I understand why some of you have stopped praying. So does Paul. Pastors regularly write to me about the untimely deaths in their churches of faithful men and women. Wives tell me their stories about unfaithful husbands. Men weep over a lost job and prolonged unemployment. Families grieve over a stillborn infant or a rebellious teenager.

What makes such incidents especially disturbing is that they all occur notwithstanding persistent and fervent prayer that they not occur. Why is it that a man or woman prays for relief or deliverance or for some essential blessing to alleviate intense aggravation but hears nothing? In humble faith, with sincerity of heart, not for a moment doubting that God is able both to hear and answer their prayers, they pray. But heaven is silent, or so it seems. I once heard a bad joke along those lines:

"What's 'God'?" asked an inquiring soul.

"Oh, well, you know when you close your eyes and ask for something?" his friend responded.

"Yeah."

"Well, God's the one who doesn't answer you."

It's a bad joke, but it rings all too true for many people. People in Paul's day faced the same temptation to quit that we do. But too much was at stake. Though defeated at the cross, Satan is still active. The weakness of the flesh abides. The threat of schism in the body of Christ is ever present. Great opportunities to share the gospel are at every turn. So, don't quit, says Paul! Continue steadfastly in prayer. Keep watch at all times lest you despair. Be thankful for all God has done and will do in response to your petitions.

Be Watchful in Prayer (Col. 4:2b)

The reason why Paul includes this exhortation to be "watchful" in prayer is because we are so easily distracted and we so quickly justify turning our attention to something else. Be alert, says Paul, to all the ways that your life and your flesh—and Satan himself—will do everything possible to get you off track, off focus. The phone rings. You suddenly remember an appointment for which you are already fifteen minutes late. A child cries out for attention. There are any number of distractions that can derail your commitment to prayer. Be watchful! Be alert! Stay on course!

Bathe Your Prayers in Thanksgiving (Col. 4:2c)

I believe Paul includes this qualifying phrase because he wants to instill confidence in us rather than fear and uncertainty as we pray. It's his way of saying, "Yes, by all means be faithful and fervent in your prayers. But know this: God is always and ever on his throne. The battle is ultimately his, on your behalf. Let gratitude for what God has already done and will do yet again permeate your petitions. In this way, you will never lose hope, fall into despair, or live in fear that he has abandoned you in your hour of need."

But how do we do this? What does it mean to pray "with thanksgiving"? Here are a few thoughts.

First, pray with gratitude that *God is actually there*, alive and alert and awake. We do not speak into a vacuum or to a God who is preoccupied with other, allegedly more important matters. I know how it feels when you pray and nothing seems to happen. After a while, you start believing the lie that your words, your tears, your impassioned pleas just drifted off into a black hole. What feels like the most reasonable thing to do in those horrible moments of virtual despair is to quit, to devote yourself to some task more productive and fruitful. But hear Paul's urgent plea: "Continue steadfastly in prayer" (v. 2).

Second, pray with gratitude that God not only lives and loves but also *actually listens* to what we say. He hears us! I know how much of a challenge it is to believe that is true, but it is true!

Third, pray with gratitude that the God who lives, loves, and listens is also *more than able to do above and beyond all we ask or think* (cf. Eph. 3:20). I'm so thankful that the God to whom I pray isn't a wimp or a weakling but an omnipotent and infinitely wise Father who delights in giving good things to those who ask (Luke 11:13).

Fourth, pray by thanking God that he has chosen to *include you in the process*! God could have ordained that all his will be accomplished independently of our participation. But he didn't. He has chosen to achieve his ultimate ends through means, the latter being primarily our prayers.

Fifth, pray by thanking God for all the ways he is *changing you* as you pray. Wholehearted and humble intercession transforms the intercessor. Our ideas of God are elevated. Our awareness of personal dependency is intensified. The magnitude of God's power and providence is manifest in ways that we otherwise might never behold. Our dreams, hopes, and desires are cleansed and purified as we humbly submit to his will and crucify our own.

Sixth, pray by thanking God that what you are asking him to graciously do in the lives of others *he has already done in yours*! If we are not grateful for the salvation, healing, and mercy granted us, how can we possibly be fervent and diligent in asking that God do the same for others?

Lastly, seventh, pray with gratitude to God not simply for what he has done but *for what he will do*. Thank him in advance for what he will do in response to your requests. Without being triumphalistic or sinfully presumptuous, we should pray with expectancy that whatever we ask, according to his will, God will do. Thank you, Lord!

The bottom line is this: It's hard to be fearful when you are immersed in gratitude. Thankfulness turns the human soul toward heaven and away from self. Thankfulness, by its very nature, requires that we fix our focus on "that" God is, "who" God is, and "what" God has done and will do. Thankful prayer is necessarily theocentric.

I'm sure you recall the incident in 2 Chronicles 20 where Jehoshaphat and the kingdom of Judah came under siege by the Moabites and Ammonites. After their prayer seeking God's assistance, the prophet Jahaziel came to them with a bizarre word of counsel: Send out the choir to confront the enemy troops and have them sing these words: "Give thanks to the LORD, for his steadfast love endures forever" (2 Chron. 20:21).

He instructs them to be thankful on the front end of the battle, before the enemy is ever engaged. On the surface, that doesn't seem very practical. Shouldn't we wait to see if God will really do what we ask and then thank him? Not always. He told them to let the reality of God's steadfast love fill your heart. Praise him for who he is. Rest peacefully in what he will do. "Stand firm," he said, "hold your position, and see the salvation of the LORD on your behalf" (2 Chron. 20:17).

God's Sovereignty in Evangelism (Col. 4:3a)

We all agree that God loves lost souls and wants them to hear the gospel of salvation in his Son. So why does he suspend the opening of an evangelistic door to them on the prayers of the Colossians? "God, why don't you directly open these doors rather than telling Paul to tell us to ask you to do so? What's the point of our asking you to do what you've already revealed is in your heart to accomplish?"

I suspect God's response to me would be: "No, Sam. That's not how I operate. Yes, of course, I could 'just do it' directly and instantaneously, without your involvement or anyone else's. But I prefer to do it when you ask me to. In fact, in most instances I won't do it unless you ask me to."

Here's another question that comes to mind: Why does Paul encourage the Colossians to pray for him? What's the point of his asking them to ask God to open a door for the word? Isn't it enough that he asks God himself? I'm assuming he did, but he evidently believed that it would greatly help his cause if others joined him in beseeching God for this blessing. Does this imply that God is more inclined to say yes to our requests if more people are united in asking him for them? That seems odd.

Let's be clear about one thing. I didn't ask these questions because I intend to solve the tension between divine sovereignty and human responsibility. I couldn't solve it even if I wanted to, and how prayer factors into the equation is way beyond my pay grade. Rather, I'm concerned about the nature of prayer. Or, more accurately, I'm concerned about the purpose of prayer. Why has God chosen to incorporate it into the way he governs the world and accomplishes his purposes?

One thing we know: *God loves to be asked*, and there's good reason for it. Consider Psalm 50:12, one of the most sarcastic verses in Scripture. God says to the Israelites: "If I were hungry, I would not tell you, for the world and its fullness are mine." If God were hungry (which, of course, he's not), he doesn't need the Israelites to provide him with a meal. "Every beast of the forest is mine," says the Lord, "[not to mention] the cattle on a thousand hills" (Ps. 50:10).

So, if God doesn't need us or our prayers, why does he create us and then command us to ask him for things? That's a pretty profound question, but it comes with a simple answer.

In Psalm 50:15, God says, in essence, "When you're in trouble, when you have needs and problems and trials and obstacles to overcome, pray to me and ask that I intervene and make provision. If you do, I'll deliver you. And in your obvious dependence upon me I will be glorified. *We both win. You get delivered. I get glorified.* You receive a blessing. And people, angels, and demons see that I'm the all-sufficient supply, the infinitely resourceful God, the one being in the universe who exists to overflow in abundant goodness to weak and needy people like you!"

It's amazing how asking a few questions about prayer drives us directly into the reason why God created the universe! God didn't create us because he was needy or lacking in some profound way. We don't supply God with anything. "The God who made the world and everything in it, being Lord of heaven and earth, does not live in temples made by man, nor is he served by human hands, as though he needed anything, since he himself gives to all mankind life and breath and everything" (Acts 17:24–25).

So, that being true, why did he make it all? He made it all so that in its (our) utter and absolute dependence on him for everything, his glory as

God might be seen and savored. Our need magnifies his supply. Our lack draws attention to his abundance. God glorifies himself by overflowing in bountiful blessings to those who otherwise deserve only death. And how do we get these blessings? By praying for them! God suspends his work on our prayers not because he can't do it alone but because our prayers highlight our dependence and his supply. We are humbled as dependent, and he is exalted as depended upon!

Not only does he get the glory for being depended upon, but we get the gladness for being dependent! There is no greater joy than getting what God gives (and he is himself, of course, the greatest gift). And there is no greater glory than for God to be giving. Jesus commanded his disciples to pray, and here's why: "Whatever you ask in my name, this I will do, that the Father may be glorified in the Son" (John 14:13). Although there are undoubtedly other reasons why God chose to incorporate our prayers in the accomplishment of his purposes, his glory is preeminent.

Earlier, I asked why Paul felt it important to enlist the prayers of the Colossians on his behalf. It's not because God is stingy and a multitude of intercessors might have greater success in prevailing on God's otherwise reluctant heart than Paul alone. Once again, it's all about God's glory. We saw this earlier in 2 Corinthians 1:11 where Paul wrote, "You also must help us by prayer, so that many will give thanks on our behalf for the blessing granted us through the prayers of many."

Note carefully why it's important that the Corinthians pray for him. It is so that "many will give thanks" for the "blessing" that God grants to him in response to their prayers. God's glory is more readily seen, known, and savored when "many" rise in unified gratitude for what he has done than if only one or a few do. So, when we pray for one another, we get gladness in receiving what God gives, and God gets glory for giving what we get.

Before I move on, a brief word is in order regarding the issue of both "open" and "closed" doors (Col. 4:3; see also Acts 14:27; 1 Cor. 16:8–9; 2 Cor. 2:12). The "door," evidently, is closed. This may suggest political opposition, social, cultural, and educational barriers to sharing the faith, adverse weather that hinders travel, or any number of factors that make evangelism difficult from a human perspective. It may be that Paul is asking God to grant him favor with those who have the authority to give him access to certain arenas of activity or platforms from which he might declare his message. In any case,

Paul believed that God was sovereign over all such circumstances and that he could remove obstacles, overcome resistance, and restrain the enemies of the faith when asked to do so by his people.

That an apostle, no less, would ask ordinary Christians like these Colossians to pray for his evangelistic success is stunning. Paul refused to trust in his skill or eloquence or theological knowledge alone. He needed the intercessory support of other believers. It's almost as if he's saying, "I'm helpless if you don't ask God to help me." And it's even more amazing when we remember that Paul had never met these people!

The Content of Our Message: the Mystery of Christ (Col. 4:3b)

And what might Paul or you and I do should the door be opened? We should have one goal, one solitary purpose: to proclaim the mystery of Christ. The word *mystery* doesn't mean what it does in a P. D. James novel or in a Sudoku puzzle. Paul typically uses this word when he has in mind a truth formerly hidden but now made known in Jesus Christ.

The "mystery" of Christ is the revelation of what God has done in and through his Son to make possible atonement for sin and its forgiveness. That the Word should become flesh (John 1:14) is a mystery now made known for our salvation. That God was in Christ reconciling the world to himself (2 Cor. 5:19) is a mystery now revealed for our justification. That faith alone in the crucified Messiah is the power of God unto salvation (1 Cor. 1:18) is a mystery now made known for our eternal welfare.

Where Christ is not proclaimed, the gospel is not known. No matter how psychologically soothing a sermon may be, if the mystery of Christ is not center stage, the gospel has not been preached. The focus of our message is not self-esteem, social justice, the plight of the poor, or world peace (as important as those issues are in their own right), but Jesus Christ crucified and risen for the salvation of lost souls.

The Clarity of Our Message (Col. 4:4)

Finally, and this may well be the strangest thing of all in Paul's request of the Colossians, he asks them to ask God that he might grant Paul clarity in how he should speak. "Pray that God will work in me," says Paul, "that I might have the words to speak in the most persuasive manner and at the most appropriate time. Ask God to operate in my heart and mind and soul so that my message will ring true and reverberate with passion, conviction, and courage." Stunning, isn't it, that a man of Paul's spiritual caliber felt so dependent on the prayers of others for his effectiveness in ministry (cf. Rom. 15:30–31)!

His request of the Colossians raises an interesting question: What precisely might hinder his clarity of speech or prevent him from proclaiming the gospel in the way he desired? It may be that he anticipated trick questions from a hostile crowd and needs the assistance of the Spirit to see through their deception and speak truth into the fog of error. It may be that he sensed the importance of using just the right illustration, parable, or analogy to make a point that would penetrate a closed and calloused heart with the truth that brings light and life. Paul, no doubt, sometimes felt confused and needed the quickening ministry of the Spirit in his mind. "Pray that God would clear my head of intellectual cobwebs and overcome any sluggishness of speech that would be unworthy of the gospel I proclaim. Pray that the Father would fill me with the Spirit of boldness and confidence and drive from me all fear of man and concern for my own reputation or physical safety."

Conclusion

Let's face it: prayer is simultaneously both one of the most rewarding and satisfying privileges we have as Christians as well as one of the most frustrating and confusing of spiritual experiences. Knowing that we are partners with God in implementing and fulfilling his will is rewarding. Experiencing the dramatic and often miraculous answer to our prayers is fulfilling. But prayer can also be incredibly frustrating when heaven seems silent, almost indifferent to our passionate pleas for help. It is also confusing when we ask why God even bothers to ask us to ask him to do what he already wants done. What's the point of prayer?

I certainly have no delusions about answering all your questions concerning prayer. I can't, and no one else can either. But one thing I do know: prayer is the Christian's life-support system. Without it, we will suffocate spiritually. Without it, we will wither and die. Without it, we will never see victory in our lives or in the life of the church. Without it, we will never experience divine healing or revival or the defeat of the devil or intimacy with Jesus. Without prayer, there simply is no Christianity. That's the way God set it up, whether we like it or understand it or not.

Allow me to repeat myself: it is dangerous and ultimately destructive to you and me if we ever fall into the trap of thinking that God will do for us apart from prayer what he has ordained to do for us only through prayer.

My aim in this book is quite practical in nature. I want to challenge you to commit yourself to a life of consistent, persistent prayer. I want to help you, as best I can, become active and energetic in praying for one another, for the salvation of lost souls, for divine healing, for heaven-sent revival, for victory in spiritual warfare, and for an increase in your intimacy with the Lord Jesus.

"But, Sam, prayer is so hard! It's an unrelenting battle, a struggle for which I feel so profoundly inadequate," you might say. Yes, I know. I'm often encouraged in my own intercessory struggle by the example of others. Consider David Brainerd (1718–47), missionary to the American Indians, who, for a season, lived in the home of Jonathan Edwards. Brainerd frequently wrote in his *Diary* of "wrestling" with God in prayer. The entry for Monday, April 19, 1742, reads in part,

> God enabled me so to agonize in prayer, that I was quite wet with sweat, though in the shade, and the wind cool. My soul was drawn out very much for the world; I grasped for multitudes of souls.[2]

On the next day, Brainerd wrote:

> I think my soul was never so drawn out in intercession for others as it has been this night. Had a most fervent wrestle with the Lord tonight for my enemies.[3]

Again,

---

2. Jonathan Edwards, *The Life of David Brainerd*, ed. Norman Pettit (New Haven, CT: Yale University Press, 1985), 162.
3. Edwards, *The Life of David Brainerd*, 162.

[I] was enabled to cry to God with a child-like spirit, and to continue instant in prayer for some time. Was much enlarged in the sweet duty of intercession. Was enabled to remember great numbers of dear friends and precious souls, as well as Christ's ministers. Continued in this frame, afraid of every idle thought, till I dropped asleep.[4]

This sort of striving and struggling with God in prayer is proper so long as it does not degenerate into a conflict of wills. The function of prayer is not to bend God's will to ours, or to wrench from him what he is reluctant to give. We must never believe ourselves capable of overpowering the Creator or forcing his hand. That being said, when was the last time you had "a most fervent wrestle with the Lord" on behalf of those you know and love, not to mention those who have not seen you face-to-face? Would that God might energize us in the struggle, empower us to agonize in our intercession, and stir us to strive without ceasing in prayer for one another.

---

4. Edwards, *The Life of David Brainerd*, 260.

PART 3

COMING CONFIDENTLY TO THE THRONE OF GRACE

CHAPTER 16

When Young Ravens Cry

Since then we have a great high priest who has passed through the heavens, Jesus, the Son of God, let us hold fast our confession. For we do not have a high priest who is unable to sympathize with our weaknesses, but one who in every respect has been tempted as we are, yet without sin. Let us then with confidence draw near to the throne of grace, that we may receive mercy and find grace to help in time of need. (Heb. 4:14–16)

Allow me to set the stage, so to speak, for what we read here in Hebrews 4:14–16, especially verse 16, on which we will focus most of our attention.

All of us are in need. All of us face situations with other people that stretch our wisdom to the limit. All of us encounter obstacles and land mines in life that we don't know how to navigate. All of us find ourselves in relational circumstances with other people that anger us, frustrate us, and leave us feeling alone and wounded. We all hurt physically. Some live with crippling doubt or paralyzing anxiety. Some fear the future while others regret the past.

And it really doesn't matter what your biggest problem is today. It doesn't matter whether it is like that of the person sitting next to you in church or if yours is unique. It doesn't matter if it's recent, you've been saddled with it for years, or it happened thirty minutes before you began reading this book. The only thing that matters is that you have great need, and you know it, and that you turn to the only person and place where genuine, life-changing help can be found. And that's what this passage of Scripture instructs us to do.

Two Truths / Two Exhortations

In verses 14–16, there are two exhortations, each grounded in a profound spiritual truth. In both cases, the reason is stated first, then followed by the exhortation.

The first spiritual truth is found in verse 14a: "Since then we have a great high priest who has passed through the heavens, Jesus, the Son of God." There it is. Did you notice that word *since*? We could as easily render it "because," that is to say, "*because*" we have Jesus as our great high priest. That's the reason, the basis, the foundation, and the grounds for the exhortation to follow.

Having just been told in verses 12–13 that the Word of God pierces and divides and discerns our hearts and thoughts and intentions, having been told that we are all laid bare and exposed to the God to whom we must give an account, there is a strong likelihood that some will recoil in fear. The fear of judgment and the fear and apprehension of standing in an infinitely holy God's presence might paralyze some. So, our author says, "No, no, don't be afraid. You must remember that Jesus is your high priest. He is the Son of God and has passed through the heavens and has taken his seat at the right hand of God, there to intercede on your behalf. He's your advocate. He's your defense attorney. He's your eternal friend."

And what is the exhortation that is based on it? It's there in verse 14b: "*let us hold fast our confession.*" Because Jesus is our great high priest, we have all the more reason to hold firmly our confession of faith in him. We see this same urgent appeal in Hebrews 3:6 and 3:14, where our author spoke of holding fast our confidence firm to the end. In other words, don't despair in your faith; don't give up hope; don't abandon your confidence in Christ. Why? Because he is your great high priest!

The second spiritual truth is found in verse 15. Try to understand why our author says what he does about Jesus in this verse. In speaking of Jesus as our "*high* priest" it almost sounds as if he's detached from us, distant from us, indifferent toward the needs, worries, and fears of ordinary people like us. But no, says our author, he's not that kind of high priest. Let me tell you what he's like and why you can trust him and why he can be counted on to understand your deepest struggles and pain. Having been tempted just like us, he can sympathize with us in our struggles. He knows what you're feeling and facing in life.

Jesus, our high priest, is not like the priests of the old covenant, such as Aaron, who were sinners and had to offer sacrifices for their own transgressions. No, Jesus was tempted just like us and can, therefore, sympathize with our weaknesses, but he never yielded to temptation.

We see this same truth in Hebrews 2:18: "For because he himself has suffered when tempted, he is able to help those who are being tempted." But doesn't the fact that he *didn't* sin mean he *can't* truly identify with me and know deeply the struggles with sin that I face? Or, as one young woman put it to me: "If Jesus never sinned, then he doesn't know what temptation is like. He lived a sheltered life and is out of touch with how strong temptation can be." I surprised her when I responded by asserting that, actually, it is only the person who *never* yields to temptation who actually knows how strong it can be. If you are tempted and quickly sin, you never get to the point where you feel the full force and nefarious nature of sin's appeal. You lose too soon. It is precisely because Jesus never yielded to temptation that he felt its full strength. By not giving in to the lie that sin speaks to us, he continued to feel its relentless assault far beyond the point where you and I typically give in. In other words, it isn't that Jesus doesn't understand what we face when temptation comes our way. It is *we* who will never understand what *Jesus* experienced when temptation came his way.

There is an important difference between the *expressions* of sin and the *essence* of sin. Expressions change over time. Jesus wasn't tempted to pull out a gun and shoot someone in cold blood. He wasn't tempted to cheat on his income taxes. He wasn't tempted to watch pornography on the Internet. He wasn't tempted to exceed the limit on his credit card by purchasing things he really didn't need. These particular expressions are unique to our century. But the essence of sin hasn't changed. Jesus was tempted with unrighteous anger, greed, lust, hatred, and every other sinful temptation that we face. And he faced them all without yielding and thus knows the battle each of us faces. He doesn't roll his eyes at your pain or shrug his shoulders indifferently or in ignorance of what you are enduring.

That's the second spiritual truth that serves as a reason, basis, or foundation for a crucial exhortation. And that exhortation is found in Hebrews 4:16: "Let us then with confidence draw near to the throne of grace." The word *then* is actually a weak translation. The word means "therefore." Again, it is "because" we have a high priest who knows what we face and feel in our battle with temptation that we "therefore" must draw near to the throne of grace when we're in a mess and need help.

In this chapter, we will only examine the second of these two exhortations, the one in verse 16.

Answering Four Crucial Questions

So let's look at this from the perspective of four questions.

(1) Where Are We to Go?

How many times have you cried out in desperation, "I just don't know where to turn! I don't know whom to trust! I don't have any place left to go! Where can I find the grace I need?" Here we are told: "Draw near to the throne of grace."

What comes to mind when you envision a *throne*? A king? A sovereign ruler? Yes, God is the great monarch of the universe, the eternal potentate, premier, and president of the cosmos all wrapped up in one. Knowing this ought to create expectancy in our hearts. We are not coming to a cosmic welfare agency for a meager handout or to the back door for scraps off someone's dinner plate. When we need grace for our souls we are coming to the *throne* of the King of kings! "In prayer," said Spurgeon, "we stand where angels bow with veiled faces; there, even there, the cherubim and seraphim adore, before that selfsame throne to which our prayers ascend."[1]

Some people, on the other hand, are more intimidated than encouraged by the idea of a throne. The regal atmosphere, the power and dignity associated with one who sits on a throne, might put hesitation in more than a few hearts. That is, until we see that this is a throne *of grace*. Our author could have, but didn't, say the throne "of God" or the throne "of heaven." Make no mistake. It is certainly a throne to which we come. But it is grace that awaits us there. It is grace that sits enthroned. It is not a throne of law, criticism, or judgment, but of grace. This throne exists to dispense grace to those who seek it. Its purposes are gracious. The utterances spoken there are gracious. The answers to prayer received there are all of grace.

---

1. Charles Spurgeon, "The Throne of Grace," in *Spurgeon's Expository Encyclopedia*, vol. 12 (Grand Rapids: Baker, 1996), 206.

This being a throne of grace means our prayers will always be heard. Though they often seem empty and frivolous to us, perhaps poorly constructed and poorly conceived, even badly spoken, God hears us. If this were a throne of justice or a throne of grammatical precision, we might have reason to worry, but it is a throne of *grace*! God doesn't care much for stately etiquette, courtly manners, or palatial proprieties as earthly rulers do. The latter are quick to judge for one social *faux pas*. God only looks for humility and desperation in those who would petition him. So, come. Ask him for grace to love him, to obey him, to enjoy him. Come falteringly and failingly, and, by all means, come frequently.

What if we can't put words to our wants? Because this is a gracious throne, *God will read your desires without the words*. When my daughters were young and struggled to articulate their desires and needs, I didn't berate them or denounce their feeble efforts. I would help them any way I could, even by suggesting the very words they longed to utter. Will our heavenly Father do less for us? Spurgeon put it this way:

> He [God] will put the desires, and put the expression of those desires into your spirit by His grace; He will direct your desires to the things which you ought to seek for; He will teach you your wants, though as yet you know them not; He will suggest to you His promises that you may be able to plead them; He will, in fact, be Alpha and Omega to your prayer, just as He is to your salvation; for as salvation is from first to last of grace, so the sinner's approach to the throne of grace is of grace from first to last.[2]

Because it is a throne of grace, nothing is required of you but your need. Your ticket to this throne is not works, but *desperation*. God doesn't want sacrifice or gifts or good intentions. He wants your *helplessness* in order that the sufficiency of his grace, at work on your behalf, might be magnified. This is a throne for the spiritually bankrupt to come and find the wealth of God's energizing presence. "This is not the throne of majesty which supports itself by the taxation of its subjects, but a throne which glorifies itself by streaming forth like a fountain with floods of good things."[3]

---

2. Spurgeon, "The Throne of Grace," 210.
3. Spurgeon, "The Throne of Grace," 210.

(2) How Often Should We Come?

The verb translated "let us draw near" conveys the sense of an approach that never ends. It is to be a daily, dare I say, hourly approach. We are constantly to come near to God. There is never a time when it is inappropriate. There is never a time when he is unavailable. There is never a circumstance that makes approaching the throne of grace a bad idea.

This notion would have been entirely foreign to those steeped in the rituals of the old covenant Levitical system. Under the old covenant, the only person allowed into God's presence was the high priest, and even in his case, he could draw near to God only on one day of the year, the Day of Atonement. Although the high priest represented the people, they were still locked out of God's presence. Their approach was forbidden. But here we are invited, indeed commanded, to come always and at every point of need.

(3) How Should We Approach God?

Our author answers this second question with one word: *confidence*. Confidence in what? Confidence in God, of course. The confidence that comes from knowing we have a great high priest who knows our thoughts, our hurts, our worst fears, and our deepest desires. But I want to suggest that this confidence is grounded not only in what God has done but in *who we are because of what God has done*. The psalmist said of God that "he gives to the beasts their food, and to the young ravens that cry" (Ps. 147:9). Could it be that this is what Jesus had in mind when he said, "Consider the ravens: they neither sow nor reap, they have neither storehouse nor barn, and yet God feeds them. Of how much more value are you than the birds!" (Luke 12:24). This is marvelous logic indeed.

The raven is but a bird, whose death means little. We, on the other hand, are immortal souls. No raven, as far as I know, will ever be redeemed, resurrected, or raptured. Could God hear its cry but turn a deaf ear to yours? No raven was ever formed in the image of God. If you heard the cry of a hungry raven simultaneous with the cry of an abandoned and starving infant, to which would you first give aid? I know, it's a silly question. But we are not better than God, are we? If we have the good sense to first help the one who bears the divine image, will God do less?

Be it noted that Jesus refers to a *raven*, not a hawk or falcon or eagle or cardinal or robin or any such bird of beauty. It is to the lowly and seemingly useless raven that he appeals. If God would provide for the needs of such an insignificant bird, will he not happily and generously provide for yours? So, come to the throne of grace with confidence.

Let's stay with this analogy for a moment. Consider the cry of the raven. It speaks no words, articulates no phrases, formulates no arguments. Its cry is purely of instinct. The raven makes no appeal to grace and knows nothing of the high priest, Jesus. In fact, Jesus didn't die for a single raven, yet the Father graciously cares for their needs. How much more, then, shall he graciously care for yours?

Nowhere are ravens commanded to cry to God, yet we are repeatedly exhorted to do so. We have the divine warrant to come to this gracious throne. Ravens aren't told to come, yet they never go away empty. You and I come as invited guests. How, then, shall we be denied by him who has issued the invitation?

The cry of the raven is at best that of an unthinking animal. Ours is the cry of the precious Holy Spirit within us (cf. Rom. 8:26ff.). When the ravens cry to God they do so alone, but we cry jointly with our heavenly intercessor, the Lord Jesus Christ (Heb. 7:25). If the mere chattering of a single bird prevails upon God, how much more shall the petitions of his blood-bought child who can clench a request with the biblical plea, "Father, do it for Jesus' sake!"

So, come to the throne of grace *with confidence*.

(4) What Would You Expect to Find at a Throne of Grace?

Grace, of course! But more than that, *mercy* too! Finding sympathy and understanding is one thing, but we need power, energy, and sustaining strength in the inner man. The purpose of this prayer isn't primarily that we might feel better but that we might *get grace* that will help us in our moment of need. When we come boldly and confidently to the throne of grace in prayer, God doesn't just feel sorry for us. His response isn't, "Oh my, what a pathetic creature you are. You really got yourself into a mess this time, didn't you? Shame on you!"

No! No! God doesn't berate you when you come to him. The first thing out of his mouth isn't, "Well, where have you been? I guess you thought you could get along well enough without me until things got really bad. What do you expect from me now? Do you expect that after ignoring me all this time, I'll just let bygones be bygones and give you whatever you ask?" If that were God's response, our author couldn't possibly have described this as a throne of grace.

He doesn't make fun of you either. He doesn't mock you or ridicule you or openly compare you to other Christians who are much more consistent in their prayer lives.

So, what is this "grace" that we get when we come to the throne of God? Well, it isn't the sort of grace that merely tells us what to do. This is the grace that energizes and empowers us to do what God has told us to do. Grace doesn't merely point us in the direction of holiness; it infuses power that we might actually walk in that way. Grace is more than words of exhortation or cheers of encouragement. Grace is more than reasons to obey or arguments to persevere. *Grace is power. Grace is energy. Grace is God at work in us to change us.* Grace changes how we think, giving plausibility and sense to ideas once believed to be false. Grace changes how we feel, bringing joy in Jesus and revulsion for sin. Grace changes how we choose, creating new and deeper desires for what we once found unappealing. Grace changes how we act, equipping and energizing the soul to do what we have failed to do so many times before.

If we are to have hope for holiness, we must have the heart-changing, mind-changing, will-changing work of divine grace that is sovereignly bestowed when heart-weak, mind-weak, will-weak people ask for it from the only place it may be found: the throne of grace.

If I may, for a moment, direct your attention to Philippians 2:12–13, I think you'll see what I mean. There Paul speaks of "God who works in you, both *to will* and *to work* for his good pleasure" (2:13). If we are to resist temptation, if we are to say no to sin, walk in sexual purity and integrity of heart, *God* must be *at work* in us. When Paul says that God works in us so that we might "will" what is right, he has in mind a volitional resolve on our part. God energizes our minds and hearts to want to work his will. This is grace! This is the Holy Spirit creating in us a desire and a love and an inclination to happily embrace whatever pleases the Father (cf. Ps. 119:36).

When Paul says that God works in us so that we might "work" what is right, he again has in mind divine grace that brings to effectual fruition the behavioral end toward which our will is inclined. In other words, the continuous and sustained working *out* on the part of the Christian is the *gracious product* of the continuous and sustained working *in* on the part of

God. We not only *desire*, we also *do*, by virtue of the dynamic, antecedent activity of *grace* in our souls.

This is the grace that constitutes the help that God so freely supplies in response to the humble prayer of those who rely on him for holiness. God helps by imparting to our souls a new taste for spiritual things that we might relish and savor the sweetness of Christ above all rival flavors. He helps by infusing our hearts with a new disposition, a fresh way of thinking, a passion for the joy of enjoying him. This *help* is *grace*! Without it we are hopelessly consigned to living out the impulses of the flesh that will invariably lead us into the deceitfulness of sin (cf. Heb. 3:12).

If we are to find in Jesus the fairest of ten thousand, if we are to revel in the joy he so generously supplies, our hearts must be fed with grace. If we are to see in him surpassing excellency and for that reason say no to the passing pleasures of sin, our hearts must be fed with grace. If we are to be fed with grace, we must come boldly to the throne on which it is seated, poised and ready to help us in our time of need, and we must ask.

And if you and I are to find answers to our questions, strength to face today, patience to endure next week, power to overcome Satan's seductions, and hope to stay on the right track until Jesus comes back, we must come to the throne of grace. *Don't bring with you anything other than your need of Christ.* Don't come with promises and reminders of past triumphs. Don't come with money or some other form of bribery. Don't come with apologies or regrets. Come empty and needy with an open hand and open heart, and let God fill you with grace and mercy to help you in your hour of need.

PART 4

LEARNING ABOUT PRAYER FROM JAMES

CHAPTER 17

Asking God for Wisdom to Make Sense of the Seemingly Senseless

> If any of you lacks wisdom, let him ask God, who gives generously
> to all without reproach, and it will be given him. But let him ask
> in faith, with no doubting, for the one who doubts is like a wave
> of the sea that is driven and tossed by the wind. For that person
> must not suppose that he will receive anything from the Lord; he
> is a double-minded man, unstable in all his ways. (James 1:5–8)

The primary theme of the epistle of James is that *Christianity is not just a body of doctrines to believe but also a life to be pursued in the power of a living faith.* In other words, James, perhaps more so than any other New Testament book, calls on us to practice daily what we profess to believe. In fact, James will go so far as to say that *a work-less faith is a worth-less faith.* In true, genuine Christianity, that experience of the soul that we call "faith" is alive, energetic, and productive. James will argue in chapter two that whereas faith alone justifies us in God's sight, such faith is never alone. It is always accompanied by the fruit of the Holy Spirit or obedience.

The greatest threat to the vibrancy and sincerity of our faith is suffering. Nothing will cause us more quickly to question the goodness of God, indeed, the very existence of God, than chronic, unrelenting pain. The non-Christian world doesn't experience this sort of disconnect. For those who deny the existence of God, pain, hardship, tragedy, and disappointment are ultimately meaningless. They are pointless. But for the Christian, who believes that God created all that exists and that he providentially governs everything that happens, trials and challenges often cause us to wonder: "God, are you there? God, do you care? God, can I trust you with my life?"

In James 1:2 he tells us how to respond to adversity: count it all joy! That's easier said than done. Sometimes it feels downright impossible. James knows that as well as anyone. That's what I appreciate about him. If he's anything, he's a realist. This man is no pie-in-the-sky, ivory-tower theologian, detached from the harsh realities of life in a fallen world or dropping pious nuggets of abstract theory on the heads of suffering men and women. Not for a moment!

James knows from experience that responding to pain and suffering with joy is perhaps the greatest challenge we face as Christians. He knows this doesn't come naturally. He knows when the human heart is engulfed and surrounded by dark clouds of tragedy and disillusionment, the experience of joy can seem a million miles away. People who have suffered greatly often describe it as a dense fog that blinds them to anything but the immediate experience of fear and anger. They can't see through the fog to anything that remotely approaches a good God, a beneficial purpose, or anything that feels redemptive.

We all know from personal experience that the ability to look on trials and tribulations as an occasion for joy, rather than bitterness, is God given. It is not something we instinctively embrace. It is a divine gift. And here is the good news: *it's ours for the asking!* That is James' point in chapter one, verses 5–8 of his letter.

If you are among the countless Christians who struggle to see your suffering and heartache from God's perspective, if you see no value in the countless obstacles you confront each day, if you live in constant confusion about what God might be up to in your life, pray! Ask him for help! Ask him for insight! Ask him for wisdom! Ask him to supply you with spiritual eyes to see what he's trying to accomplish in your life.

Let's be honest with each other. There are times in all our lives when despite what James says in verse 2, we simply can't "count it all joy" because the trials we encounter are so random, so seemingly senseless, and, worst of all, so undeserved, that we find it virtually impossible to "know" what James says in verse 3 we should know. In other words, James clearly indicates that the key to enduring trials with joy is our ability to "know" or "understand" that God's purpose in them is to transform us to look more like Jesus. But some trials are so overwhelming and persistent that we can't see anything but the trial. It blinds us to anything God might be up to.

What are we to do when that happens? Is our case hopeless? Does God just cut us loose in frustration and turn his attention to those Christians who are able to understand what he's up to in their lives? No! You aren't hopeless. Your situation is not beyond God's ability and willingness to redeem. Here is what James says you are to do: pray!

God-Given Wisdom (James 1:5a)

Before we look at what James actually says, I know precisely what you *wish* he had said. I know because I wish that he had said it too. Would that James had said, "Hey folks, if you can't quite comprehend God's purpose in your trials, don't worry; just ask him to remove them. Come on, God, push delete on those painful circumstances. Make them disappear. You can do it. Come on, come on, I know you can!" Alas, that is not what James says. So, what does he say? Let's look.

First, the "wisdom" that God promises to give us when we pray is the insight we need to make sense of what otherwise appears to be senseless suffering. We can't wrench this promise from its context and apply it to every other problem we face. So, be careful before you appeal to this text to find assurance that God will always tell you which of several people you should marry, or that God will always tell you which of three job opportunities you should select, or that God will tell you which stock is worthy of your financial investment.

The promise is for wisdom to "know" your trials are not without meaning or value. God can use them for your ultimate welfare. And once you "know" that, you will find the strength to "count it all joy" when those trials come your way.

Now, don't be misled. I'm not saying you shouldn't pray for discernment and guidance when it comes to finding a spouse, a job, a worthy investment for your money, or any such decisions you face. But that's not what this text is about. Later, in James 4:2, we are told to pray about everything and that the reason we so often go without is because we simply fail to ask. In James 5, he will tell us to pray for healing when we are sick. Paul in Philippians 4:6 exhorts us to let our "requests be made known to God," and there are no restrictions on what we should or shouldn't pray for. But here in James 1, the context must be observed.

Second, the promise of wisdom to discern God's plan and purpose and reason for our trials does not mean he will always grant us perfect understanding of why things happen the way they do. Rarely do we have exhaustive knowledge of why tragedies occur or how all the pieces of life's jigsaw puzzle fall into place. What God promises is sufficient wisdom to help us know and rest confidently in the fact that trials serve a greater purpose in our lives.

In relation to this, let me say one more thing. *Exhaustive or comprehensive knowledge isn't the cure-all that many think it is.* When you experience sudden and undeserved tragedy, knowing where it came from and what purpose it serves doesn't always diminish the pain you feel. I've spoken to and prayed with a lot of people who suffered the loss of a loved one in a car accident or from cancer, or people who have lost their jobs for no justifiable reason. I've asked them, "If you were given perfect and comprehensive insight into why this happened and what benefits will come to you from having endured it, would it make it any less painful and distressing?" Nine times out of ten they say no.

So, what precisely does he mean by the word *wisdom*? Some define it as the ability to select worthy ends and the most effective means of achieving them. J. I. Packer has said that wisdom is "the power to see, and the inclination to choose, the best and highest goal, together with the surest means of attaining it."[1] Someone else said that whereas "knowledge" is the ability to take things apart, wisdom is the ability to put them together again.

For James, "wisdom" is both intelligence and insight, both understanding and application, both theory and practical moral discernment. In James 1:5, it is that perception, insight, discernment, or quality of mind that enables the Christian to confront and submit to life's hardships with attitudes and actions consistent with God's will. *It is the God-given ability to take the scattered, chaotic, and seemingly senseless trials and afflictions of life and understand them as God's way of producing Christian maturity.*

I once read about a woman who worked for Warren Wiersbe, former pastor of Moody Bible Church in Chicago. She suffered a stroke, and her husband went blind. Wiersbe told her, "I'm praying for you." She said, "What

---

1. J. I. Packer, *Knowing God* (Downers Grove, IL: IVP Books, 1993 [1973]), 90.

are you praying for?" He responded, "I'm praying for God to help sustain and strengthen you." She said, "Good, but pray also that I'll have the wisdom not to waste all this." That's what James is talking about.

The Necessity of Prayer (James 1:5b)

Don't overlook the fact that God doesn't give wisdom willy-nilly or randomly or irrespective of whether we ask him for it. If you need and want wisdom, you must ask for it! Someone once said that "God will have everything fetched out by prayer." Simply put, as I've said numerous times in this book, *we must never assume that God will give us apart from prayer what he has promised to give us only through prayer.* Don't ever make the mistake of thinking: "Well, of course God will help me understand this mess I'm in. He's God. That's what he's in business for. So, I'll get on to more important matters and not waste my time asking him for something that he's sure to give me anyway."

The Giving God (James 1:5c)

The wisdom we need comes only from God. This isn't the wisdom that one gains from pursuing a PhD or reading a book on management and leadership skills. As Proverbs 2:6 indicates, it is "the LORD [who] gives wisdom." Of course, God may choose to utilize any number of means to impart wisdom to us, but we must never lose sight of the fact that wisdom is a gift of God.

So, notice three things about God in this verse. First, he gives "generously." However, perhaps "generously" isn't the best rendering of this word. It may mean something more like "single-minded," "sincere," "undivided," or "wholehearted." In other words, God isn't conflicted about whether to give. He gives with singular intentionality. The assurance spoken of here, that God will most assuredly give us what we ask, echoes the words of Jesus in Matthew 7:7: "Ask, and it will be given to you." Jesus grounds that promise in the character of God: if we, being evil, happily give good gifts to our children, how much more will God, who is incomparably good, give good things when his children ask (Matt. 7:11). So too James grounds his assurance to us in the generosity and goodness of God.

Second, he gives indiscriminately, which is the point of the word *all* in verse 5. He doesn't just give to tall people or redheaded little girls or people with good-paying jobs or people whose suffering is far worse than most others. Whatever the nature of your affliction, regardless of your station in life, God gives.

Third, he does this "without reproach" (v. 5c). What an interesting choice of words. What does it mean? I think several things are in mind. It means that God will not mock us for asking. He won't scold us, make fun of us, or throw it back in our faces that we had the audacity to ask him for wisdom. God will never respond to our request for wisdom by saying, "What's the matter with you? Can't you figure this out on your own? You dummy! You idiot! How much longer do I have to put up with you? Oh, all right, since you've asked, I'll answer and provide you with the wisdom you need. But you ought to be ashamed of yourself for not having made sense of life on your own."

When you come to him in prayer, God doesn't think, *Good grief. Not you again! Haven't I already done enough in your life?* In other words, wrapped up in the phrase "without reproach" is the idea that God will not berate us by constantly reminding us in the days ahead of what he did in times past. So don't come to God in prayer fearful that if he answers you, he will constantly remind you of it for the rest of your life and make you feel guilty for having the audacity to have asked in the first place.

One thing that James doesn't address is the *means* God might employ to impart this wisdom. We must look elsewhere in Scripture for that. Perhaps the principal means he uses is the Scriptures. He expects us to immerse ourselves in the revelation of his Word. Our minds ought to be shaped by the values, principles, and truths of God's Word before we ever pray for wisdom. And then God can say: "Don't you recall what I said about this in Romans 5? Do you remember what Solomon said to you in Proverbs as he wrote under the inspiration of the Holy Spirit? Surely you learned some lessons from studying the life of David in the Old Testament." In this way, God awakens wisdom in us for the challenge of facing our trials. Here is how the psalmist put it:

> I have more understanding than all my teachers,
>> for your testimonies are my meditation.
> I understand more than the aged,
>> for I keep your precepts. . . .
> Through your precepts I get understanding;
>> therefore I hate every false way. (Ps. 119:99–100, 104)

God also uses the insights and maturity of other Christians to impart wisdom to us. Sometimes the only way we can gain wisdom is by trial and error, by facing down our trials and persevering through them.

The Characteristics of Fruitful Prayer (James 1:6–8)

James 1:6–8 remind us that God is not a heavenly vending machine who delivers provided the right amount of spiritual coinage is inserted. *The promise of answered prayer is premised on the proper attitude in those who ask.* James focuses our attention on two things: the presence of faith and the absence of doubt. C. S. Lewis frames the problem this poses in a strikingly unsettling way:

> How is it possible at one and the same moment to have a perfect faith—an untroubled or unhesitating faith as St. James says (1:6)—that you will get what you ask and yet also prepare yourself submissively in advance for a possible refusal? If you envisage a refusal as possible, how can you have simultaneously a perfect confidence that what you ask will not be refused? If you have that confidence, how can you take refusal into account at all?[2]

This "faith" that must characterize our prayers is not faith in general or even faith in Christ. It is contrasted with "doubt" and thus refers to our confidence in God's ability and willingness to answer prayers that are in harmony with his nature and purpose for our lives. So "faith" means the sort of confidence or trust that says, "I know in my heart that God can do this for me. I know in my heart that he's the kind of God who absolutely loves to do things like this for his children." There's nothing here to suggest that by "faith" James means that we presumptuously claim in advance that God will always do what we ask him to do. This is no name-it-and-claim-it "faith."

Well, if that's the case, what then does he mean when he says we should pray "with no doubting"? The word basically means to "differentiate" or "judge" or "dispute," but here it has the meaning of "dispute with oneself." He has in mind those times when we find ourselves debating with ourselves. There's a division in our hearts: on the one hand, we believe God is good

---

2. C. S. Lewis, *Letters to Malcolm: Chiefly on Prayer* (Boston: Mariner, 2012), 58–59.

and generous, but on the other hand, maybe he's not as good or generous as we've been led to think. Maybe God fulfills his promises, but then again maybe he doesn't.

Notice in verse 8 he refers to this sort of person as "double-minded" (v. 8a). The word for "double-minded" is literally "*double-souled.*" This particular word has never appeared in Greek literature until now. James probably coined the word himself. There is a sense in which he is describing what might be called *spiritual schizophrenia!* Such a man is the pattern for Bunyan's "Mr. Facing-both-ways" in *Pilgrim's Progress*. He is like the mythological horseman who mounted his horse and promptly rode off in both directions!

The doubt he has in view is compared to the waves of the sea swelling up and subsiding, never having the same shape or size but varying from moment to moment both in direction and strength. It's as if one day we are full of confidence in the importance and necessity of wisdom from God, and the next day we are seduced by the world around us into thinking that we can figure it out all on our own. One day we are consciously dependent on God alone only to wake up the day after with a determination to look to the ways and wisdom of the world and its secular values to help us thrive.

But the Bible blesses the person who pursues God with a single-minded sincerity, a heart undivided and undistracted. As the psalmist says, "Blessed are those who keep his testimonies, who seek him with their whole heart" (Ps. 119:2).

Of course, he doesn't mean we will never experience any degree of doubt. No one can banish all doubt from their minds. We are, after all, weak and fallen people, and life has a way of questioning pretty much everything. Rather, the idea is of sustained consistency over time. Even when doubt occasionally intrudes into our thinking, by God's grace we maintain our overall confidence in who he is and what he enjoys doing.

Some of you live in constant fear that the slightest tinge of doubt may inadvertently creep into your thought process and ruin everything! You struggle and strain to squeeze every vestige of doubt from your brain, like wrenching water from a sponge. When you finally feel confident that you've arrived, a wayward thought suddenly erupts in the back of your mind, or a question arises in your heart. "Darn it! Just when I thought I had this thing under control and boom, doubt reappears. Not a big doubt, but a doubt. I've spoiled everything. God obviously won't hear my prayers now."

Think of your mind or heart as if it were a house. You've been diligent to shut every window and seal it tightly. You closed every door and locked it securely. Nothing can get in. Then suddenly you discover that doubts are sneaking in through some tiny air vent in the attic, and you've failed yet again! And to make matters worse, you know yourself well enough to realize you won't be any different tomorrow. No matter how confident you may grow, doubts will always appear like those pesky weeds in your front yard that you thought you'd pulled up by their roots. Nothing you do will make them disappear forever.

No! That is not what James is saying. No human being has ever lived without experiencing those sorts of battles with doubt, and no human being will ever live without them. God knows that and is gracious, patient, kind, generous, and always ready to give us the wisdom we need.

I don't believe James is denouncing honest, intellectual doubts. He has in mind the person who wavers between God and the world, shifting allegiance and loyalty, at one moment looking to God for guidance and the next reading the *National Enquirer* for information about what to do. Asking God questions about why something happened or why something else didn't isn't necessarily a bad form of doubt. Saying to him, "I don't understand" is okay. He knows you don't and can see straight through the false spiritual façade you create when you pretend to know what you don't know. To say, "God, I'm really confused right now. Your ways make no sense to me," is not sinful doubting.

The sort of "doubt" that is unavoidable and not inconsistent with "faith" is found in the so-called "Psalms of Lament." A good example is how David cried out to God in Psalm 13:1: "How long, O LORD? Will you forget me forever? How long will you hide your face from me?" Are you there? Do you care? Psalms of Lament essentially contain three parts: (1) I'm all alone and I'm hurting. (2) Our enemies, both yours and mine, are winning. And (3) God, you don't care! And yet in virtually every one of these psalms, the psalmist ends by reaffirming his confidence in God. He calls to mind everything God has done in the past. He anticipates joyfully worshiping with God's people again in the future.

Conclusion

Several things can be said in summary of James 1:2–8. First, we won't get very far in the Christian life until we recognize that trials, afflictions, and hardships are absolutely necessary for Christian growth. A life of perpetual, unbroken ease, comfort, and prosperity may sound appealing, but it will produce only spiritual midgets.

Second, we must also embrace the truth that these trials are designed by God to produce in us a spirit or attitude of perseverance, a disposition never to quit. This, in turn, initiates the believer into a process of growth and character development that will culminate in a mature, wholly developed individual who looks, talks, thinks, and acts like Jesus!

Third, knowing this is what makes possible our ability to "count" as "all joy" what we might otherwise resent and resist.

Fourth, if you still don't get it, if none of this makes sense, if you can't see or understand how any of this fits together into a coherent whole, don't give up hope! Don't despair! Instead, come to God in prayer, confident that he is a good and generous God and loves nothing more than to answer the heartfelt, faithful prayers of his children, and ask!

CHAPTER 18

Suffering, Healing, and the Prayer of Faith

S o, let's be honest with each other about why we seem to have lost confidence in the practical effectiveness of prayer. When I talk with all kinds of Christians, I hear comments like these:

> Come on, Sam, we live in a digital world where religious rituals from medieval times, like prayer, simply don't fit in. Enlightened and educated people might grudgingly concede that there is a supernatural world, but it plays no meaningful or practical role in daily living.

> Children pray, and it's cute. But to think that God actually involves himself in our lives in response to our requests is far-fetched, to say the least.

> Honestly, I would pray if I thought it might do some good. But nowadays, it's a lot easier to just do it yourself without depending on God and whether he's in the mood to help.

I assume most of you read *Huckleberry Finn* when you were younger. Today, it is on the politically incorrect list of banned books in many sectors of our society. But Huck Finn's experience with prayer rings all too true among Christians in the local church. Listen to him:

> Miss Watson she took me in the closet and prayed, but nothing come of it. She told me to pray every day, and whatever I asked for I would get it. But it warn't so. I tried it. Once I got a fish-line, but no hooks. It warn't any good

to me without hooks. I tried for the hooks three or four times, but somehow I couldn't make it work. By and by, one day, I asked Miss Watson to try for me, but she said I was a fool. She never told me why, and I couldn't make it out no way. I set down one time back in the woods, and had a long think about it. I says to myself, if a body can get anything they pray for, why don't Deacon Winn get back the money he lost on pork? Why can't the widow get back her silver snuff-box that was stole? Why can't Miss Watson fat up? No, says I to myself, there ain't nothing in it.

"*There ain't nothing in it.*" Sadly, that sums up how many Christians feel about prayer, although they would never let another Christian know that's how they think. There are many reasons why Christians don't pray more: scriptural ignorance, busy and exhausting lives, a failure to understand God's character, and countless other reasons. But beneath and behind them all is the lingering bogeyman of why we don't pray: "There ain't nothing in it." Or to put it in simpler terms: "It doesn't work. I tried praying, but heaven was silent. If God really cared about me and my problems, I would have heard or seen something from him by now. No, Huck was right: *There ain't nothing in it.*"

I suspect that some of you agree with Huck Finn. I don't. And that isn't because I have the job of writing a book about prayer. It's because I've seen God do amazing and miraculous things in response to prayer. It's because I really do believe that what he says in his Word about prayer is true. You don't have to go any further than the book of James to get a sense of the importance, urgency, and power of prayer. We saw it in the opening chapter:

If any of you lacks wisdom, let him ask God, who gives generously to all without reproach, and it will be given him. (James 1:5)

And again, in chapter four:

You do not have, because you do not ask. You ask and do not receive, because you ask wrongly, to spend it on your passions. (James 4:2b–3)

And then we have this remarkable closing paragraph to the letter, where James is consumed with the power of prayer:

> Is anyone among you suffering? Let him pray. (James 5:13a)

> Is anyone among you sick? Let him call for the elders of the church, and let them pray over him. (James 5:14a)

> And the prayer of faith will save the one who is sick. (James 5:15a)

> Therefore, confess your sins to one another, and pray for one another. (James 5:16a)

> The prayer of a righteous person has great power as it is working. (James 5:16b)

> Elijah . . . prayed fervently that it might not rain, and for three years and six months it did not rain on the earth. (James 5:17)

> Then he prayed again, and heaven gave rain, and the earth bore its fruit. (James 5:18)

James couldn't be more precise or passionate about the power of prayer. Or perhaps we should say, the power of God, for it is not in our praying but in the one to whom we pray that power is found. So, if you really want to embrace Huck Finn's conclusion that prayer is useless because "there ain't nothing in it," you must take the next step and declare, *"there ain't nothing in it, because there ain't no one there."* But if there is someone there, if God exists and is who he claims to be, then nothing makes more sense than prayer, even when we don't always get what we want.

Private, Personal Prayer (James 5:13)

James first describes in verse 13 what I'm calling private, personal prayer. This is our responsibility to consistently pray for our own needs, whether anyone else ever knows or joins to intercede on our behalf. He asks, "Is anyone among you suffering?" The word translated "suffering" (NIV, "in trouble") refers to any kind of harm that burdens you. He does not specify either the cause or character of the suffering. This is a general reference to any form of oppression, persecution, emotional turmoil, depression, marital strife, spiritual anguish, financial strain, or physical affliction. Any discomfort of soul, spirit, or body is in view. When you suffer for whatever reason, pray!

This kind of praying can take place anywhere at any time. You can pray for relief from your troubles and difficulties while you're driving to work, walking in the neighborhood, playing golf, singing in a church service, or reading a book. This sort of prayer is open-ended and always appropriate.

If you're in a season of life when there are innumerable reasons to be "cheerful," pepper your prayers with praise. We can do both simultaneously. Even when you are stressed and hurting, for whatever reason, due to whatever cause, you also have much to celebrate. So, pray and praise at the same time!

How Suffering Stimulates Prayer

I've already mentioned the various excuses people give for not praying. To be perfectly honest, I've got a few of my own. "I don't have the time." "Life is too busy." "I never know what to say." "It seems so fruitless. Nothing ever comes of it." But the one justification for a prayerless life that I hear most often is an appeal to suffering. People are convinced that God is angry with them. "He's fed up. He's had enough of me. I'm hurting right now, so why would God want to hear from me, much less grant my requests?"

We can all understand this reaction. Suffering, whatever form it takes, is probably the greatest threat to our belief in the goodness of God. It blinds us to anything valuable he may be producing in our lives. It numbs our hearts and anesthetizes our souls. All feeling for God slowly slips away. Suffering leads to all sorts of questions: "What did I do to deserve this? I know I'm a sinner, but what I'm experiencing right now feels way out of proportion to anything I've done."

Scripture has a lot to say about suffering and its purpose, but my concern is its relationship to prayer and the way it so often renders us silent before God. Consider this one text of Scripture that I hope will be of encouragement to you amid whatever pain or deprivation you may be going through at present.

> In the whole land, declares the LORD,
>   two thirds shall be cut off and perish,
>   and one third shall be left alive.

> And I will put this third into the fire,
>> and refine them as one refines silver,
>> and test them as gold is tested.
> They will call upon my name,
>> and I will answer them.
> I will say, "They are my people";
>> and they will say, "The LORD is my God." (Zech. 13:8–9)

I'm asking you to forego the debate over how or when this prophecy will be fulfilled. Let's not get sidetracked by arguments over eschatology. Instead, consider why God takes his beloved children through hard times, through unimaginable suffering and anguish. Is there no purpose to it at all? Is our pain and distress senseless, or does God have a purpose in it?

The apostle Peter uses similar language to portray the suffering many were experiencing in the first century.

> In this you rejoice, though now for a little while, if necessary, you have been grieved by various trials, so that the tested genuineness of your faith—more precious than gold that perishes though it is tested by fire—may be found to result in praise and glory and honor at the revelation of Jesus Christ. (1 Peter 1:6–7)

Peter goes on to describe how this experience of hardship produces in us greater "love" for Jesus, more stable and solid belief in him, and, above all else, "joy that is inexpressible and filled with glory" (1 Peter 1:8).

My point in citing Peter's words is to highlight that there is always a "so that" in our various trials. Zechariah certainly agrees. Look again at the passage cited above and see what comes through the refining fire of suffering: "*They will call upon my name, and I will answer them.*"

God's purpose in our suffering is not to create despair, but desperation; not feelings of abandonment but profound need that only he can meet. His aim in our hardship is to awaken and ignite in our hearts a relentless and enduring pursuit of him in prayer. The response of the remnant (the "third" who survive) is not one of anger, resentment, or deconstruction. Instead, they pray! They "call" on the name of the Lord, and he answers them! It says something about our stubborn and self-sufficient hearts that it takes suffering to wake us and remind us that only God is worthy of our devotion, that only God can empower us to endure to the end.

The lesson for us all here is never to look on our pain, disappointment, and opposition from an unbelieving world as a reason to turn away from God. Instead, pray! Call on the name of the Lord. In ways that only his infinite wisdom can fathom, he will answer us and bring light out of our darkness, hope out of despair.

The Physically Suffering and the Prayer of the Elders (James 5:14–15)

This is an extremely rich and densely packed passage, and I'm in no hurry to rush through it. Let's look at it closely.

> Is anyone among you suffering? Let him pray. Is anyone cheerful? Let him sing praise. Is anyone among you sick? Let him call for the elders of the church, and let them pray over him, anointing him with oil in the name of the Lord. And the prayer of faith will save the one who is sick, and the Lord will raise him up. And if he has committed sins, he will be forgiven. Therefore, confess your sins to one another and pray for one another, that you may be healed. The prayer of a righteous person has great power as it is working. Elijah was a man with a nature like ours, and he prayed fervently that it might not rain, and for three years and six months it did not rain on the earth. Then he prayed again, and heaven gave rain, and the earth bore its fruit. (James 5:13–18)

"Is anyone among you sick?" (v. 14a). The fact that James singles out the "sick" assumes that he has something in mind different from the "suffering" he just mentioned in verse 13. This person is extremely ill, most likely bedridden. We see this in three things. First, the fact that James tells this person to "call" for the elders does suggest that they are in extremely bad shape. There is a second reason we are right in thinking so. It's found in the phrase, "let them pray over him" (v. 14b). This is unusual. We don't typically read in the New Testament about praying "over" someone. The preposition translated "over" is a separate word in the original text, not included in the verb "to pray." In fact, this is the only place in the entire New Testament where the preposition "over" is used in conjunction with praying for someone. You can pray "for" someone and not necessarily pray "over" them. The word *over* suggests that this person is lying on their back, unable to initiate any movement toward other people or the elders of the church.

Yet another reason I think James is talking about an extraordinarily serious affliction is what he says in verse 15, namely, that "the Lord will raise him up." This suggests that the person was laid low, as it were, or stretched out on a bed. If they are healed, it involves raising them up from where they were lying prostrate.

The nature of the sickness in view here is physical or bodily. You might think that goes without saying, but such is not the case. You won't find many defending the view that this is "sickness" of a nonphysical nature. Most who argue for it are cessationists who are uncomfortable with the reality of healing and how this applies to the church in our day.

One author suggests that James has in view emotional distress and spiritual exhaustion experienced by God's people in their deep struggle with temptation and their relentless battle with besetting sin. It is true that the word *sick* in verse 14 (*astheneō*) can mean "weak" in faith or spiritually fatigued (cf. Rom. 14:1–2; 1 Cor. 8:11–12; 2 Cor. 13:3), as is also the case with the other Greek word translated "sick" in verse 15 (*kamnō*; cf. Heb. 12:3). It is also true that the Greek words in verses 15–16 translated "restore" (*sōzō*), "raise up" (*egeirō*), and "heal" (*iaomai*) may legitimately refer to the restoration or renewal of spiritual and emotional vitality. However, when *astheneō* means spiritual weakness, usually the context or a qualifier such as "weak *in faith*" (Rom. 14:2) or "weak *in conscience*" (1 Cor. 8:7) makes that clear. Moreover, in the material most relevant to James (the four Gospels), *astheneō* almost always refers to physical illness. The same is true for *kamnō*. And *iaomai*, when not used in an Old Testament quotation, always refers to physical healing. As far as *sōzō* and *egeirō* are concerned, both are appropriate descriptions of physical healing (*sōzō* in Matt. 9:21–22; Mark 5:34; 6:56; 10:52; Luke 7:50; 17:19; and *egeirō* in Mark 1:31; 2:9–12; Acts 3:7).

That being said, James would not want you to think that if your affliction is emotional or spiritual in nature you should not ask for others to pray for you. We already saw in verse 13 that regardless of the nature or cause of one's affliction, prayer is appropriate.

Why are the "elders" singled out? Most likely, it is because they are representatives of the entire church. When a sheep is wounded or in danger, it most naturally seeks out the aid of its shepherd, which is how elders are described in 1 Peter 5:1–2. It is also assumed that the elders of a church are men of maturity, spiritual insight, prayerfulness, compassion, etc. As such, they would be likely candidates (but not the only ones, of course) to receive from God the necessary gifting to minister healing to the sick.

There is another qualification to put on this statement. Don't ever conclude from this passage that only elders are to pray for the sick. Don't ever think that other believers, both male and female, of all ages can't or shouldn't pray for one another. Notice in verse 16 that James exhorts all believers to "pray for one another." Some of the most powerful and effective intercessors and prayer warriors that I have known were never elders or pastors in a local church. So, remember this: if an elder or the board as a whole isn't available, you aren't falling short or missing a thing if you ask other Christians to pray for your healing. All of us, regardless of whether we hold office or are or are not on staff at a church, are responsible for praying for others.

Why are the elders called on to pray for the sick rather than the "healers" or those with the spiritual gift of healing? People we refer to as cessationists, who don't believe that miraculous gifts like healing and prophecy still exist today, make much of this. Their argument goes something like this:

> The fact that James calls for the *elders* to pray rather than the *healers* or those with the spiritual gift of healing proves that this particular supernatural power was already on its way out from the life of the church. It proves that God only intended for divine healers to operate in the life of the *early*, first-century church. Or if healing does continue today, it happens only rarely and never through a particular person with the spiritual gift of healing.

My response to that is *there is no such thing as "the gift of healing." There never has been.*[1] I say this both because of the way Paul describes this spiritual phenomenon and the misconceptions surrounding it. The significant thing about 1 Corinthians 12:9, 28 is that both the word *gift* and the word *healing*

---

1. I have addressed this issue in considerably more detail in my book, *Understanding Spiritual Gifts: A Comprehensive Guide* (Grand Rapids: Zondervan, 2020).

are plural and lack the definite article, hence the translation: *"gifts of healings"* (unfortunately the ESV renders it in both instances as "gifts of healing"). Evidently, Paul did not envision that a person would be endowed with one healing gift operative at all times for all diseases. His language suggests either many different gifts or powers of healing, each appropriate to and effective for its related illness, or each occurrence of healing constituting a distinct or separate gift in its own right.

I've had the opportunity on numerous occasions to meet people who have what appears to be a healing anointing for one particular affliction. Some can pray more effectively for those with back problems, while others see more success when praying for migraine headaches. This may be what Paul had in mind when he spoke of "gifts" of "healings."

One of the principal obstacles to a proper understanding of healing is the erroneous assumption that if anyone could ever heal, they could always heal. But in view of the lingering illnesses of Epaphroditus (Phil. 2:25–30), Timothy (1 Tim. 5:23), Trophimus (2 Tim. 4:20), and perhaps Paul himself (2 Cor. 12:7–10; Gal. 4:13), it is better to view this gift as subject to the will of God, not the will of people. Therefore, a person may be gifted to heal many people, but not all. Another may be gifted to heal only one person at one particular time of one particular disease.

When asked to pray for the sick, people are often heard to respond: "I can't. I don't have the gift of healing." But if my reading of Paul and James is correct, there is no such thing as *the* gift of healing, if by that one means the God-given ability to heal everyone of every disease on every occasion. Rather, the Spirit sovereignly distributes "a" *charisma* or "gift" of healing for a particular occasion, even though previous prayers for physical restoration under similar circumstances may not have been answered, and even though subsequent prayers for the same affliction may not be answered. In sum, "gifts of healings" are occasional and subject to the sovereign purposes of God.

Few doubt that Paul had a "gift" for healing. But his prayers for Epaphroditus weren't answered, at least not at first (see Phil. 2:25–30). Clearly, Paul could not heal at will. Aside from Jesus, no one else could either! There is doubt whether even Jesus could (read John 5:19; Mark 6:5–6). Some would conclude from Paul's failure to heal his friend that "the gift of healing" was "dying out" at this juncture in the life of the church (despite that late in his ministry, in Acts 28:9, Paul apparently healed everyone on the island of Malta who came to him). It seems better to conclude that healing was always subject to God's will, not man's. No one, not even Paul, could always heal all diseases. If Paul was distressed that Epaphroditus was ill, almost unto death, and that initially, his prayers for him were ineffective, I doubt seriously if the apostle would have drawn the same conclusions that modern cessationists do. Paul understood the occasional nature of gifts of healings.

The fact that healing is an expression of divine "mercy" (Phil. 2:27) means that it should never be viewed as a "right." Healing is not the payment of a debt. God does not *owe* us healing. We don't deserve healing. I believe we should have faith for healing. But there is a vast difference between faith in divine mercy, on the one hand, and presumption based on an alleged right, on the other.

The word *mercy* is the same one used in the Gospels to describe why Jesus healed people when he was on the earth. God's motive for healing hasn't changed! The primary reason God healed through Jesus prior to Pentecost and why he continues to heal after Pentecost is because he is a merciful, compassionate God. God is no less merciful, compassionate, or caring when it comes to the physical condition of his people after Pentecost than he was before Pentecost.

The elders are described as "anointing him with oil in the name of the Lord" (James 5:14c). Aside from Mark 6:13, this is the only passage in the New Testament that recommends the use of oil for the sick. Why "oil"? Some believe he recommended it as a *medicinal aid* (see Luke 10:34). Oil was frequently used in the ancient world for medicinal purposes. This may account for James' use of the verb *aleiphō* ("to anoint"), which emphasizes the actual physical action of pouring. Another word that means "to anoint" (*chriō*) is usually employed when the purpose of the anointing is religious or symbolic. However, the distinction between these two verbs should not be pressed, for their meanings often overlap. But if the oil was strictly medicinal, why is it *alone* mentioned as a helpful remedy for the sick? Oil was certainly beneficial, but no one claims it was appropriate for *every* illness. Also, if the purpose of oil was strictly medicinal, why was it necessary for the elders to do the anointing? Would not others, or perhaps the suffering individual himself, have already done this to alleviate his suffering?

More likely the oil has *religious/spiritual* significance in this passage. If so, it would probably represent the Holy Spirit and his ministry of consecration whereby an individual or some object is set aside for God's service (cf. 1 Sam. 16:13; Isa. 61:1; Acts 4:27). In other words, the anointing here is a physical action with symbolic significance. We are probably to understand this as the consecrating or setting aside of this person for God's special attention and a way of directing everyone's faith to the power of the Holy Spirit.

What is "the prayer of faith" (James 5:15)? "The prayer of faith" isn't one that we pray whenever *we* want to. It is a unique prayer, divinely energized on occasions when it is God's sovereign purpose to impart a gift for healing. James was careful to place the definite article ("the") before both "prayer" and "faith" (hence, "*the* prayer of *the* faith"). One prays *this* prayer only when prompted by the Spirit-wrought conviction that God intends to heal the one for whom prayer is being offered. This is more than merely believing that God is able to heal; this appears to be faith that he, in this case, is not only willing to heal but plans to heal *right now*. Only when God wills does God sovereignly bestow the faith necessary for healing. When God chooses to heal, he produces in the heart(s) of those praying the faith or confidence that such is precisely his intent. The kind of faith to which James refers, in response to which God heals, is not the kind that we may exercise at our will. It is the kind of faith that we exercise only when God wills.

It may well be that the "faith" James describes is the "gift of faith" mentioned in 1 Corinthians 12. The "gift of faith" is a special faith that "enables a believer to trust God to bring about certain things for which he or she cannot claim some divine promise recorded in Scripture, or some state of affairs grounded in the very structure of the gospel."[2] In other words, it is the "God-given ability, without fakery or platitudinous exhortations to believe what you do not really believe, to trust God for a certain blessing *not* promised in Scripture."[3] Thus the "gift of faith" is that *mysterious surge of confidence* that rises within a person in a particular situation of need or challenge and that gives *an extraordinary certainty and assurance that God is about to act through a word or action.*

---

2. D. A. Carson, *Showing the Spirit: A Theological Exposition of 1 Corinthians 12–14* (Grand Rapids: Baker, 2019 [1987]), 48.

3. Carson, *Showing the Spirit*, 48n65.

Consider these two texts that I believe are in the same way describing how the spiritual gift of faith operates:

> And Jesus answered them, "Have faith in God. Truly, I say to you, whoever says to this mountain, 'Be taken up and thrown into the sea,' and does not doubt in his heart, but believes that what he says will come to pass, it will be done for him. Therefore I tell you, whatever you ask in prayer, believe that you have received it, and it will be yours." (Mark 11:22–24; cf. Matt. 17:20–21; 21:21–22)

> And if I have prophetic powers, and understand all mysteries and all knowledge, and if I have all faith, so as to remove mountains, but have not love, I am nothing. (1 Cor. 13:2)

The spiritual gift of faith, like the other *charismata*, is not given to every member of the body of Christ. However, any member of the body of Christ is a potential candidate for the experience of this manifestation of the Spirit. The gift of faith should probably be regarded, more so than most other gifts of the Spirit, as occasional or spontaneous rather than permanent or residential.

When I was pastoring in Ardmore, Oklahoma, quite a few years ago, a young couple came to me before the service and asked that the elders of our church anoint their infant son and pray for his healing. After the service, we gathered, and I anointed him with oil. At two weeks of age, he had a serious liver disorder that would require either immediate surgery or, more likely, a transplant. As we prayed, something very unusual happened. As we laid hands on this young child and prayed, I found myself suddenly filled with an overwhelming and inescapable confidence that he would be healed. It was totally unexpected. Not wanting to be presumptuous, I tried to doubt but couldn't. I prayed confidently, filled with a faith unshakable and undeniable. I said to myself, "Lord, you really are going to heal him."

I then did something that I had never done before nor have I done since, although I've prayed for hundreds if not several thousand people. I was absolutely *certain* God had healed him, and I told them so. They were shocked by my confidence. The next morning the doctors had no explanation for a liver that was functioning perfectly. He was totally healed and is a healthy young man today.

I asked his mother to describe what happened in more detail. She sent me the following letter in 2011. I've taken the liberty to change the names, but everything else is left precisely the way she wrote.[4]

> When Ricky was born, we assumed he would have physiological jaundice. All but our firstborn had it, from what we assumed was a blood incompatibility between my husband's AB positive and my A- DU positive blood type. Ricky did have jaundice, and within 24 hours like we predicted. The doctors can do two types of blood work for jaundice: indirect bilirubin and direct bilirubin. I am not sure which one is the number we hear so often with jaundice. Once that particular number gets to a certain point, lights are used. The other number indicates how the liver is working to get rid of the bili. If that number is low, meaning that the liver is doing its job, then the higher number will soon go down and everything will be fine—sometimes without lights at all. Not all doctors even do the second number. Well, the doctors were doing the number on Ricky. He had the same blood type as me and should not have had any physiological jaundice at all. What I didn't know was that the number was slowly creeping up, meaning that Ricky's liver was not working!
>
> We were in Norman, Oklahoma, and I got a call from the doctor's office. Ricky was just a few days shy of two weeks. He had been such a great baby! I would literally have to wake him up to feed him (actually—not that great of a thing, I found out). His count had reached a critical level and the office had already set up an appointment with a pediatric gastroenterologist for Monday. I asked the doctor what the concern was and his reply was that Ricky either had a liver that was not going to work and he would need a transplant, or he had a blockage that could be fixed through surgery. For the first time I looked at Ricky with objective eyes. He was a bluish color and he had not gained any weight since he was born. He was very lethargic (remember—the good baby—never cried!) and only ate when I made him eat! It hit me like a ton of bricks. I had a really sick baby and I hadn't even known!
>
> We called you and asked if the elders would pray over Ricky. We went to church the next morning, and after church we went to your office with

---

4. I first shared this story in my book, *The Beginner's Guide to Spiritual Gifts* (Minneapolis: Bethany House, 2015).

the elders. Ricky was born at 11:58 A.M. two weeks earlier—so he was probably as near to exactly two weeks old when you did that. You told us as we left that Ricky would be just fine. I know you must have had a special word from God. **WHAT DID HAPPEN TO YOU FOR YOU TO BELIEVE THAT?** The next morning I got Ricky up and he was WHITE! He had been that awful blue color. He even had a fat roll under his chin! He looked great! I never had any special feeling come over me, but I knew I was looking at a baby that was very healthy! We took him in and the specialist did various blood tests on him. He had his chart and said that Ricky looked great to him—but his chart indicated that he was actually very sick. The doctor had records for over a week on Ricky's blood work. He also told us that he would call us the next day and let us know what the results were and what we needed to do. He called that evening! He was very excited that the news was good. He said that Ricky appeared to be totally normal at this point. I asked him how that could happen and he said that he had no answers for me because Ricky had been very sick. I told him that we had the entire state of Oklahoma praying for him and at that point he revealed that he was a Christian! He told us that prayer was the only way that this happened and now he understood why Ricky was okay. It was a miracle! In fact, Ricky weighed more that day than the day he was born—so he had gained a lot overnight. He has never had any health issues since. Prayer is a mighty, wonderful thing!

There is so much more for us in this passage in James 5, calling for two additional chapters to address its many truths.

CHAPTER 19

Healing Prayer and the Two "One-Anothers"

John Wimber, a friend of mine who founded the Vineyard movement, died in 1997. John was the manager and contributed to the Righteous Brothers' musical arrangements in their early years. When he came to faith in Christ, he attended a church with his wife, Carol. After the service, John greeted the pastor and asked him a simple question:

> "Sir, I enjoyed the service, but when are we going to do the stuff?"
>
> "The 'stuff'?" the pastor asked, in a somewhat bewildered tone of voice. "What do you mean by the 'stuff'?"
>
> "You know," said John, "the 'stuff': healing the sick and casting out demons and prophesying. The 'stuff'!"
>
> "Oh, I see what you mean," said the pastor. "We don't do the stuff. We preach about it. We believe what the Bible says about it. But we don't do it."[1]

Well, I am fully committed not only to believing the "stuff" but also to "doing" it. And so, in this chapter, we turn our attention yet again to James 5 and the subject of the healing of the body.

A Brief Review

In the preceding chapter on James 5, we looked at several things of great importance. I pointed out that the language used here most likely portrays a

---

1. Wimber, obviously frustrated, is reported to have said in response to the pastor, "So, I gave up drugs for *this*?"

person who is physically ill and bedridden, perhaps even near death, who calls for the elders of the church to pray for them. We talked about the symbolic use of oil as pointing to the person/power of the Holy Spirit and examined what James means by "the prayer of faith."

Most importantly, I explained that in the New Testament, contrary to widespread, popular opinion, there is no such thing as "the" spiritual gift of healing. No one is ever portrayed as possessing the power to heal all people of every disease at any time. Rather, the Holy Spirit sovereignly bestows to one person a gift for healing a particular disease while then bestowing to yet another person yet another gift for the healing of yet another disease. Healing is never in our back pocket, so to speak, as if we control it and use it according to our will. Rather, multiple gifts for a variety of separate healings are bestowed by God according to his will.

Five Essential Truths

Let me say one more thing before we begin. My reason for paying meticulous attention to the text of James 5 is to increase and intensify your faith in God's power to heal in response to prayer. I want you to *believe* what James says so that you will *behave* in a way that will lead to the healing of the sick. I don't want you merely to *believe* in the stuff: I want all of us to be actively and energetically engaged in *doing* the stuff!

There are some statements in Scripture that are so profoundly un-profound (no, that's not a word, but it works here) that they are easily overlooked. One of them is James 4:2b–3, where James tells his audience that "you do not have, because you do not ask. You ask and do not receive, because you ask wrongly, to spend it on your passions." Here is what James is saying:

> If you don't have what you think you need it is because you don't come to God and ask him for it. And when you do come and ask, you pray with wrong motives. You want God to give you things so that you might use them to satisfy your selfish desires. You don't pray for what you need to experience more of God, or so that you might be less selfish and more giving, or so that you might be a blessing to others. In order to get what you selfishly want and covet and desire, you turn to God and ask him to supply it.

This is stunning. James portrays men and women wanting something (or someone) that satisfies, and then coming to God not because *he* satisfies, but only to ask him for the means to get something else. Once we get it, we turn away from God to find our satisfaction in whatever thing he gave us. This is why James will describe people in the next verse as "adulterous" (v. 4a)!

In essence, James portrays God as our heavenly husband to whom we come asking for money to pay for a visit to a prostitute! "God is our husband," says Piper, "and the world is a prostitute luring us to give affections to her that belong only to God."[2] James has in mind people who use prayer to try to get from God something they desire more than God. They are like the wife who demands money from her husband so she can visit an adulterous lover.

We need to be careful, though, that we do not misuse this passage. James is not saying that prayer gets us whatever we want. He is saying that if we don't get what we most need, it is largely because we have neglected the divinely ordained means for receiving what God may well be willing to give. As we've seen repeatedly in this book, other factors must be considered, such as praying in Jesus' name, praying in accordance with God's will, abiding in Christ, asking for those things that serve to make known God's glory, etc.

We now turn our attention to what James says in verse 5:15, extending through verse 16. And there are five things that warrant our close study.

First, James says in verse 15 that "the prayer of faith will save the one who is sick, and the Lord will raise him up" (v. 15b). He doesn't mean that this person was an unregenerate unbeliever. The word *save* is often used in the New Testament to describe not merely spiritual forgiveness of sins and deliverance from eternal condemnation, but it is also used to describe physical healing of the body. There are countless examples of this in the New Testament, but one verse should be enough. It concerns the woman who suffered from a discharge of blood for over twelve years. We read in Matthew 9 that,

> she said to herself, "If I only touch his garment, I will be made well." Jesus turned, and seeing her he said, "Take heart, daughter; your faith has made you well." And instantly the woman was made well. (Matt. 9:21–22; see also Mark 6:56; 10:52; Luke 17:19)

---

2. John Piper, *A Hunger for God: Desiring God through Fasting and Prayer* (Wheaton, IL: Crossway, 1997), 78.

The word translated "made well" that occurs three times is the same Greek word found in James 5. We could as easily translate Matthew's text: "'If I only touch his garment, I will be *saved*.'... 'Take heart, daughter; your faith has *saved* you.'... [And] the woman was *saved*." This is confirmed by what we see in the next phrase, which says that God will "raise him up," that is to say, he will physically raise him up from his sickbed.

Second, James says that "if he has committed sins, he will be forgiven" (James 5:15c). James is in harmony with Jesus (John 9:1–3) and Paul (2 Cor. 12:1–10) that not all sickness is the direct result of sin. Sometimes it is (1 Cor. 11:27–30; Mark 2:1–12), but not always. The "if" in verse 15 is not designed to suggest the one who is sick may *never* have sinned. The meaning is that if God should heal him in answer to prayer, this indicates that any sins of the sufferer, which might have been responsible for this particular illness, were forgiven. In other words, *if* sins were responsible for his sickness, the fact that God healed him physically would be evidence that God had forgiven him spiritually.

Third, James says that before you pray for one another, you should "confess your sins to one another" (v. 16a). The New Testament never singles out any special group of "priests" who are uniquely privileged or empowered or have greater and more consistent access to God. All Christians are priests. James has in mind mutual confession; not of all individuals to one priest, but of each individual to every other individual as the need may present itself. So how does this work? Here are some suggestions for how to confess your sins to one another.

To begin, this "confession" can happen anywhere at any time. It can happen over coffee or lunch with a friend. It can happen in your small group if you choose to confess in the presence of several people. It can happen with two or three of your closest friends. It can happen in smaller prayer sessions. It can happen after a church service, with the help of one or several of the prayer ministry members in your local body.

But note carefully that it is confession "to one another" and not just to God. Certainly, there is the need for confessing sins to God, but James has in mind taking this a step further and making it known to another Christian. Not a non-Christian. Not a golfing buddy or the lady next door. It is one Christian to another or to several other Christians.

Although James does not specify when or where, or to how many this confession should be made, it seems reasonable to think that the first and best way to obey this command is to do it privately rather than publicly. I don't think James is suggesting that all the members of a local church stand up in front of the rest and publicly confess their sins. It may be that on occasion a few need to do this, but James is probably thinking of a more private, one-on-one situation.

The first and most obvious way in which we might fulfill this command is by confessing to the person against whom we've committed the sin. If "Joe" has sinned against "Mike," it is much easier for him to tell "Bob," "I sinned against Mike when I slandered him to a group of people just to make myself look good." It is much more difficult for "Joe" to go to "Mike" directly and say to him, "Mike, I need to confess to you that I sinned against you. I spoke ill of you in front of others, all to make myself look good. Would you please forgive me for this?"

Quite honestly, sometimes we are willing to tell someone else a sin we committed as a way of avoiding having to confess face-to-face to the person we sinned against. But what good is it to confess your sin against "Mike" simply by telling "Bob" about it? That enables you to "confess" without also repenting and asking for forgiveness from the person you offended. I don't think James means that if your struggle is with lust you should go to the woman or man who is the focus of your lust and say, "I need to confess to you that I often lust for you. I have sexual fantasies about you." No. That should be confessed to a third party. And it may be best that you not mention the name of the person for whom you lust.

People often ask, "Do I need to confess my sins to someone I know, or can it be to a stranger?" Again, oftentimes, people prefer to confess to someone who doesn't know them. It's easier. It's safer. It's less likely you'll feel ashamed or embarrassed because a total stranger has no prior expectations of your behavior. Some are disinclined to confess to someone who already knows them out of fear they might lose face or suffer loss of respect. But if this is in your heart, it may be an indication that you aren't entirely sincere or humble or broken. If you are still self-protective, one might wonder if you are being entirely honest with the Lord and with others about your sins. What good is that sort of confession?

I think the best way to fulfill James's counsel is first, if possible, to confess your sins to the person against whom they've been committed. Ask their forgiveness. But second, if your sinful struggles are more general and less directed to a particular person, speak to a friend or several of them and open up your heart in honest contrition. Some sins are more self-referential in the sense that they can be present in your life and no one else would know about them. I have in mind things such as envy, unbelief, greed, selfishness, idolatry, jealousy, drunkenness, and pride.

If someone confesses their sin to you, you are under strict obligation never to repeat the content of that confession or the person's sin to anyone else. There are two exceptions. First, it may be that the person confessing gives you permission to tell others. Second, if they confess to you that they have committed a physical or sexual assault against a minor, you are obligated by law to report this to the authorities. It may be best that you report this to a pastor or an elder who will then assist you in making the report to the proper legal authorities.

What should you do if someone comes and says, "I've been sexually unfaithful to my spouse"? First, process this with a pastor or elder or your small group leader. Second, the likelihood is that you would need to return to this individual and say to them, "It's important that you not conceal this any longer from your spouse. You should go to them immediately and confess to them also. If you don't, I will do so myself." Give them a reasonable time frame within which to make this happen.

Fourth, after confessing your sins, "pray for one another" (v. 16b; this is the second significant "one another" in our passage). Notice the word "therefore" with which verse 16 opens. In other words, he is saying: "*Since* God can heal the sick when we pray for them, as verse 15 makes abundantly clear, be diligent to pray for one another."

What we learn from verse 16 is that *it isn't just the elders who are responsible to pray for the sick*. The entire body of Christ, men and women, young and old, are instructed to pray "for one another" so that "you," the people in the local church, "may be healed." You must never think that you are excused from praying for the sick simply because you are not an elder. The word translated "one another" is all-inclusive: everyone in the body of Christ is responsible to pray for everyone else.

Ask God to increase your faith and confidence in his ability. Ask God to impart a gift for this particular healing. Ask God to be merciful and kind and compassionate. Ask God to release his power into this person's body and to restore it completely to its former condition of health.

Note carefully that James does not simply say, "Expect God to heal you." He holds out the possibility of healing, but *only after* we confess our sins to one another and pray for one another.

But why is confession so important? Why would God seemingly suspend healing on it? There are several ways to answer this.

If your sin is one of bitterness, resentment, or unforgiveness, there is an undeniable emotional and psychological release that comes with confession. These sinful energies in the soul can eat away at you like an acid, poisoning your heart, bringing depression and anger, blinding you to the truths of God's grace. It's almost as if such sins release a toxin into your spirit. They sour the soul. They likely cause you to doubt God's goodness and power.

If the sin is one of unforgiveness or resentment, you may need to speak directly to the other person involved. "I need to confess to you that I've not forgiven you for what happened. I still hold anger and bitterness in my heart toward you for what you did, and I often find myself wishing that bad things would come your way. That is evil. It is sinful for me to think of you in this way. I don't want to think or feel this way ever again. Will you forgive me for failing to forgive you? Will you forgive me for holding this against you?"

One more thing should be noted. It is horribly inconsistent and presumptuous of us to continue in unrepentant sin all the while asking God to heal our bodies. It's as if we are saying, "God, I'm enjoying my sexual immorality too much to give it up, but while I've got your attention, could you help me with this deep pain in my back?" Or, "Lord, I genuinely resent Steve/Sally. And I intend to continue to hold resentment in my heart. But since you're merciful, would you go ahead and heal me of diabetes?"

What this tells us is that God has chosen to suspend healing mercy on the repentance of his people. When the hurting doesn't get healed, it may be a result of stubbornness and spiritual insensitivity more than because "God doesn't do that sort of thing anymore." Simply put, we should never expect that God will heal us while we hypocritically nurture in our hearts unforgiveness, anger, spite, greed, and lust without sensing any need to confess such sins or to turn from them.

Fifth, what reason do we have to believe that any of this will make any difference at all? The reason is found in the last half of verse 16—"The prayer of a righteous person has great power as it is working" (v. 16c). Do you believe that? If not, why not? Is God misleading us by having James write this? Surely not.

So, what does James mean by the word *righteous*? In one sense, all born-again believers are "righteous" through faith in Christ. God has imputed or reckoned to you the righteousness of his Son. Every Christian can lay hold of this promise. On the other hand, he also wants us to understand that if we choose to live "unrighteously" by willfully resisting God's will and selfishly refusing to repent or confess our sins, we shouldn't expect that our prayers will accomplish much (see James 4:2–3).

But if we humbly acknowledge our sins and seek by God's grace to live in accordance with his revealed will, there simply is no limit to what God will do for us in response to our prayers. Never forget, there is "great power" in and through prayer because we pray to an omnipotent and almighty God!

Conclusion

Finally, we must be willing to bear the stigma of *perceived* failure. While it isn't failure, it may be "perceived" by others as failure. We have succeeded when we have obeyed the Scriptures to pray for the sick. Whether or not they are healed rests with God. John Wimber once said, "I decided long ago that if one hundred people receive prayer and only one is healed, it is better than if none receive prayer and no one is healed."[3] I agree.

---

3. John Wimber, *Power Healing* (San Francisco: Harper & Row, 1986), xviii. If you are bothered by the fact that prayer does not always result in healing, I address the possible reasons in, "Why Doesn't God Always Heal the Sick?" in *Tough Topics: Biblical Answers to 25 Challenging Questions* (Wheaton, IL: Crossway, 2013), 303–8; as well as in *Understanding Spiritual Gifts: A Comprehensive Guide* (Grand Rapids: Zondervan, 2020), 254–59.

CHAPTER 20

Prayer, Healing, and Elijah Our Example

T he responses I hear when I ask someone to pray for the sick that they might be healed are varied:

"But I'm not an *elder*. And James says the sick should call for the *elders* to have them pray."

"But I'm not a *pastor*. I'm not on *staff* at our church. Isn't it the responsibility of pastors to pray for the sick? Isn't that what we pay you guys to do?"

"But I'm not very *eloquent*. I wouldn't even know what to say, and if I were to say anything at all, I'd probably stumble over my words and make a fool of myself."

"But I'm not a *theologian*. I don't know much about doctrine, and I'd probably say something heretical if I were to pray for the sick."

"But I'm not a very *mature* Christian. I'm weak. I struggle with doubt. I struggle with fear. I struggle with various temptations. I'm just not qualified to pray for the sick. Why would God ever listen to the prayers of someone like me? Why should I ever think that he might answer my prayers by healing someone?"

Those aren't all the answers I've heard, but it's a representative list. I mention them because I'm convinced that James heard the same sort of objections when he urged people in the first century to be diligent in their prayers for one another for healing.

Let's be honest. What we've been looking at in James 5:13–16 is daunting.

It's challenging and more than a little frightening. When you read these verses, the instinctive human reaction is to conclude that James simply must be talking about a special class of Christians: supersaints or holier-than-thou type folk, the sort who never, or at least rarely, sin. Surely James would lay this responsibility only on the shoulders of those believers who virtually glow or vibrate with the presence of God. Surely, so we conclude, he can't mean me.

But he does mean you. If you are a believer in Jesus, you are included in this exhortation to mutual prayer for one another, all with a view of being healed physically of whatever affliction, pain, or disease from which people typically suffer.

As I said, James undoubtedly faced the same sort of objections that I faced regularly at Bridgeway, where I served as lead pastor for fourteen years. The reason I know this is because of what we read in verses 17–18. He points us to an example we should follow to motivate all believers to engage in this ministry of intercessory, healing prayer. He directs our attention to someone that everyone in the church, both in the first and twenty-first centuries, has heard of, someone whose experience of the power of prayer is undeniable and can serve as a model for us all. And who might that be? Elijah!

> Elijah was a man with a nature like ours, and he prayed fervently that it might not rain, and for three years and six months it did not rain on the earth. Then he prayed again, and heaven gave rain, and the earth bore its fruit. (James 5:17–18)

Just so you know, it's quite common in the Bible for an author to encourage and motivate his audience by appealing to the example of someone with whom they're familiar. Jesus did it on several occasions, one of which is in John 13, where he celebrated the Last Supper with his disciples:

> A new commandment I give to you, that you love one another: just as I have loved you, you also are to love one another. (John 13:34)

The apostle Paul didn't hesitate to encourage his disciples to imitate his life, insofar as he himself imitated Jesus. Of the numerous instances of this, I give you only one, where Paul pointed to himself and his habit of working with his own hands so that he wouldn't be a burden to others. After reminding them that he had every right to be supported for his ministry in their midst, he said this to the church at Thessalonica:

> It was not because we do not have that right [to be supported financially by you], but to give you in ourselves an example to imitate. (2 Thess. 3:9; see also Heb. 13:7 and all of Hebrews 11)

Already in James, in 5:10–11, our author directed the attention of his readers to certain Old Testament prophets and especially to Job as an example of steadfastness that we should imitate.

That's all well and good, you say, but why Elijah? Is he really the best example of someone who prayed fervently and with power? It would appear there were other Old Testament figures who stand out more noticeably as men and women of prayer.

God himself pointed to *Moses* and *Samuel* as two of the most prolific intercessors in the Old Testament (Jer. 15:1; see especially Num. 11:1–3; 21:6–9; 1 Sam. 7:1–14; 12:16–18). One also thinks of *Joshua* (Josh. 10:7–14), *Hezekiah* (2 Kings 19:14–20, 35–37), *Jehoshaphat* (2 Chron. 20:1–25), *Ezra* (Ezra 9:5–15) and *Nehemiah* (Neh. 1:5–11). If you had asked me, I would have pointed first and foremost to *Daniel* and his fervent and fearless prayer life (see Dan. 9:3–19).

So why Elijah? What do we know of this man?

Elijah the Prophet

At first glance, Elijah strikes us as *the least likely example* for James to cite if his goal was to encourage us to pray expectantly. Let me remind you of this great prophet.

We read in 1 Kings 17:17–24 that Elijah was instrumental in raising from the dead the son of a widowed lady from Zarephath. Perhaps the most famous incident in his life was his confrontation with the 450 prophets of the pagan deity Baal on Mt. Carmel. Elijah was determined to call the people of God to exclusive allegiance to Yahweh, so he proposed a test. He told the prophets of Baal to sacrifice a bull on one altar and he would do the same on another. The prophets were told to cry out to Baal to ignite with fire their sacrifice, and Elijah would do the same in crying out to God. You must see this for yourself to fully appreciate both the humor and the tragedy of it all:

And they took the bull that was given them, and they prepared it and called upon the name of Baal from morning until noon, saying, "O Baal, answer us!" But there was no voice, and no one answered. And they limped around the altar that they had made. And at noon Elijah mocked them, saying, "Cry aloud, for he is a god. Either he is musing, or he is relieving himself, or he is on a journey, or perhaps he is asleep and must be awakened." And they cried aloud and cut themselves after their custom with swords and lances, until the blood gushed out upon them. And as midday passed, they raved on until the time of the offering of the oblation, but there was no voice. No one answered; no one paid attention. (1 Kings 18:26–29)

Elijah then instructed the people to drench his sacrifice with twelve jars of water. He then prayed to God to show them all who really is God.

And at the time of the offering of the oblation, Elijah the prophet came near and said, "O Lord, God of Abraham, Isaac, and Israel, let it be known this day that you are God in Israel, and that I am your servant, and that I have done all these things at your word. Answer me, O Lord, answer me, that this people may know that you, O Lord, are God, and that you have turned their hearts back." Then the fire of the Lord fell and consumed the burnt offering and the wood and the stones and the dust, and licked up the water that was in the trench. (1 Kings 18:36–38)

I can almost hear some of you saying to yourselves:

Sam, stop! You aren't encouraging us in the least. In fact, you are *discouraging* us from thinking that our prayers will make a difference. My goodness: Elijah is a prophet and worked great signs and wonders and miracles. If ever there were a supersaint, a man filled with the grace and power of God, it had to be Elijah. How in the world can you and James point us to *him* as an example to be followed?

Let me make it even more difficult for you. We are told in Malachi 4:5 that Elijah is the man whose "appearance" was to be a prophetic prelude to the coming of the Messiah. Of course, we know that the reference was actually to John the Baptist, who embodied the ministry and message of

Elijah (see Mark 9:11–13). We must also deal with the fact that just as Moses was representative of the revelation of Law, Elijah was representative of the Prophetic Books. And was it not Elijah who, with Moses, appeared on the Mount of Transfiguration?

Aside from Enoch, Elijah is the only person who never tasted physical death; God took him into the glory of heaven apart from dying. Jewish tradition taught that Elijah would come at just the right time to deliver the righteous man from his afflictions. This may be why many thought Jesus was crying out to Elijah from the cross (see Matt. 27:46–49; Mark 15:34–36). Indeed, in the opinion of many in the first century, Elijah was considered almost *semidivine*.

Why in the world would James point us to a man who is so obviously different from all the rest of us? Why direct our attention to a man who was so singular in the supernatural? Why try to motivate us to pray by giving as an example a man who clearly is in a class all by himself?

The answer is quick in coming:

> "You're wrong," says James. "All of you are *wrong*. Elijah is *not* special. Elijah is *not* unique. Elijah is *not* someone who lives above the temptations of the flesh. Elijah is *not* a special case who lived at a special time. Elijah is *not* different from you. Elijah is *not* semidivine. Elijah is *not* in a class all by himself. He's just a man. He's just like you and me. He's normal. He's ordinary."

James says it in one simple phrase: "Elijah was a man [not a 'god'] with a nature like ours" (James 5:17a). He most likely has the experience of 1 Kings 19 in view. Let's read it together:

> Ahab told Jezebel all that Elijah had done, and how he had killed all the prophets with the sword. Then Jezebel sent a messenger to Elijah, saying, "So may the gods do to me and more also, if I do not make your life as the life of one of them by this time tomorrow." Then he was afraid, and he arose and ran for his life and came to Beersheba, which belongs to Judah, and left his servant there.
>
> But he himself went a day's journey into the wilderness and came and sat down under a broom tree. And he asked that he might die, saying, "It is enough; now, O LORD, take away my life, for I am no better than my fathers."

And he lay down and slept under a broom tree. And behold, an angel touched him and said to him, "Arise and eat." And he looked, and behold, there was at his head a cake baked on hot stones and a jar of water. And he ate and drank and lay down again. And the angel of the LORD came again a second time and touched him and said, "Arise and eat, for the journey is too great for you." And he arose and ate and drank, and went in the strength of that food forty days and forty nights to Horeb, the mount of God.

There he came to a cave and lodged in it. And behold, the word of the LORD came to him, and he said to him, "What are you doing here, Elijah?" He said, "I have been very jealous for the LORD, the God of hosts. For the people of Israel have forsaken your covenant, thrown down your altars, and killed your prophets with the sword, and I, even I only, am left, and they seek my life, to take it away." (1 Kings 19:1–10)

There, you can see it: contrary to everything you've been told or believed until now, Elijah is not different from you. He struggled with the same weaknesses, fears, and doubts. He battled hesitation, unbelief, timidity, frustration, disappointment, and depression. Listen to me. Elijah was a weak and broken man, just like you and just like me and just like the people in the first century to whom this letter by James is addressed.

The Fallacy of the "Cluster" Argument

Many who are skeptical of divine healing today and tell us we have little reason to expect that God will do miraculous things in response to our prayers appeal to what I have called the "cluster" argument. Here is what I mean. They argue that signs, wonders, and miracles were not customary phenomena even in biblical times. Rather, they were clustered or concentrated at critical moments of revelatory activity in redemptive history, specifically, during the days of Moses and Joshua, during the ministries of Elijah and Elisha, and in the time of Jesus and the apostles. Excluding these periods in biblical history, supernatural events were isolated and quite rare.

This is simply false. I have responded in detail to this argument elsewhere, but for our purposes here, I'll be brief and say only one thing.[1]

---

1. If interested, you can read my response to the cluster argument in, "A Third Wave View," my contribution to the book, *Are Miraculous Gifts for Today? Four Views* (Grand Rapids: Zondervan,

When I read the Old Testament, I discover a consistent pattern of supernatural manifestations in the affairs of humanity. In addition to the multitude of miracles during the lifetime of Moses, Joshua, Elijah, and Elisha, we see numerous instances of angelic activity (just read Genesis!), supernatural visitations and revelatory activity, healings, dreams, visions, and the like. One example would be that period when Daniel was taken captive into Babylon along with the rest of the Jewish people. If you read the book of Daniel, you see multiple miracles and instances of deliverance and dreams and visions and other supernatural phenomena.

Consider the assertion of Jeremiah 32:20. There we read: "You [God] have shown signs and wonders in the land of Egypt, and to this day in Israel and among all mankind, and have made a name for yourself, as at this day." This text alerts us to the danger of arguing from silence. The fact that from the time of the Exodus to the Babylonian captivity fewer instances of signs and wonders are *recorded* does *not* mean they did not occur. Jeremiah insists they did. One might compare this with the danger of asserting that Jesus did not perform a particular miracle or do so with any degree of frequency simply because the Gospels fail to record it. The apostle John tells us explicitly that Jesus performed "many other signs in the presence of the disciples" which he did not include in his gospel account (John 20:30), as well as "many other things that Jesus did" that were impossible to record in detail (John 21:25).

So, the first thing we see is that Elijah should not be viewed as having lived and ministered at a special and unrepeatable time when God was performing great miracles, such that we should not expect the same in our day. But even more important than that is the mere fact that James cites Elijah's example in a context where he is encouraging us to pray for healing.

The point of James 5:17–18 is to counter the argument that Elijah was somehow unique or that because of the period in which he lived, he could pray with miraculous success, but we cannot. James wanted his readers to know that Elijah was just like you and me. He was a human being with weaknesses, fears, doubts, and failures, no less than we. In other words, James said, "Don't let anyone tell you Elijah was in a class by himself. He wasn't. He's just like you. You are just like him. Therefore, pray like he did!"

1996), 186–90. For an even more detailed response, see Jack Deere, "Were There Only Three Periods of Miracles?" in *Surprised by the Power of the Spirit* (Grand Rapids: Zondervan, 1993), 253–66.

Don't forget the context: James appealed to the example of Elijah to encourage us when we pray for the sick! The point is that we should pray for miraculous healing with the same faith and expectation with which Elijah prayed for both the beginning and the end of a three-and-a-half-year drought. Thus, as John Piper has said, "This text does not limit powerful praying for divine healing to the elders, and it encourages us rather than discouraging us to think of our praying in the same category with a great miracle worker of the Bible."

What Happens When We Pray Fervently

James refers to two occasions on which Elijah prayed. First, he prayed, and there ensued three and a half years of drought and famine (see 1 Kings 17:1). Again, he prayed, and it rained cats and dogs (see 1 Kings 18:41–46)! You might wonder, "Why in the world would anyone pray that it not rain for such a long period of time?" The reason is that the drought that ensued was an expression of God's judgment against King Ahab, his wicked wife Jezebel, and the people of Israel for their rampant idolatry, immorality, and evil deeds.

But it is also of significance that Baal, the Canaanite deity, the 'god' of Ahab and Jezebel, was believed to be the god of rain and fertility. When it rained, people conceived of it as Baal "impregnating" the earth, which in due course bore its fruit in the form of crops. Elijah's prayer and the resultant drought, therefore, were a direct confrontation with and defeat of Baal.

Some have asked the question of why James says it was three and a half years (as we also see in Luke 4:25) when, according to 1 Kings 18:1ff., it was three years. Most likely, there were six months of drought that preceded Elijah's declaration. This would have made Elijah's declaration of drought even more substantial and meaningful since it would have come at the end of the dry season and at the beginning of the rainy season when everyone typically expected the rain to fall.

Why was Elijah's prayer used mightily of God on these occasions? The answer is found in two statements made by James. First, he was "righteous" (5:16b). Second, he prayed "fervently" (5:17a). Literally, "he prayed with prayer," or he really prayed; no halfhearted, half-baked verbal dart aimed at heaven. His prayer was sustained, sincere, and relentless. If the prayers of this man, of like passions with us, can be used by God to control the forces of nature, surely God is well pleased to use our petitions to heal our bodies and to fulfill our daily needs.

But what precisely does James 5:16 mean? Let's look at it more closely and focus on the variety of ways it has been translated. James writes:

> The prayer of a righteous person has great power as it is working. (ESV)

> The effective prayer of a righteous man can accomplish much. (NASB 1995)

> The prayer of a righteous person is powerful and effective. (NIV)

Who is this "righteous person"? In one sense, it can refer to all men and women who have trusted Christ. By God's gracious act he has imputed or reckoned the righteousness of Jesus to those who put their faith in his life, death, and resurrection. This, of course, is simply what we know as the truth of justification by faith alone. But the righteousness in view here is more likely the obedient life of the believer. James doesn't mean that sinless perfection is a requirement for effective prayer. After all, he directs our attention to Elijah, "a man with a nature like ours" (v. 17). And that "nature" we all possess is one that is often given over to sin and doubt and fear. James has in mind a person who is committed to living in obedience to the will of God and is quick to confess and repent when they fail to do so.

The most likely rendering of the second half of the verse would be: "the prayer of the righteous is able to do much" (or has power or is competent). The final word in the sentence is a present tense participle of the verb *energeō*, which means to work, accomplish, achieve, or be effective (and yes, this is the verb from which we derive our English words *energy* and *energetic*). It agrees in gender and case with the word *prayer*, and thus likely functions as an adjective. If we should ask what kind of prayer James has in mind, his answer would be: prayer that is working or effective. But the position of this participle at the end of the sentence suggests that it may function adverbially, as seen in the ESV rendering: "as it is working."

There is also the question of whether the participle is middle voice or passive. If middle, the proper rendering would be, "The prayer of a righteous person is powerful in what it is able to do." If passive, it would read, "in what it is enabled to do," or "when it is made effective," presumably by the Holy Spirit (or perhaps by the faith of the one praying). On this latter view, "James would subtly introduce a qualification to the effectiveness of prayer: only when God 'energizes' the prayer as it is offered in accordance with his will will it be effective."[2] But Moo ultimately questions the cogency of this interpretation and believes the participle is middle voice, hence: "as it powerfully works."

I think Dan McCartney best captures the point James is making:

> It is best to take the participle as modifying 'is powerful,' explaining not under what conditions it is effective, but in what way prayer has power: it is powerful because it effects change. James's point is that prayer causes things to happen, as the example of Elijah in 5:17–18 demonstrates. It causes things to happen because God responds to it.[3]

Commentators continue to disagree on the precise translation, but I don't think that should hinder us from finding here a clear affirmation of the power of prayer. When the man or woman who loves God's revealed will and relies on the Spirit to live in accordance with it, their prayer can do great things and accomplish much, especially when it comes to praying for the sick to be healed.

---

2. Douglas J. Moo, *The Letter of James* (Grand Rapids: Eerdmans, 2000), 247.

3. Dan G. McCartney, *James*, Baker Exegetical Commentary on the New Testament (Grand Rapids: Baker Academic, 2009), 258.

PART 5

CONCLUDING THOUGHTS

CHAPTER 21

Controversial Texts and
Challenging Questions about Prayer

There are numerous baffling biblical texts and challenging questions about prayer that I haven't addressed in other chapters. So, let's tackle a few of them here.

The So-Called "Law of Agreement"
and Matthew 18:15–20

In an article in *Charisma* magazine (May 2014), a Tennessee pastor cited the words of Jesus in Matthew 18 to support the practice of "agreement" in prayer as a way of increasing the probability of receiving what we ask. "Before His death and resurrection," he writes, "Jesus gave a hint about miracle power in Matthew 18:19–20." He then cites the words of Jesus to the effect that "if two of you agree on earth about anything they ask, it will be done for them by my Father in heaven. For where two or three are gathered in my name, there am I among them."

One would be hard-pressed to find a text so frequently cited and so dear to the hearts of Christian men and women as this one. Of course, all biblical texts should be precious to us. But they are precious and powerful only to the extent we interpret them in light of their context and in accordance with what the original author intended to teach.

This Tennessee pastor exhorts us to "read this promise and see its potential. If we can agree," so he suggests, "anything becomes possible!"

I am somewhat hesitant to take issue with this interpretation, if for no other reason than that my theological hero, Jonathan Edwards, embraced it in support of his efforts in the eighteenth century to mobilize a global concert of prayer among Christians.[1] Unity of mind and agreement of purpose is of great value in the life of the local church, and nothing I say about how this text in Matthew has been abused should detract from that truth.

But the simple fact remains that Jesus was not talking about the so-called "law of agreement" or in any way suggesting that if we can put aside our differences and come to unity in that for which we pray we will see "miracle power" released where "anything becomes possible." So, what was Jesus saying? The only way to answer that question, as I said, is to read this passage in context. Let's look at where it falls in the eighteenth chapter of Matthew's gospel:

> If your brother sins against you, go and tell him his fault, between you and him alone. If he listens to you, you have gained your brother. But if he does not listen, take one or two others along with you, that every charge may be established by the evidence of two or three witnesses. If he refuses to listen to them, tell it to the church. And if he refuses to listen even to the church, let him be to you as a Gentile and a tax collector. Truly, I say to you, whatever you bind on earth shall be bound in heaven, and whatever you loose on earth shall be loosed in heaven. Again I say to you, if two of you agree on earth about anything they ask, it will be done for them by my Father in heaven. For where two or three are gathered in my name, there am I among them. (Matt. 18:15–20)

Clearly, Jesus is addressing the subject of church discipline.[2] He presents the procedural steps for what is to be done when a professing Christian sins. The first step is private rebuke (v. 15). If unsuccessful, this is to be followed by plural rebuke (v. 16; cf. Deut. 19:15). If plural rebuke fails, which is to say that the person remains in denial or unrepentant regarding their misbehavior, there follows public rebuke and eventually separation (v. 17), a decision

---

1. See his treatise, "Some Thoughts Concerning the Revival," in *The Great Awakening*, ed. C. C. Goen (New Haven, CT: Yale University Press, 1972), 520–21.

2. See especially D. A. Carson, "Matthew," *The Expositor's Bible Commentary*, 8:403–4; and J. Duncan M. Derrett, "Where Two or Three Are Convened in My Name ...': A Sad Misunderstanding," *ExpT* 91 (1979–80): 83–86.

that the church may be confident has divine approval (v. 18). So, if Matthew 18:19–20 is taken as a reference to prayer, its application must at least be restricted by the immediately preceding context (vv. 15–18).

However, I'm not persuaded that Jesus is saying anything directly about prayer, much less about the so-called "law of agreement."

The "two" people in verse 19 who come to an agreement are, likely, the same "two" people mentioned in verse 15, namely, the offender and the person against whom the offense has been committed.[3] Furthermore, the verb translated "ask" in verse 19 does not necessarily mean to ask in prayer. It may well refer to the "pursuing of a claim." Similarly, the word translated "anything" need not be taken in the sense of "any legitimate object of petitionary prayer" but in the sense we see in 1 Corinthians 6:1 where Paul has in mind "any judicial matter" that has come before the church for adjudication.

If this is correct, Jesus would have been describing a situation in which two people involved in a dispute come to an agreement on the matter that has divided them. Presumably, this will have occurred based on the church's judgment, referred to in verse 18. In such cases our heavenly Father will approve and ratify the decision (literally, "it shall come to be from the Father," or perhaps, "it shall be allowed, granted, sanctioned"). Therefore, the "two or three" mentioned in verse 20 who are "gathered" or who come together in the name of Jesus are probably the two disputants themselves, along with the third party who was called in as an outside witness (v. 19).

Thus, Jesus is most likely not promising that God will answer any prayer that two people agree upon, as if to suggest that the same prayer uttered by only one believer is less pleasing to God. Rather, Jesus would be saying that when two Christians involved in a personal dispute resolve their differences, God sanctions or approves the matter. The verdict of heaven, so to speak, is consonant with that of the church, before whom the matter was adjudicated (see 1 Cor. 5:4).

Although we should avoid being dogmatic in the interpretation of this passage, caution must prevail in any attempt to derive from it a law or eternal principle to the effect that if two believers of one mind pray for the same thing at the same time, they may be assured of seeing their request fulfilled.

---

3. Derrett believes that the "two or three" are the judges called by the church to settle the matter, but Carson has a persuasive response in "Matthew," 404.

That being said, I am certainly not opposed to corporate prayer. Far less do I mean to indict as unbiblical the so-called "prayer chain" or the "day of prayer" in which believers converge to bring their petitions *en masse* to the throne of grace. I am only suggesting that if this sort of joint supplication is undertaken, the participant should not do so based on Matthew 18:19–20.

Even less appropriate is the use of this passage in "The Wedding Song" made popular by Paul Stookey (of Peter, Paul, and Mary fame) in 1970. Although I would hope that love prevails any time two Christian people come together, that is not what Jesus is promising here. If this song was sung at your wedding, please don't be angry with me!

Finally, why is it important that we take time to carefully and thoroughly examine a passage in terms of context and authorial intent? The simple answer is that it will protect us from believing something God hasn't said and from trusting in a promise he never made. My concern is that many will adopt the notion of a "law of agreement" and pray with the expectation (dare I say, presumption?) that if they can only get one or two others to agree with them on some matter, God is obligated to answer their request accordingly. When he doesn't, confidence in God and his Word is undermined. Of course, he may answer their prayers, but if he does, it isn't because he is honoring a "promise" allegedly stated in Matthew 18.

If Jesus Is Coming Back Soon, Why Pray?

It is widely reported that the great sixteenth-century Protestant Reformer, Martin Luther, once said, "If I knew for sure that Jesus was coming back tomorrow, I'd plant a tree today." Luther wasn't trying to be cute, nor did he think that his words were contradictory. He was simply pointing out that no amount of speculation, confidence, doubt, or belief about when Jesus might return should ever undermine the fulfillment of our basic ethical obligations or lead us to abandon the routine responsibilities set forth for us in Scripture.

Sadly, many Christians through the centuries have taken an altogether different and unbiblical approach to this problem. Convinced that Christ was to return soon, they abandoned their daily tasks and embraced a form of hyperspirituality that served only to bring reproach on the name of Christ and disaster to their own lives. How often have we heard and seen something like this:

The end of all things is at hand! Therefore, let's shave our heads, adorn ourselves in white robes, and run to the hills!

Christ is coming back soon! Therefore, let's sell our possessions, quit our jobs, and turn our backs on a culture that is hell-bound!

The end of human history is just around the corner! Therefore, let's refuse to bathe, learn how to cry on cue, and contort our faces in a show of deep concern for the plight of all lost souls!

We are certain that Jesus is coming back before we die! Therefore, let's set a specific date for Jesus' return, write it up in a bestselling book, and then make sure we've got an excuse for why he doesn't return on the day we said he would, to protect our reputations!

The end of all things is at hand! Therefore, let's abandon the local church, launch a parachurch movement that will gather thousands of followers, and forget about higher education, paying our taxes, getting married, having children, and mowing the grass!

The second coming is surely on the horizon! Therefore, let's host a seminar and work hard at identifying the Antichrist and figure out ways that 666 applies to all the people we don't like!

Well, not exactly. Peter's advice is of a different spirit:

The end of all things is at hand; therefore be self-controlled and sober-minded for the sake of your prayers. Above all, keep loving one another earnestly, since love covers a multitude of sins. Show hospitality to one another without grumbling. (1 Peter 4:7–9; italics mine)

Did you see the word *therefore* in verse 7? It is *because* the end of all things is at hand that we are to pray for one another, love one another, be hospitable to one another, and serve one another. I want us to think about how we should react to the reality of Christ's impending return. I want us to think about what kind of person God wants us to be in view of the end of all things.

But we need to begin at the beginning: What does Peter mean when he says in verse 7: "The end of all things is at hand"? Many liberal skeptics have pointed to texts such as this as proof that Christianity is false, and the Bible is in error. After all, the second coming of Christ didn't occur in the first century when Peter and his readers lived. Others believe "the end of all things" refers to the events of AD 70, the destruction of Jerusalem and its temple, all of which marked the end of the Jewish age and the judgment of God against an apostate nation that had rejected the Messiah. But does it make sense to describe the events of AD 70 as "the end of *all* things"? Furthermore, how could that event possibly be such a motivating factor to those living in northern Asia Minor? These to whom Peter writes are largely gentile believers living in Pontus, Galatia, Cappadocia, Asia, and Bithynia (see 1:1–2).

The New Testament writers believed that with Christ's death, resurrection, and exaltation to the right hand of the Father, the "last days" have dawned. See Acts 2:17; 2 Timothy 3:1; Hebrews 1:1–2; 1 John 2:18. But Peter didn't know if the last of the last days or the end of the end times would come in his lifetime. Christ's death and resurrection mark the beginning of the end, although neither Peter nor we know when the end of the end will come.

Yet another reason why I'm persuaded that Peter did indeed have in mind the end of history at the second coming of Christ is because of what we see in verses 5–6 regarding the final judgment of all mankind. "They will give account to him who is ready to judge the living and the dead. . . . The end of all things is at hand; therefore . . . !"

One might think that the reality of the end would lead Peter to call for extraordinary deeds of great power, works that would capture the attention of the world and gain for us fame and glory. No. It's the simple, basic tasks of everyday life that must be pursued: praying for one another, loving one another, hosting one another, and serving one another.

Our first responsibility, in view of the impending end of all things, is to pray for one another. Peter here calls for mature and level-headed intercessors (v. 7b). *Self-controlled* and *sober-minded* are words that are virtually synonymous and should be taken together. Both are essential to effective intercession. Simply put: Keep a cool head! Keep your wits about you. Don't get caught up in wild-eyed, irresponsible fanaticism where you think the ordinary rules of Christianity no longer apply. Maintain spiritual and mental discipline in a time when others cast common sense aside and forget who they are.

The idea is not simply "so that you may pray" but "so that you may pray more effectively and intelligently." Some who feel called to intercession make the mistake of thinking this justifies fanaticism, neglect of routine responsibilities of life, or withdrawal into monastic solitude. Others shake and bake and fall down and are swept away into flights of religious euphoria and physical manifestations. Thinking about the end of all things has led some to lose their composure, to forsake common sense, to ignore the Scriptures, and to act irrationally. But Peter wants us to know that one can be a faithful and fervent intercessor without losing perspective or composure.

Use the nearness of the end as an opportunity for prayer, but don't lose your heads in the process! What we desperately need today are self-controlled, level-headed, mature, sober-minded intercessors.

Is There Such a Thing as "Wordless" Prayer?

> To pray successfully without words one needs to be "at the top of one's form." Otherwise the mental acts become merely imaginative or emotional acts—and a fabricated emotion is a miserable affair.
> (C. S. Lewis, *Letters to Malcolm: Chiefly on Prayer*, 11)

The answer to that question depends entirely on what we mean by "wordless." Not all prayer has to be audible. In other words, there is undoubtedly a thing called "unspoken" prayer in the sense that we remain silent. But that doesn't mean our prayers are devoid of words. If you doubt this, consider Hannah who is described as "speaking in her heart; only her lips moved, and her voice was not heard" (1 Sam. 1:13). In fact, when Eli accused her of being drunk, she said she had been "pouring out" her "soul before the LORD" (v. 15). There was no sound, but there was certainly prayer. Hannah's appeal to the Lord was in the form of words, but they remained unspoken, staying silent within her heart. Have we not all at some time done this very thing? Not wanting others to hear our requests, not wanting to be disruptive in a gathering of friends, we articulate our needs to God but in a way that no one else can hear them.

If you have any doubt about whether God knows your unspoken

thoughts, inner desires, fears, faith, and prayers, consider these texts which
are unmistakably clear:

> And you, Solomon my son, know the God of your father and serve him with
> a whole heart and with a willing mind, for the LORD searches all hearts and
> understands every plan and thought. (1 Chron. 28:9a)

> He who disciplines the nations, does he not rebuke?
> He who teaches man knowledge—
>> the LORD—knows the thoughts of man,
>> that they are but a breath. (Ps. 94:10–11; cf. 1 Cor. 3:20)

> Sheol and Abaddon lie open before the LORD;
>> how much more the hearts of the children of man! (Prov. 15:11)

> Even before a word is on my tongue,
>> behold, O LORD, you know it altogether. (Ps. 139:4)

> The heart is deceitful above all things,
>> and desperately sick;
>> who can understand it?
> "I the LORD search the heart
>> and test the mind,
> to give every man according to his ways,
>> according to the fruit of his deeds." (Jer. 17:9–10; cf. 1 Kings 8:39;
>> Jer. 11:20; 16:17; 18:23)

> O LORD of hosts, who tests the righteous,
>> who sees the heart and the mind. (Jer. 20:12a; cf. 1 Sam. 16:7)

> And the Spirit of the LORD fell upon me, and he said to me, "Say, Thus says
> the LORD: So you think, O house of Israel. For I know the things that come
> into your mind." (Ezek. 11:5; cf. Isa. 66:18; Matt. 9:4)

> And he said to them, "You are those who justify yourselves before men, but
> God knows your hearts." (Luke 16:15a)

> And they prayed and said, "You, Lord, who know the hearts of all, show which one of these two you have chosen." (Acts 1:24; cf. Acts 15:8; Rom. 8:27; 1 Thess. 2:4)

> And no creature is hidden from his sight, but all are naked and exposed to the eyes of him to whom we must give account. (Heb. 4:13; cf. John 2:25; Rev. 2:23)

I trust that these texts (and many more like them) are enough to persuade you that God knows your thoughts and desires without you having to speak a single syllable.

Let's return to the issue of so-called "wordless" prayer. By this, many have in mind what is also called "centering" prayer in which they make no use of their minds, articulate no words, but remain still before God. No, this is not the same as biblical meditation. In so-called "centering" prayer, the rational faculty is bypassed. The mind is emptied of thought. But when we meditate on the Lord, our minds are engaged with God, his beauty, his gracious activity, and our thoughts are filled with words and images rooted in Scripture. Thus, "centering" prayer has more in common with eastern forms of meditation wherein the mind remains empty. I see no justification for this in Scripture.[4]

I'm not suggesting that sitting quietly and inaudibly before the Lord is always wrong. It may well serve to prepare us for meeting God in prayer, a way of calming our hearts in his presence. I'm simply saying that it isn't prayer. Prayer is conversing with God.

But we must also consider Romans 8:26–27. Paul says this:

> Likewise the Spirit helps us in our weakness. For we do not know what to pray for as we ought, but the Spirit himself intercedes for us with groanings too deep for words. And he who searches hearts knows what is the mind of the Spirit, because the Spirit intercedes for the saints according to the will of God.

All Christians feel weak at times and wish that there was a way in which our unspoken requests could be made known to God. Simply put, we all need

---

4. I address this issue and the nature of biblical meditation in my book, *Pleasures Evermore: The Life-Changing Power of Enjoying God* (Colorado Springs: Navpress, 2000), 185–207.

the help of the Holy Spirit. The word *likewise* (v. 26a) connects what he's about to say with what has gone before. He encouraged the believer in Romans 8:18 in view of the surpassing glory that will replace our current suffering. Similarly, in verses 19–25 he again encourages the believer to persevere by pointing to the fact that even the material creation is groaning in anxious anticipation of our redemption, because when we receive our glorified bodies at the return of Jesus, the material creation will also experience its final redemption and the curse of futility imposed on it because of Adam's sin will be lifted. The earth and everything in it will be renewed (see Rev. 21–22). So, verses 18–27 constitute one long exhortation designed to encourage believers to persevere amid hardship and suffering. To that, Paul now adds that even when you feel weak and wordless in your prayer life, the Holy Spirit himself intercedes on your behalf to make certain that your deepest desires and needs are brought to the Father in heaven.

The word *weakness* refers not to physical exhaustion or to intellectual confusion but to our not knowing "what we ought to pray for" (NIV). We know that there is much more that needs to be articulated, but we can't figure out precisely what it is. But it is uplifting to know that my limitations, my lack of knowledge, my inability to decipher precisely how and for what I should pray is no reflection on God's power (cf. Eph. 3:20–21). Paul is not talking about style or posture or manner or length but of content in prayer. We are ignorant of what we or others may need, ignorant of what God has promised, and unable to put into words the cry of our hearts. But the Holy Spirit takes up where we, because of weakness, leave off. If we do not know what to pray for, the Spirit does. He intercedes for us "through wordless groans" (Rom. 8:26b NIV).

Is this groaning of the Holy Spirit literal or physically audible, or could it be metaphorical? The "groaning" of the material creation is clearly metaphorical. We humans literally and audibly groan as we wait in anxious expectation to be set free from the perishable and painful bodies in which we now live. But Paul says that God the Holy Spirit would also groan as he identifies with our deep, profoundly emotional, yet inarticulate yearning for answers to prayers that we feel too weak and ignorant to utter.

As our intercessor (vv. 26–27), he intercedes for us "with groanings too deep for words." The single Greek word behind this translation is used only here in the New Testament (*alalētois*). Does it mean ineffable, that is, incapable of being expressed in human language (cf. 2 Cor. 12:4)?[5] If so, the groans may well be audible, though inarticulate. Or does it mean simply unspoken, never rising to the audible level at all? If the former is correct, the groanings are probably ours, which the Holy Spirit inspires and prompts within us. But the latter is more likely. The groans are from the Holy Spirit himself. He is the one who "intercedes for us." Douglas Moo explains:

> While we cannot, then, be absolutely sure . . . , it is preferable to understand these "groans" as the Spirit's own "language of prayer," a ministry of intercession that takes place in our hearts (cf. v. 27) in a manner imperceptible to us. . . . I take it that Paul is saying, then, that our failure to know God's will and consequent inability to petition God specifically and assuredly is met by God's Spirit, who himself expresses to God those intercessory petitions that perfectly match the will of God. When we do not know what to pray for—yes, even when we pray for things that are not best for us—we need not despair, for we can depend on the Spirit's ministry of perfect intercession "on our behalf." . . . [According to verse 27] God, who sees into the inner being of people, where the indwelling Spirit's ministry of intercession takes place, "knows," "acknowledges," and responds to those "intentions" of the Spirit that are expressed in his prayers on our behalf.[6]

Thus, it is the Spirit who prays, not us. If praying in tongues is included in Paul's thought in verses 26–27, it is in no way exclusively concerned with tongues.[7] Paul may well include tongues in the reality of the Spirit's groans within and for us, but he would not restrict the latter to praying in tongues. In other words, Romans 8:26–27 is a glorious truth that applies across the board to all Christians, those who pray in tongues and those who do not. We must not overlook the context of verses 18–27 in which all Christians suffer in this present time, all Christians groan under the curse imposed by sin, and all Christians therefore struggle in their weakness to know precisely how and

---

5. The word for "inexpressible" is found in 1 Peter 1:8 (*aneklalētos*). It is significant that Paul does not use that word here.

6. Douglas J. Moo, *The Epistle to the Romans* (Grand Rapids: Eerdmans, 1996), 526–27.

7. For a clear defense of the interpretation that Paul is indeed addressing the experience of praying in tongues, see Fee, *God's Empowering Presence*, 575–86. See also, John Bertone, "The Experience of Glossolalia and the Spirit's Empathy: Romans 8:26 Revisited," in *Pneuma: The Journal of the Society for Pentecostal Studies* 25, no. 1 (Spring 2003): 54–65.

what to bring to God in prayer. The promise of the Spirit's work on our behalf in verses 26–27 thus applies to every believer, every child of God, regardless of what spiritual gift they either have or don't have.

Instead of our weakness in prayer bringing discouragement to our hearts, Paul reminds us that "the Spirit helps us in our weakness" (Rom. 8:26a). The only other place in the entire New Testament where this verb *help* is used is in Luke 10:40 where Martha asks Jesus to tell Mary to "help" her in the kitchen. So, the Spirit helps us by taking our unexpressed desires and petitions, communicating them perfectly to the Father. But does this refer to our groanings, or to the groanings of the Holy Spirit, or in some sense to both? Could it be that the Holy Spirit stirs and elicits these groanings in us such that they are in some sense both his and ours?

Some argue that these can't be the groanings of the Spirit because the Spirit is communicating directly with our heavenly Father. Why would the Spirit need to make use of groanings? The Spirit knows what he is asking on our behalf, and the Father certainly knows what the Spirit is saying. God the Father knows the mind of the Spirit, and the Spirit knows what the will of God is for each of us (v. 27). There is no confusion or uncertainty.

But Paul isn't talking about how the Spirit regularly speaks to the Father. He describes an altogether unique experience when the Spirit intercedes with the Father on our behalf when our hearts and minds are incapable of articulating in prayer what we want him to know. So, I am led to conclude that these "groanings" are both ours and those of the Holy Spirit. The Spirit awakens in us or stirs in our hearts groanings with which he then identifies and makes his own. He then carries these groanings to the heart of the Father on our behalf. Such groanings occur in our "hearts" (v. 27), not in our mouths. You can't hear them or feel them. Rather, as God searches the hearts of his children (v. 27), he finds unuttered, unexpressed groanings produced in us by the Spirit.

These requests and needs are taken up by the Spirit in the form of deep groanings and carried by him to the Father. The Father, in turn, understands perfectly what these groanings mean because when the Spirit conveys them to God on our behalf, he does so in a way that perfectly conforms to God's will. The mind of the Spirit and the mind of the Father are in perfect harmony. So here is the sequence or process that Paul is describing. In our weakness, we don't know what to pray for—the Holy Spirit awakens in us and stirs up groans—the Spirit in turn makes our groans his own, groans that can't be put into words—these groans are then taken by the Spirit to God the Father—God the Father knows perfectly what the Spirit is saying because the Spirit only asks the Father, on our behalf, for things that align with his will.

The "groans," then, are not prayer. They are the result of our inability to find the words to express what we need most from God.

Thoughts on the Most Difficult and Challenging Text in Scripture on Prayer

> The New Testament contains embarrassing promises that what we pray for with faith we shall receive. Mark XI:24 is the most staggering. (C. S. Lewis, *Letters to Malcolm*, 57).

There is hardly a more challenging issue when it comes to prayer than how it relates to faith. And no text more directly raises this question than Mark 11. Here it is:

> As they passed by in the morning, they saw the fig tree withered away to its roots. And Peter remembered and said to him, "Rabbi, look! The fig tree that you cursed has withered." And Jesus answered them, "Have faith in God. Truly, I say to you, whoever says to this mountain, 'Be taken up and thrown into the sea,' and does not doubt in his heart, but believes that what he says will come to pass, it will be done for him. Therefore I tell you, whatever you ask in prayer, believe that you have received it, and it will be yours. And whenever you stand praying, forgive, if you have anything against anyone, so that your Father also who is in heaven may forgive you your trespasses." (Mark 11:20–25)

C. S. Lewis expands on his comment about Mark 11:24 being "the most staggering" promise in the New Testament related to prayer:

> Whatever we ask for, believing that we'll get it, we'll get. No question, it seems, of confining it to spiritual gifts; *whatever* we ask for. No question of a merely general faith in God, but a belief that you will get the particular thing you ask. No question of getting either it or else something that is

really far better for you; you'll get precisely it. And to heap paradox on paradox, the Greek doesn't even say "believing that you *will* get it." It uses the aorist, *elabete*, which one is tempted to translate "believing that you *got* it."[8]

Before we try to unravel this "staggering" promise, I need to explain the connection between the cursing of the fig tree and the power of faith when we pray. Peter points out the withered tree, and Jesus responds by urging his followers to exercise faith in God, the sort of faith that moves mountains. In those days, moving or casting a mountain into the sea was proverbial for the miraculous. After all, why would any Christian want to make a mountain fall into the sea? The point of our Lord is to highlight the fact that otherwise humanly impossible things, things that require supernatural and miraculous power, can occur when prayer is filled with faith.

The instantaneous and miraculous destruction of the fig tree serves as an object lesson to the disciples of what can be achieved by faith in God's power. It is as if Jesus says to Peter, "Pete, your comment tells me that you are amazed by the sudden and supernatural withering of the fig tree. But if you have faith in God, all things are possible through prayer." So, the withered fig tree is used by Jesus not only to teach us about the dangers of hypocrisy but also about the power of prayer!

Several things must be considered if we are to make sense of what Jesus says. We must first recognize that the "belief" or "faith" here is not a case of a Christian forcing himself to believe what he does not really believe. It is not a wrenching of one's brain, a coercing of one's will, a contorting of one's expectations to embrace as real and true something that one's heartfelt conviction says otherwise, what C. S. Lewis refers to as "a feat of psychological gymnastics."[9] Jesus is not telling us that when doubts start to creep in you should put your hands over your ears, close your eyes, and say to those doubts, over and over again, "Lalalalala, I can't hear you. Lalalalala, I can't hear you!" That's not faith. That's "make-believe." That's spiritual pretending.

On the other hand, we are responsible to take steps that will facilitate the deepening of faith in our hearts. We can do things, by God's grace, that will expand our confidence in God's goodness and his greatness and help

---

8. Lewis, *Letters to Malcolm*, 57–58.
9. Lewis, *Letters to Malcolm*, 60.

diminish if not drive out our doubts. As I study and meditate on the character of God, my confidence in what he can do increases. As I reflect and ponder the grace and kindness of God, my confidence in his goodness grows and intensifies.

Clearly, there are other factors that must be taken into consideration when we ask God for things in prayer. In other words, we can't read this passage in Mark 11 as if it stood alone, unrelated to everything else we read in Scripture about prayer. Elsewhere we are told that faith is not the sole condition for answered prayer. We must ask God with the right motives (cf. James 4:1ff.). Husbands must treat their wives with gentleness and kindness and understanding (1 Peter 3:7). We must clean the slate, so to speak, in our relationships with others. This is the point of the final verse in this passage. If you harbor unforgiveness in your heart toward others, it isn't likely that God will answer your prayer, no matter how much alleged faith you think you have (see Matt. 6:14–15). And we must ask in accordance with God's will. It doesn't matter if I am somehow able to banish all doubt from my mind and convince myself that I've already received what I asked for; if what I'm asking isn't consistent with the will and character of God, the answer will be no.

No amount of faith will force God's hand to do something that is contrary to our welfare. It doesn't matter how persuaded you are or how much faith you have; you simply don't want God to answer every prayer you pray! Look with the benefit of hindsight on some of the things you once believed you needed and were convinced that God would give you. Yikes! Thank you, Lord, for saying no to many of these prayers. It would have been devastating had you said yes. And we must never forget that sometimes God says no to prayers that are offered up in faith because he has something even better in store for us that he plans on giving at a more appropriate and suitable time.

My point is simply that it is irresponsible and insensitive to suggest, based on this passage, that if someone doesn't receive from God what they asked for, it is because they are at fault for failing to have enough faith. The absence of faith may well be a factor, but it is not the only factor. There are other things that may more readily account for unanswered prayer.

I am persuaded that *the only way anyone can fulfill the condition set forth by Jesus in Mark 11 is if God himself chooses to impart to us the faith he requires.* Faith, ultimately, is a gift from God. When God wants to bless us with a miraculous answer to our prayer, he will take the initiative to cultivate and build the fulfillment of the condition he requires into our hearts. He will sovereignly banish all doubt from our hearts and will enable us to believe that we have already received it. It isn't an issue of my willpower but of God's gracious initiative and determination to empower me to do what I otherwise could never accomplish in my own strength (see esp. Phil. 2:12–13; Heb. 13:20–21).

The key to understanding and experiencing the promise of Mark 11 is to pray and seek God for what only God can do. Ask him to equip you with unshaking confidence that he will give you what you need. Begin by asking God for an extraordinary, powerful faith. Ask God that he might work in us the confidence that he is pleased to bless. So, in sum, the absence of all doubt and the presence of unwavering faith described here are not in our power to produce, apart from God. He alone can meet the conditions that he requires of us. So, pray that he will.

Will God Always Hear Our Prayers?

No. Perhaps I shouldn't be so blunt in answering that question, but we need to be aware of the circumstances under which God himself says he will not hear or respond to our prayers. Several texts make this crystal clear.

> If I had cherished iniquity in my heart,
>> the Lord would not have listened.
> But truly God has listened;
>> he has attended to the voice of my prayer. (Ps. 66:18–19)

> Blessed be God,
>> because he has not rejected my prayer
>> or removed his steadfast love from me! (Ps. 66:20)

To "cherish" iniquity more literally means to "aim for" or "look forward to" and has in view coming to God in prayer hoping that he will provide an opportunity to commit some sin. Should we ever try to use God to justify our sin, we can be assured that he will not listen. Unconfessed sin for which there has been no repentance, and the willful determination to persist in it, is a surefire way to silence heaven. While the psalmist is not suggesting that sinless perfection is a condition for answered prayer, a hard-hearted devotion to sin is almost a guarantee that our prayers will be "rejected" (v. 20). On the flip side, a broken, repentant, and contrite heart assures us that God will attend "to the voice" of our petitions.

Much the same thing is in view in several other Old Testament texts where idolatry and egregiously wicked behavior are found in God's people. In Proverbs, we read that because God's people "hated knowledge and did not choose the fear of the LORD" (Prov. 1:29),

> then they will call upon me, but I will not answer;
>> they will seek me diligently but will not find me. (Prov. 1:28)

Calloused disregard for the plight of the poor is yet another reason why God may not hear and respond to our prayers:

> Whoever closes his ear to the cry of the poor
>> will himself call out and not be answered. (Prov. 21:13)

The effect on God of unrepentant sin and bloodshed is made clear in Isaiah 1:15. There God himself declares,

> When you spread out your hands,
>> I will hide my eyes from you;
> even though you make many prayers,
>> I will not listen;
>> your hands are full of blood.

It is nothing short of stunning that God's people can lift their hands to him in a show of desperation and need and offer up "many" prayers, and yet God refuses to listen.

God told Jeremiah in no uncertain terms not to "pray for this people, or lift up a cry or prayer for them, and do not intercede with me, for I will not hear you" (Jer. 7:16). The reason is that by their idolatrous practices they "provoke me to anger" (7:18). We see this tragic truth yet again in the prophecy of Micah, where the Lord declares that "they will cry" to him, "but he will not answer them; he will hide his face from them at that time, because they have made their deeds evil" (Mic. 3:4).

We often make the mistake of thinking that the sort of sin that shuts the ears of God to our prayers are openly defiant and sexually perverse sins that all can see, but the apostle Peter disagrees. When men fail to live with their wives "in an understanding way" (lit., "according to knowledge") and refuse to "honor" "the woman as the weaker vessel," their prayers are "hindered" (1 Peter 3:7).

If you want your prayers to be heard and not hindered, you must live with your wife in a certain way. There must be an effort to identify her most basic needs and meet them with love and humility. There must be a kindhearted tenderness in view of her weaknesses and a commitment to provide what will enable her to flourish in her relationship with the Lord. We men must devote ourselves to whatever will empower our wives to come alive and feel the dignity of being a female. There must be a recognition that she is a fellow heir of the grace of life and an accompanying bestowal of honor rather than any belittling or demeaning. When we husbands live like this (with understanding, tender care, and honor), our prayers will not be hindered. If we do not live like this, our prayers will fall on deaf ears. Grudem says it well:

> No Christian husband should presume to think that any spiritual good will be accomplished by his life without an effective ministry of prayer. And no husband may expect an effective prayer life unless he lives with his wife "in an understanding way, bestowing honor" on her. To take the time to develop and maintain a good marriage is God's will; it is serving God; it is a spiritual activity pleasing in his sight.[10]

---

10. Wayne A. Grudem, *The First Epistle of Peter: An Introduction and Commentary* (Grand Rapids: Eerdmans, 1988), 146.

Conclusion

What follows is less of a conclusion and more of a challenge. I trust you will receive this in the spirit in which I intend it. I don't want to come across as a bully, demanding things from you. After all, I have no spiritual authority over your life. My heart is that you will use what follows to examine the posture of your own soul when it comes to the importance of prayer. If you've read this book carefully, you know by now how critically important prayer is in the life of a child of God. My aim in this "conclusion/challenge" is to press this point, calling upon each of us to examine our hearts as to the depth of our commitment to seek the Lord in prayer. Are we willing to pay whatever price is necessary to maintain a life of consistent, constant intercession? And I know of no better story in Scripture to issue this challenge than that of Daniel.

I assume you all know the broad outlines of the story of Daniel. According to Daniel 6:1–3, Darius "planned to set him over the whole kingdom" (v. 3). This infuriated "the high officials and the satraps" (v. 4) who undoubtedly were envious of the favor the king has shown to Daniel. They sought to find some ground or basis to accuse him and undermine his influence with Darius. One gets the impression that there was repeated monitoring of Daniel's activity. Perhaps coworkers, secretaries, subordinates, janitors, etc. watched his every move and recorded his every word. They would have examined his personal financial records and scrutinized his work history. Their motivation was a mixture of several factors. As just stated, envy was certainly driving them. Furthermore, Daniel was a holdover from the Babylonian regime, whereas these men were of the Medo-Persian kingdom. Their dislike for his godliness no doubt provoked them to dispose of him. But Daniel "was faithful, and no error or fault was found in him" (v. 4b).

This determination on their part reveals two things: First, they knew about Daniel's spiritual and religious commitment, especially his devotion to prayer. He had not hidden his faith to survive or thrive "in the office." Second, they were persuaded his commitment was so deep that he would rather face death than compromise. They concluded that the only way to catch Daniel in some misdeed would be to enact a law of state that would violate a law of his God. In other words, the only way to implicate Daniel in a crime is to formulate a law that requires him to sin. They reasoned this way: "We must bring the law of Darius into conflict with the law of Yahweh. Then Daniel's devotion to his God will give us opportunity to charge him with civil disloyalty to Darius. We must make it impossible for Daniel to be simultaneously innocent before his God and obedient to the state."

They decided to enact a law that prohibited anyone from praying to anyone other than Darius himself. It is strangely ironic that the only way they can make Daniel appear immoral is by deceitfully exploiting his morality! They take advantage of his integrity to portray him as dishonest. They were determined to make his own high degree of commitment to God work against him. Would that we were all of such character that this would be the only way to ensnare us in the appearance of unrighteousness.

As soon as Daniel heard about the new law, he immediately "went to his house where he had windows in his upper chamber open toward Jerusalem. He got down on his knees three times a day and prayed and gave thanks before his God, as he had done previously" (v. 10). How should we characterize Daniel's response? Was he guilty of tempting God? Was his response one of religious ostentation? Was Daniel a spiritual show-off? Was he characterized by a martyr complex? Was he lacking in wisdom and common sense? Why did he not pursue a different course of action, such as ceasing to pray for the period of the decree? After all, what is one month without prayer when compared to a lifetime to serve God? Or he could have prayed silently, and if not silently, then secretly.

The reason why Daniel persisted in his practice is not difficult to understand. Here is how Leon Wood explains it:

> If he should pray elsewhere, those knowing him and his habits, including especially his hostile colleagues, would think that he had ceased, and this would spoil his testimony before them. He had been an open witness

before, both in word and life practice; he must continue now lest all that he had done before to influence others to faith in the true God should be for naught. The existence of a continued testimony was more important than the existence of his life![1]

In other words, if Daniel were suddenly to cease praying in his customary fashion, he would have been labeled a hypocrite, a "convenient Christian." Goldingay rightfully comments that "when prayer is fashionable, [then] it is time to pray in secret (Matt. 6:5–6), but when prayer is under pressure, to pray in secret is to give the appearance of fearing the king more than God."[2] Daniel no doubt realized what was going on and knew that if they failed in this plot, they would certainly try another until they succeeded. One final observation: Could it be that one reason he was so successful before men in public is that he was so dedicated to God in private prayer?

Well, you know how the story ends. Daniel is cast into the den of lions, where he is preserved alive through the intervention of an angel sent by God. What's most important is whether prayer and our devotion to seek God are as important to us as to Daniel. I seriously doubt if any of us will face a den of lions for having been caught praying in public. As far as Daniel was concerned, the lions were the least of his worries. Preeminent in his heart was his commitment to pray no matter the cost. Can you and I say the same thing about ourselves?

---

1. Leon Wood, *A Commentary on Daniel* (Grand Rapids: Zondervan, 1973), 163.
2. John E. Goldingay, *Daniel*, Word Biblical Commentary (Dallas: Word, 1989), 131.

Prayer and the Sin unto Death[1]

> If anyone sees his brother committing a sin not leading to death, he shall ask, and God will give him life—to those who commit sins that do not lead to death. There is sin that leads to death; I do not say that one should pray for that. (1 John 5:16)

Whenever we hear words like, "There is sin that leads to death," we instinctively ask, "Have I committed it?" Let's be honest: statements like this in Scripture are scary and often throw people into the depths of fear, anxiety, and even depression. For such folk, virtually every misstep in life, every wayward thought, every indecisive moment potentially becomes the grounds for their exclusion from the kingdom of God. They experience little, if any, of that "joy" that Scripture portrays as the essence of Christian living. Often they become obsessed not simply with the first, more general question of "Can a *Christian* commit the sin unto death?" but with the more specific and personal concern: "Have *I* committed the sin unto death?" As you can well imagine, the problems posed by this passage are innumerable, and therefore, so are the interpretations placed upon it. Here are the more cogent views and my critical interaction with each.

---

1. What follows is adapted from my chapter, "Can a Christian Commit the Sin unto Death?" in *Tough Topics 2: Biblical Answers to 25 Challenging Questions* (Ross-shire, Scotland: Christian Focus, 2015), 77–90.

Sin unto Death Is Apostasy

This first interpretation of the passage is one proposed by many Arminians, those who believe a Christian can apostatize from the faith (i.e., fall from grace) and lose their salvation. I. Howard Marshall represents this position. The principal elements in his explanation of the text are these.

The "brother" about whom John speaks is a genuine, born-again believer, as the usage of the term brother in 1 John would appear to demand (see 1 John 2:9, 10, 11; 3:10, 12[twice], 13, 14, 15, 16, 17; 4:20[twice], 21; 5:16). The kind of "death" John has in mind is spiritual, eternal death, even as the "life" with which it is contrasted is spiritual and eternal.

That "sin" that leads to death or results in death is any sin that is incompatible with being a child of God. What sins qualify? According to 1 John, "Sin that leads to death is deliberate refusal to believe in Jesus Christ, to follow God's commands, and to love one's brothers. It leads to death because it includes a deliberate refusal to believe in the One who alone can give life, Jesus Christ, the Son of God."[2]

On the other hand, sin or sins that do not lead to death "are those which are committed unwittingly and which do not involve rejection of God and his way of salvation. The sinner is overcome by temptation against his will; he still wants to love God and his neighbor, he still believes in Jesus Christ, he still longs to be freed from sin."[3] Marshall makes this distinction between deliberate apostasy ("sin that leads to death") and unwitting transgression ("sin that does not lead to death") on the basis of the Old Testament distinction between "unintentional" or "unwitting" sins, for which atonement was possible, and "deliberate" or "high-handed" sins, for which the Levitical sacrificial system provided no forgiveness (see Lev. 4:2, 13, 22, 27; 5:15, 17–18; Num. 15:27–31; Deut. 17:12).

Christians can commit both types of sin. If someone sees a brother committing sin that does not lead to death, one should pray for him, and God will use the prayer to give him life. However, if someone sees a Christian brother engaged in open refusal to repent and believe, he is on his way to death. John did not require (but neither does he forbid) that anyone pray for

---

2. I. Howard Marshall, *The Epistles of John* (Grand Rapids: Eerdmans, 1978), 248.

3. Marshall, *The Epistles of John*, 248.

him. Consequently, some Christians may, in fact, apostatize from the faith by committing sin that leads to their eternal death. The doctrine of eternal security is obviously incompatible with this view.

Several comments should be made about this interpretation. First, the text does not say that the "brother" commits sin that leads to death. John refers to a brother only regarding sin that is not to death. Second, if the sin of the Christian brother is not the kind that leads to death, why must we pray that God would give him life? Marshall's answer is that "there is always the danger that a person who sins unconsciously or unwittingly may move to the point of sinning deliberately and then of turning his back completely on God and the way of forgiveness. Because of this danger, it is essential that Christians pray for one another lest any of their number cross the line that leads to open and deliberate rejection of the way of life. No sin is of such a kind as to prevent forgiveness, provided that we repent of it. We are to pray for our brothers that they will repent of all sin. When we do this, we have God's promise that he will hear our prayers."[4] But John does not say that the brother was about to "cross over" some such line. Indeed, he says just the opposite. It was to the brother who was *not* committing sin unto death that God promised to give life.

Furthermore, it would be difficult to think of another New Testament author who affirms the doctrine of eternal security with any greater conviction or frequency than the apostle John (John 6:37–44; 10:11–18, 27–30; 17:1–2, 7–12; 1 John 5:18). Other texts likewise deny what Marshall affirms (Rom. 8:29–39; 1 Cor. 1:4–9; Phil. 1:6; 1 Thess. 5:23–24; 2 Thess. 2:13–15; 2 Tim. 2:19; 1 Peter 1:5; Jude 24). Finally, why would John not require us to pray for an apostate? Marshall says it is because "where a person himself refuses to seek salvation and forgiveness there is not much point in praying for him."[5] But isn't that a description that applies to everyone in the world who is not a Christian? Are we not to pray for unbelievers at all?

Raymond Brown, a Roman Catholic scholar, seems to argue for a position similar to Marshall's. Those who sin unto death, he says, are "former brothers and sisters who have opted to be children of the devil by going out to the world that prefers darkness to light. Since Jesus refused to pray for

---

4. Marshall, *The Epistles of John*, 248–49.
5. Marshall, *The Epistles of John*, 249.

such a world (John 17:9), the author's adherents should not pray for those who belong to the world (1 John 4:5). When his readers came to faith and joined the Johannine community of 'brothers,' they passed from death to life (1 John 3:14). By leaving the Community the secessionists have shown that they hate the 'brothers' and have reversed the process by passing from life to death. In that sense theirs is a sin unto death."[6] But then, in a footnote Brown balks, saying that it is unclear "whether the author would admit they ever had life, since he says that the secessionists never really belonged to the Community (1 John 2:19)."[7] Stephen Smalley also argues for a position in many ways identical to Marshall. Whereas John "expected his readers to walk in the light as sons of God . . . he did not ignore the possibility that some believing but heretically inclined members of his community might become apostate. . . . We conclude that John attributes the possibility of 'sin which does not lead to death' to believers, but 'mortal sin' to unbelievers who are, *or believers who have become, antichristian*."[8]

Blasphemy of the Holy Spirit

Others say the "sin unto death" is blasphemy against the Holy Spirit. This view finds its most able proponent in John Stott. His arguments are as follows.

The brother about whom John speaks is not a Christian man. The term *brother* is being used in "the broader sense of a 'neighbor' or of a nominal Christian, a church member who professes to be a 'brother'" but who in reality is a counterfeit.[9] He appeals to 1 John 2:9–11 for an example of this broad use of the term. Also, how can a Christian with eternal "life" (1 John 3:14) be given "life" as John affirms? "How can you give life to one who is already alive? This man is not a Christian, for Christians do not fall into death when they fall into sin."[10] Stott agrees with Marshall that both the "life" and "death" of which John speaks are spiritual and eternal in nature.

However, neither individual in verse 16 is a Christian. The individual in

---

6. Raymond E. Brown, *The Epistles of John*, Anchor Bible (Garden City, NY: Doubleday, 1982), 636.

7. Brown, *The Epistles of John*, 636n17.

8. Stephen S. Smalley, Word Biblical Commentary, *1, 2, 3 John* (Waco: Word, 1984), 299 (emphasis mine).

9. John R. W. Stott, *The Epistles of John: An Introduction and Commentary* (Grand Rapids: Eerdmans, 1976), 190.

10. Stott, *The Epistles of John*, 189.

verse 16b who commits "sin that leads to death" is no more a believer than the "brother" of verse 16a. He is, most likely, one of the false teachers about whom John has been warning his readers, a counterfeit Christian who is exposed by his eventual departure from the church (1 John 2:19). The sin which "leads to death" is the blasphemy of the Holy Spirit (Matt. 12:22–32). It is deliberate, open-eyed, and persistent rejection of Jesus Christ. Sin that leads to death, therefore, is not some solitary sin but a settled state of sin. It is the high-handed and obstinate repudiation of the claims of Christ as made known in the gospel. Although John did not forbid us to pray for someone who blasphemes the Holy Spirit, he did not recommend it because he could not be certain that God would answer it.

Again, several observations are in order. First, although it is possible, I think it is highly unlikely that John would here refer to a non-Christian as a "brother." Most commentators agree on this point. Second, if both men in verse 16 are nonbelievers, men who reject and disbelieve the gospel of Jesus Christ, how are we to know which one has committed sin that does not lead to death, and which one has committed sin that *does* lead to death? How are we supposed to differentiate between an unbeliever and a so-called "hardened" unbeliever in order that we might pray for the former but not the latter? If John was supposed to be giving us guidance for knowing when and when not to pray, he was uncharacteristically fuzzy about it.

Third, Stott's view must also face a problem that plagues every interpretation. When we read verse 16 in the light of its immediately preceding context (verses 14–15), it seems John was describing a particular kind of prayer we could know would always be answered. In other words, prayer for a brother whose sin is not unto death is always according to God's will. Consequently, John assured us that in response to such prayer God would give life to the errant brother. If this is correct, the implications are astounding, for it would mean that any non-Christian for whom we pray, assuming that he has not sinned unto death, will be saved and given eternal life. Even were we to interpret "brother" as referring to a Christian, the problem remains. In the latter case, it would imply that any sinning Christian for whom we pray will be restored and renewed. This, however, ascribes more to the power of prayer than the rest of Scripture would allow. Although it is not a final authority, experience itself teaches us that not every believer for whom we intercede responds and repents.

Also, what about the man who commits sin that leads to death? In Stott's view, John was saying that he does not recommend we pray for him because it is doubtful if that prayer will be answered. If "sin that leads to death" is blasphemy of the Holy Spirit, as Stott argues, then whoever commits this sin will never be saved. But if it is never God's will to give life to a man who is committing sin unto death, why doesn't John explicitly forbid prayer for him? The fact is, whereas John does not require that we pray for this man, neither does he prohibit such prayer. But why doesn't he forbid it if, by definition (on Stott's view), the sin he has committed is unforgivable?

Donald Burdick, although not agreeing in every particular with Stott (he said the "brother" is a believer), suggests that one reason why God may not answer prayer for the man sinning to death is because "the stubborn will of the sinner may not bend. God," says Burdick, "though sovereign, chooses not to coerce the will and thus violate the integrity of the personality he created in his own image."[11]

But God's effectual grace in converting the sinner is persuasive, not coercive. More importantly, if Burdick's point is valid, why would it not also apply to the brother who commits sin not unto death? Why should we think that God's activity regarding the brother not sinning to death is any less "coercive" or any less a "violation" of the integrity of his personality than God's activity with regard to the man whose sin *is* unto death? Sin is a stubborn, rebellious act of one's will, both in the believer and unbeliever, regardless of who commits it. The alleged coercion or violation that concerns Burdick, irrespective of its degree or intensity, is coercion and violation, nonetheless.

Perhaps a way to avoid this problem is to understand John to be saying that giving life to brethren who do not sin unto death is something that God often desires to do. Therefore, we should pray to that end. There is no guarantee that it is always God's will to answer such prayers, even though the language of verse 16a is seemingly unconditional. But even this does not explain why John does not forbid prayer for those who, by definition (on Stott's view), can never be forgiven of their sins (for remember, blasphemy of the Holy Spirit is, according to Jesus, "unforgivable").

---

11. Donald W. Burdick, *The Letters of John the Apostle: An In-Depth Commentary* (Chicago: Moody Press, 1985), 408.

Finally, if the man who commits sin unto death is a non-Christian, he is already dead. What, then, could John have meant by saying that if he sins deliberately and persistently, that is, if he blasphemes the Holy Spirit, he will *die*? Stott agrees that the man is already dead, but by persisting in unbelief, he will die the "second death" (Rev. 20:11–15). "Spiritually dead already, he will die eternally."[12]

Sins Within and Sins Without

This third view is difficult to label. It is somewhat of a mediating position between the views of Marshall and Stott. David M. Scholer is its most convincing defender. Scholer agrees with Marshall that the "brother" is a Christian man, and that "death" is spiritual and eternal in nature. He also agrees with Marshall that "sin that leads to death" must be identified and defined from within the epistle of 1 John itself. It consists primarily of hating the brethren and denying that Jesus is the Christ.

However, unlike Marshall, he insists that *believers* do *not* commit sin that leads to death. Nowhere in the passage, Scholer strenuously claims, is it ever said that a true believer, a "brother," commits sin that leads to death. Believers do commit sin that does not lead to death (1 John 1:8; 2:1), and the Christian community is to intercede for them. Prayer for such sinning Christians will be used by God to renew and reconfirm the "life" they already have in Christ (1 John 3:14).

John is not primarily concerned with the sins of unbelieving outsiders, such sins that lead to death, and therefore does not speak in order that anyone should pray about it. "Prayer," says Scholer, "is not absolutely forbidden concerning the matter, nor is it said that one who commits the 'sin unto death' is forever beyond the hope of becoming a member of the believing community. But throughout 1 John there is a radical separation between the believing community and the unbelieving world so that prayer for the unbelieving world would not be a 'normal' or 'effective' practice."[13] Scholer proceeds to interpret 1 John 3:6, 9 and 5:18 in the light of 5:16–17. Simply put, the "sin" that Christians cannot commit is not a reference to the practice of

---

12. Stott, *The Epistles of John*, 190.

13. David Scholer, "Sins Within and Sins Without: An Interpretation of 1 John 5:16–18," in *Current Issues in Biblical and Patristic Interpretation*, ed. Gerald Hawthorne (Grand Rapids: Eerdmans 1975), 243.

sin in general or persistence in sin. Rather, the sin the believer can't commit is "sin that leads to death," namely, hatred of believers and denial of Jesus.

Essential to this view is a rephrasing of the closing statement in verse 16. The New American Standard Bible 1995 translates this phrase, "I do not say that he should make request for this." The New International Version renders it, "I am not saying that you should pray about that." Both translations make it appear that John was recommending we not pray about the sin unto death or for the one who commits it. Scholer would translate this phrase in another way: "I am not speaking concerning that (i.e., sin unto death), in order that you should pray." In other words, John's purpose is not to enlist prayer concerning sin unto death and those who commit it, although in another context and at another time it may be legitimate to do so. Rather, it is the sin of believers, sin that is not unto death, that he is speaking about and for which he asks that his readers pray.

To sum up, "sin that leads to death" consists principally of hating believers (what John called "murder") and not confessing Jesus (what John called "lying"). This sin cannot be committed by believers for the simple reason that, by definition, this is the sin that makes one an unbeliever. Believers are guilty of sin that does not lead to death, that is, "they do break fellowship with God (1:6–2:1), but without participating in hating the brothers or denying Jesus."[14] Sin unto death is a sin of those who are "disruptive, heretical outsiders."[15] Consequently, John is not concerned here with them or their sin. His concern is with the sin of "insiders," that is, believers within the community of faith.

This view has much to commend it. First, it looks for the meaning of "sin that leads to death" within 1 John itself and interprets "brother" and "death" in keeping with their usage in this epistle. Second, this view has the advantage of restricting sin unto death to unbelievers. Like Stott's interpretation, the "death" into which the sin of these unbelievers leads them is the second, eternal death. Third, Scholer's interpretation supplies us with a cogent solution to other problem texts in 1 John, namely, those that assert that the one born of God cannot or is not able to sin. When 1 John 5:18 (literally, "no one who is born of God sins") is read in the light of 5:16–17, one can see the sense in taking verse 18 to mean, "no one who is born of God sins sin that leads to death."

---

14. Scholer, "Sins Within and Sins Without," 242.
15. Scholer, "Sins Within and Sins Without," 242.

The only problem one might have with this view is the phrase "God will give him life." To say this means "he will renew and reconfirm the life he already has" lacks explicit parallel in 1 John and is not, so far as I can tell, stated in precisely these terms elsewhere in the New Testament. But given the number of difficulties the other interpretations face, this one problem is slight by comparison.[16]

Physical Death

The interpretation of Benjamin B. Warfield deserves careful attention. Warfield agrees with Marshall on two points. The "brother" is a Christian, and it is possible for them to commit "sin that leads to death." Where Warfield disagrees with Marshall (in addition to his affirmation of eternal security, which Marshall denied) is in his belief that *the death in view is physical, not spiritual.* The New Testament does refer to believers suffering illness and occasionally physical death because of persistent and unrepentant sin (see Acts 5:1–11; 1 Cor. 5:5; 11:29–30; James 5:14–15, 19–20).

According to Warfield's interpretation, this brother is not sinning in such a way that his physical life is in jeopardy, and since he is a Christian, he already has spiritual life. What, then, could John have meant when he said that God would give him "life" in response to our prayers? Warfield writes:

We may suppose that by giving life there is meant rather the maintaining or perfecting than the initiating of life. He who lives below his privileges, in whom the life which he has received is languid or weak in its manifestations, is made by our prayers the recipient of fresh vital impulses, or powers, that he may live as the Christian should live. Hitherto living on a plane which can be spoken of only as sinful—though not mortally sinful—he will through our prayers receive newness of life.[17]

---

16. A helpful discussion of this passage that takes a view quite similar to that of Scholer is found in Robert W. Yarbrough, Baker Exegetical Commentary on the New Testament, *1–3 John* (Grand Rapids: Baker Academic, 2008), 305–14. According to Yarbrough, "sin unto death" would refer to "doctrinal convictions, ethical patterns, and relational tendencies—or any combination of these three—which belie one's claim to know the God of light (1:5)" (310). Thus "sin unto death" is "simply violation of the fundamental terms of relationship with God that Jesus Christ mediates" (310).

17. Benjamin B. Warfield, "Praying for the Erring," *Expository Times* 30 (October 1918–September 1919): 537.

In saying that some sin leads to death and other sin does not, John is not giving us a criterion by which we may examine other believers' lives to determine whether we should pray for them. He differentiates between these two kinds of sin simply to tell us why it is that some of our prayers are answered, and others are not. Warfield explains:

> He is merely saying that of those whom we observe to be sinning in the community, some are, in point of fact, sinning to death, and others not; and that, in point of fact, our prayers will be of benefit to the one and not to the other. Who they are who are sinning to death, we do not in any case know. John does not suppose us to know. Only, in urging us to pray for our sinful brethren, and promising us an answer to our prayers, the gift of life to them, he warns us that there are some for whom our petitions will not thus avail. But he warns us of this, not that we may avoid praying for these unhappy ones, but that we may be prepared for the failure of our prayers in their case.[18]

That no sinner is to be excluded from our prayers is proved, says Warfield, by noting the difference between two Greek words John uses in verse 16 (the NIV translation renders both words by the single English term "pray"; whereas the ESV renders the first "ask" and the second "pray"). The word in verse 16a translated "he should pray" (*aiteō*) refers to genuine Christian prayer. But the word in verse 16b (*erotaō*), likewise translated "he should pray," does not refer to intercessory prayer. Rather it denotes the asking of questions, the seeking of information, perhaps for the purpose of debate or discussion. If this understanding of the two words is correct,

> the passage would no longer have even the surface appearance of excluding one kind of sinners from our prayers. . . . It would, on the contrary, expressly require us to pray for all sinners, intimating that though there is a sin to death, that is a matter about which we are not to make anxious inquiry before we pray, but, leaving it to God, we are for ourselves to pray for all our brethren whom we observe to be living sinful lives.[19]

---

18. Warfield, "Praying for the Erring," 539.
19. Warfield, "Praying for the Erring," 539.

The purpose of this passage, therefore, is not to set us upon the task of determining what the sin unto death is or who may or may not have committed it. The message of the apostle is that sin is deadly and that if we would have life, we must avoid it. Therefore, let us come to our brethren's aid by praying for one another. If the sin of the brother for whom we pray is sin unto death, our prayers will not be answered. His sin has taken him beyond the point at which our prayers will restore him. However, that his sin is unto death is not something we can know before we pray. On the other hand, if the sin of the brother for whom we pray is not sufficiently severe and persistent to jeopardize his physical life, God will answer our prayer and restore this brother to the fullness of joy and spiritual energy in his daily life with Christ. But again, that his sin is not the kind that leads to death is not something we can know before we pray.

Although Warfield's interpretation is intriguing, like the others, it is subject to several objections. In the first place, it is unlikely that "death" means physical death. Scholer reminds us that in 1 John "death is the state in which one is before he becomes a believer and out of which he is transferred unto life (3:14; see John 5:24). The one who does not love the brothers (that is, believers) remains in death (3:14). Those who do not love (unbelievers; see 3:9–10; 4:7–8) are not of God (3:10), are in darkness (2:11; see 1:5) and do not know God (4:8; see 4:7). Thus it is clear that a 'sin unto death' is one which signifies the complete absence of any fellowship with God."[20] Of course, this is not to say that it was impossible for John to shift his emphasis from spiritual to physical death, but only that it seems improbable for him to have done so.

Second, Warfield says that John did not mean to tell us that before we pray, we could know whether a brother's sin is unto death or not. We are to pray; if his sin is not to death, God will answer our prayer. If it is to death, our prayer will fail. But this seems overly subtle of John, if not downright obscure. A straightforward reading of verse 16 appears to indicate that the brother for whom we are to pray is the brother *whom we see* sinning the sort of sin that is not to death. If John did not expect us to be able to know whether his sin was to death, he surely chose an odd way of saying so.

Finally, there is some doubt to the validity of drawing a sharp distinction between the Greek words *aiteō* (used in verse 16a) and *erotaō* (used in

20. Scholer, "Sins Within and Sins Without," 240.

verse 16b). There are several verses in John's gospel (John 14:14; and 16:19, 23) in which the distinction most likely does apply. In 1 John 5, however, most modern commentators insist that the words are synonymous and that the apostle's shift from one to the other is purely stylistic. Note well, though, that even should one accept the distinction between these two terms as a valid one, it doesn't necessarily follow that "death" is physical. It is conceivable that all the views we have examined are compatible with this distinction.

Conclusion

I find myself a bit reluctant to conclude anything about this passage! But if push comes to shove, and I suspect many of you are waiting for my answer, I would have to endorse the view of Scholer and Yarbrough (among others who advocate this position). Therefore, my answer to the question posed in the title is no, a Christian cannot commit the sin unto death because such a sin(s) is precisely what identifies and defines a non-Christian. In any case, this text will probably persist in its (in)famous claim to be one of the most perplexing in all the New Testament until Christ returns and sets us all straight. In the meantime, hermeneutical humility is the wise course to pursue.

Can We Pray to the Holy Spirit?[1]

Can we, or can we not, pray to the Holy Spirit? Augustine (354–430) composed this prayer to the Holy Spirit:

> Breathe in me, O Holy Spirit, that my thoughts may all be holy;
> Act in me, O Holy Spirit, that my works, too, may be holy;
> Draw my heart, O Holy Spirit, that I love but what is holy;
> Strengthen me, O Holy Spirit, to defend that is holy;
> Guard me then, O Holy Spirit, that I always may be holy.

Do you agree or disagree with Augustine's direct requests to the Spirit of God? If you agree, you affirm that we can pray to the Holy Spirit. If you disagree, you deny that we can pray to the Spirit.

I will summarize the arguments made by both sides. Then I'll explain my own view.

Yes, We Can Pray to the Spirit

Scripture presents two examples of prayer directed to the Spirit. The first involves the prophet Ezekiel who, being in the Spirit (*ruach*) and set down in a valley of dry bones (the lifeless people of Israel), is commanded by God to "prophesy over these bones," with the promise that the Lord would cause

---

1. This article was written by Gregg Allison and first appeared at https://www.logos.com/grow /min-pray-to-the-spirit/, and is cited here with permission.

breath (*ruach*) to enliven them (Ezek. 37:4–5). As Ezekiel obediently prophesied, the bones became fitted with sinews, flesh, and skin, but there was no breath in them; they remained lifeless. God again addressed Ezekiel:

> Prophesy to the breath [*ruach*, "spirit"]; prophesy, son of man, and say to the breath, Thus says the Lord GOD: Come from the four winds, O breath, and breathe on these slain, that they may live. So I prophesied as he commanded me, and the breath came into them, and they lived and stood on their feet, an exceedingly great army. (Ezek. 37:9–10)

We know that the breath to whom Ezekiel prophesies is the Holy Spirit because the Lord God explains this event: "I will put my Spirit [= the Holy Spirit] within you, and you shall live" (v. 14). The key point for our discussion is that Ezekiel prophesies—that is, prays to the Spirit, who enlivens God's people—in obedience to the Lord's command.

The second example of prayer to the Spirit is part of the apostle John's blessing of the seven churches:

> Grace to you and peace from him who is and who was and who is to come, and from the seven spirits who are before his throne, and from Jesus Christ the faithful witness, the firstborn of the dead, and the ruler of kings on earth. (Rev. 1:4–5)

This apostolic benediction is Trinitarian, directed to the Father ("who is and who was and who is to come"), the Holy Spirit ("the seven spirits who are before his throne"), and the Son ("Jesus Christ"). The key point for our discussion is that John invokes a blessing (grace and peace) upon the churches from the seven spirits—that is, he prays to the Spirit as part of his benediction.

Proponents of praying to the Holy Spirit build a theological case for the practice. Simply put,

- The Holy Spirit is God, equal to the Father and the Son.
- Prayer is and should be directed to God.
- Therefore, as prayer is directed to the Father (e.g., "Our Father, who is in heaven"), and to the Son (e.g., Stephen, as he dies: "Lord Jesus, receive my spirit"), it is proper that prayer be directed to the Holy

Spirit (e.g., "the seven spirits"). Such prayer is proper in all three cases because each person of the Trinity is fully God.

- Indeed, the church confesses (Nicene-Constantinopolitan Creed, 381), I believe in the Holy Spirit, the Lord . . . who with the Father and the Son together is worshiped and glorified.

If it is proper to worship and glorify the Holy Spirit (who is—and because he is—fully God, "the Lord"), and if prayer is part of worship and extends glory to its recipient, then prayer to the Spirit (who is—and because he is—fully God) is proper.

Proponents of prayer to the Spirit agree that most prayers, following the biblical pattern, should be directed to the Father in the name of the Son and in the Holy Spirit (that is, in step with, or empowered by, the Spirit). They also acknowledge that no biblical passage instructs Christians to pray this way. Our common pattern of prayer is a theological conclusion drawn from several passages of Scripture:

- Prayer is directed to the Father: Jesus taught us to pray "Our Father" (Matt. 6:9).
- Prayer is in the name of the Son: as taught by Jesus: "Whatever you ask in my name, this I will do, that the Father may be glorified in the Son. If you ask me anything in my name, I will do it" (John 14:13–14; 15:16; 16:23–24).
- Prayer is in the Spirit: as taught by Paul: "praying at all times in the Spirit, with all prayer and supplication" (Eph. 6:18; cf. Jude 20).
- Thus, in a technical sense, even the general pattern of prayer is not strictly "biblical" but instead "theological." And wise theological thinking affirms that prayer, which is directed to God, includes the Holy Spirit.

Still, this pattern should not always be followed. For example, we should never pray, "Thank you, Father, for becoming incarnate and dying on the cross for my sins." That prayer is wrongheaded! Rather, we should pray, "Thank you, Son of God, for becoming incarnate and dying on the cross for my sins." The general idea here is that prayer is rightly directed to the person of the triune God who is responsible for the particular work at the heart of our prayer. Only the Son became incarnate and died on the cross, so prayers of thanksgiving should be directed to him for the particular works of incarnation and crucifixion.

Accordingly, an example of a prayer rightly directed to the Spirit would be (in the case of sharing the gospel with a friend), "Holy Spirit, convict Meredith of her sin, righteousness, and judgment." This proper prayer would be in keeping with Jesus' promise to send the Spirit: "And when he comes, he will convict the world concerning sin and righteousness and judgment" (John 16:8). It is not the Father who convicts of sin, and Jesus specifically noted that such a role would belong to the Spirit. Thus, this prayer is rightly addressed to the Spirit.

No, We Should Not Pray to the Spirit

Those who deny that we should pray to the Spirit have arguments as well. I'll list three of them.

First, they argue that because Scripture itself indicates the common biblical pattern of prayer, we should always follow it and never deviate from it. Thus, the two prayers used to illustrate proper praying to the Son and the Spirit should be voiced in the typical way:

> Thank you, Father, for sending your Son to become incarnate and to die on the cross for my sins. In Christ's name, Amen.

Similarly,

> Father, please send your Holy Spirit to convict Meredith of her sin, righteousness, and judgment. I pray this in Jesus' name, Amen.

Second, opponents of praying to the Spirit argue that such prayer contradicts Jesus' affirmation about the Spirit: "He will glorify me" (John 16:14). They reason that the Spirit's role is never to draw attention to himself and that praying directly to him violates Jesus' stated principle.

Third, those who oppose praying to the Spirit point to the specific role of the Spirit in our prayers, as described by Paul in his letter to the Romans:

The Spirit helps us in our weakness. For we do not know what to pray for as we ought. (Rom. 8:26)

Opponents argue that if it is the role of the Spirit to help us pray, it would seem odd that our prayers should be directed to him.

We Should Pray to the Spirit

I do pray to the Holy Spirit. So let me briefly respond to the three arguments made by opponents of such prayer.

First, there is surely nothing wrong with praying to the Father, as quoted above. This pattern of praying is correct and blessed, so if opponents advocate such praying, they should pray in this way with a good conscience!

Second, consider the full context of Jesus' affirmation of the Spirit's role: "He will glorify me, for he will take what is mine and declare it to you." One wonders how the specific role of the Spirit highlighted here—glorifying the Son by speaking about Jesus (i.e., inspiring Scripture, which focuses on Christ)—would preclude prayer to the Spirit, even something like this: "Holy Spirit, thank you for inspiring the gospel of John and revealing the glory of Jesus!" Prayer to the Spirit for his intervention through works specifically attributed to him—e.g., conviction of sin, inspiration of Scripture, regeneration, sanctification—by no means contradicts Jesus' affirmation in this passage.

Third, consider the full context of Romans 8, as well, which affirms that it is "the Spirit himself [who] intercedes for us . . . , because the Spirit intercedes for the saints" (Rom. 8:26–27). One wonders how the specific role of the Spirit highlighted here—interceding for troubled believers—would preclude prayer to the Spirit, even something like this: "Holy Spirit, you who are the Comforter (John 14:16, 26; 15:26; 16:7), please comfort me in this season of distress."

I affirm not only that we can pray to the Holy Spirit, but that we should pray to the Holy Spirit.

A Dangerous and Misguided View of Prayer

A Review of Operating in the Courts of Heaven, by Robert Henderson

I don't enjoy writing critical reviews. But sometimes it is necessary. I was alerted to this book by Robert Henderson some time ago, and the book itself was published in 2014. Evidently its influence is continuing to spread.

You've often heard the expression, "Don't judge a book by its cover." That's probably a good policy to follow. In this case, my judgment was formed not by the cover of the book but by its sub-title, which honestly caught me by unpleasant surprise. The subtitle is: "Granting God the Legal Right to Fulfill His Passion and Answer Our Prayers."

I greatly appreciate Henderson's zeal for prayer and how he stresses the important role it plays in God accomplishing his purposes. But let me say this as clearly as I can. God does not need us or anyone else to "grant" him the "right" to do what he wants to do. Even the suggestion that we have this power over God accomplishing his good pleasure is indicative of a deficient view of God. God is not hindered by anything other than the good pleasure of his own will. Let me briefly remind us all of who this God is who, according to Henderson, stands in need of our permission:

> Then Job answered the LORD and said:
> "I know that you can do all things,
> and that no purpose of yours can be thwarted." (Job 42:1–2)

The LORD brings the counsel of the nations to nothing;
　　　he frustrates the plans of the peoples.
The counsel of the LORD stands forever,
　　　the plans of his heart to all generations. (Ps. 33:10–11)

Our God is in the heavens;
　　　he does all that he pleases. (Ps. 115:3)

For I know that the LORD is great,
　　　and that our Lord is above all gods.
Whatever the LORD pleases, he does,
　　　in heaven and on earth,
　　　in the seas and all deeps. (Ps. 135:5–6)

This is the purpose that is purposed
　　　concerning the whole earth,
and this is the hand that is stretched out
　　　over all the nations.
For the LORD of hosts has purposed,
　　　and who will annul it?
His hand is stretched out,
　　　and who will turn it back? (Isa. 14:26–27)

Remember this and stand firm,
　　　recall it to mind, you transgressors,
　　　remember the former things of old;
for I am God, and there is no other;
　　　I am God, and there is none like me,
declaring the end from the beginning
　　　and from ancient times things not yet done,
saying, "My counsel shall stand,
　　　and I will accomplish all my purpose,"
calling a bird of prey from the east,
　　　the man of my counsel from a far country.
I have spoken, and I will bring it to pass;
　　　I have purposed, and I will do it. (Isa. 46:8–11)

At the end of the days I, Nebuchadnezzar, lifted my eyes to heaven, and my reason returned to me, and I blessed the Most High, and praised and honored him who lives forever, for his dominion is an everlasting dominion, and his kingdom endures from generation to generation; all the inhabitants of the earth are accounted as nothing, and he does according to his will among the host of heaven and among the inhabitants of the earth; and none can stay his hand or say to him, "What have you done?" (Dan. 4:34–35)

In him we have obtained an inheritance, having been predestined according to the purpose of him who works all things according to the counsel of his will. (Eph. 1:11)

These texts alone, among dozens of others, testify that whatever God is pleased to do, he will do, and nothing or no one can stay his hand or hinder him. To suggest that God is somehow limited or hindered from accomplishing his "passion" and will indicates a deeply flawed view of God.

Henderson's basic thesis is that "prayer is an activity that takes place in the courtroom of Heaven" (15). He contends that the primary reason our prayers go unanswered is because Christians "rush into a conflict without securing a verdict from Heaven" (16). To see our prayers answered, we must first secure from the courtroom of heaven "a legal precedent to be there" (16). We must first obtain "legal verdicts from Heaven" (18) for our prayers to be answered. We must go "into the courts of Heaven" and get "things legally in place so God's will can be done on the Earth" (41).

How does this happen? Henderson believes it occurs "when we begin to present cases from the revelation we are seeing and understanding out of the books of Heaven" (42). There are "legal arguments" that give Satan the right to rule individuals and nations and "step by step and piece by piece we take away these legalities and grant God the legal right to fulfill His Kingdom will" (43). If you're wondering where in the Bible any such notion is found, the answer is, Nowhere!

At the bottom of this unbiblical approach to prayer is the belief, by Henderson, "that what Heaven wants done cannot happen without our involvement" (44). Of course, it is true that God has chosen to accomplish his purposes in response to the prayers that he has evoked in the hearts and voices of his people. But whether God's deepest "passions" or desires or purposes are accomplished is ultimately up to God alone, and no one can hinder him from achieving his aims or thwart his predetermined plans.

As noted above, Henderson's underlying motive in this book is itself quite admirable. He is burdened that so many of our prayers appear to go unanswered. He longs to understand why and provide an approach to prayer that will greatly increase the believer's effectiveness. But the proposed solution is, in my opinion, misguided and even dangerous to the life of the believer.

As I said, it grieves me to have to write a review of this sort. I am a practicing charismatic who believes in and prayerfully pursues the exercise of all spiritual gifts. But it is precisely because I cherish the teaching of Scripture on this subject that I cringe when others who also self-identify as either Pentecostal or charismatic do such damage to our reputation by misinterpreting and misapplying Scripture.

The essence of Henderson's proposal is that "we must learn to only make war based on judgments, decisions and verdicts that are received out of the courts of Heaven" (18). He believes the fundamental problem is that "we have tried to win on the battlefield [of prayer] without legal verdicts from Heaven backing us up" (18). But is this truly what Scripture teaches? As you will see from what follows, my answer is no.

Before I delve into this general thesis, we should take note of the many texts that are seriously misunderstood and misapplied with a view to supporting it.

Luke 18:1–8

Henderson believes he finds grounds for this view from the story in Luke 18:1–8, a passage that I believe he badly misinterprets. He argues that the story of the unjust judge and the widow demonstrates that "when we pray, we are entering a courtroom" (19). The parable concerns a judge who did not fear man or God and a seemingly helpless widow who brings her request to him for justice. This parable supposedly teaches us that "all we need is a legal precedent based on a verdict from Heaven and the fight is over. We then simply put into place the verdict that has been set down" (21). Of course, there is absolutely nothing in the parable about this widow securing a "legal precedent" or a "verdict from Heaven."

People are often misled when they try to press the details of a parable and derive from them some profound theological lesson. Jesus taught his disciples in parables drawn from numerous settings in everyday life, be it the roadside (Luke 10:25–37), the banquet hall (Luke 14:12–24), the farm (Luke 12:13–21), the open country (Luke 15:1–7), one's house (Luke 15:8–10), the family property (Luke 15:11–32), the temple (Luke 18:9–14), the vineyard (Luke 20:9–18), and so on. In none of these instances does Jesus intend for us to frame our reference for Christian living based on the locale of the story. The fact that Jesus told a parable set in a courtroom does not mean that the only effective way to pray is by conceiving ourselves in the courtroom of heaven. This courtroom was on Earth.

Many have read this parable as if it is teaching that God is like the judge and we are like the widow. No. The point of the parable is to encourage us to pray without ceasing, given the fact that God is *not* like the judge, and we are *not* like the widow. Unlike the judge, God is kind and generous and quick to help us, and we are his redeemed, adopted, and well-loved children, not helpless widows with no one to advocate on our behalf. Therefore, if this helpless and defenseless widow can obtain what she needed from a heartless and self-serving judge, how much more should we, the redeemed and beloved children of God, persevere in prayer to receive what we need from a gracious and kindhearted heavenly Father!

Daniel 7:10

Henderson makes much of Daniel 7:10 and the reference to "the books" in heaven. From this text and Psalm 139:16, he draws the conclusion that "every person ever born has a book written about them" (26). But that is not what the text says. Psalm 139:16 speaks of *"God's"* book, not ours. His book is the plan he has for each of us, specifically "the days that were formed" for us, "when as yet there was none of them." With no text to prove his point, Henderson argues that "there are also books about churches, apostolic networks, businesses, ministries, cities, states, regions, and nations" (28). When you read something like this, you should always ask the question, "Where is that in the Bible?" In this case, the answer is "nowhere."

What, then, are the "books" of Daniel 7:10? The scene is undoubtedly one of judgment, and the "books" most likely is a reference to the record of evil deeds committed by non-Christians. We read that "books were opened" at the final judgment (Rev. 20:12). John says that "the dead were judged by what was written in the books, according to what they had done" (Rev. 20:12). These are not "books" about believers, or "books" that record our destiny or purpose. The "books" in both Daniel 7:10 and Revelation 20:12 contain the record of the deeds of those who have rejected Christ and thus are used as the grounds on which they are eternally judged and cast into the lake of fire.

I should also point out that the description in Daniel 7 is nowhere related to the nature of prayer. Nothing in the text would lead us to believe that discerning the "secrets" contained in these "books" is the key to seeing our prayers answered.

Hebrews 10:5–7

In this text we find Jesus Christ making use of Psalm 40:6–8 to declare that his coming to put an end to sin and accomplish God's will was "written" of him "in the scroll of the book" (Heb. 10:7). Henderson makes illegitimate use of this text by arguing that "even Jesus had a book" (26). He writes:

> There is a book in Heaven that chronicled what Kingdom purpose Jesus would fulfill in the Earth. Jesus came with a passion and a commitment to complete what had been written in the books of Heaven about Him. (26–27)

The problem is that "the scroll of the book" that was written about Jesus and anticipated his obedience and self-offering was, for David, the psalmist (who wrote Psalm 40), most likely the texts that recorded the Davidic Covenant itself (see 2 Sam. 7:12–14; Pss. 89:30–37; 132:11–12). Others suggest it was the Pentateuch, the first five books of the Old Testament. Considering Christ's coming, this "book" or "scroll" most likely expands to encompass the entire Old Testament. My point is that Henderson again tries to find a text that refers to these alleged "books" in heaven, one that even was designed for Jesus, when in fact the author of Hebrews is clearly referring to the Bible itself, in particular the Old Testament which foreshadowed and prophesied of the coming of Messiah.

Revelation 10

Henderson also appeals to Revelation 10:2 and the "little scroll" in the hand of the angel. The question is whether this "little scroll" in chapter 10 is identical to the "scroll" of chapter 5. You may recall from Revelation 5 that the scroll was sealed with seven seals. It couldn't be opened and its contents revealed until the seven seals were broken. The seventh and final seal was broken in Revelation 8:1. Now, here in Revelation 10:2, it makes sense that the scroll is finally said to be "open." The content of the scroll is God's sovereign purpose for establishing his kingdom on Earth. Therefore, the "little scroll" here in chapter 10 is likely identical to the "scroll" in chapter five, containing the substance of the book of Revelation itself.

Henderson contends that when John prophesied from the "books" (although Revelation speaks only of a single "book"), "it allowed court sessions to begin" (29). But John says nothing about court sessions beginning. John says nothing about the nature of prayer in Revelation 10. This habit of reading out of texts things that are simply not present in them is one of the major problems I have with Henderson's book.

2 Timothy 1:9

Another example of this is his misinterpretation of 2 Timothy 1:9. He argues that "Paul is exhorting Timothy to fulfill what was planned before time began" (30). But Paul nowhere exhorts Timothy to do any such thing. Paul is extolling God because he saved us in accordance with "his own purpose and grace, which he gave us in Christ Jesus before the ages began" (2 Tim. 1:9). This means, says Henderson, "that purpose and grace have been waiting on us to discover them from before time began" (30). But Paul says no such thing. We don't have to discover anything because God himself has "manifested" this sovereign and gracious purpose "through the appearing of our Savior Christ Jesus" (2 Tim. 1:10).

Romans 8:29–30

Perhaps the most distressing misinterpretation of the text is Henderson's altogether novel reading of Romans 8:29–30. I think I can confidently say that his interpretation of this text is a first in the history of Christianity. Among the hundreds of commentaries and thousands of journal articles on Romans, no one has ever proposed anything remotely like what Henderson says.

He interprets God's "foreknowledge" (Rom. 8:29) as decisions in the counsel of the Lord that include "individuals, cities, states, businesses and all the way up to nations" (36). Of course, that isn't what Paul says. Paul speaks of "those whom" God foreknew, which from the context is a reference to the "saints" (Rom. 8:27) who "love God" and "are called according to his purpose" (Rom. 8:28). Nothing is said in the text about cities or states or businesses or nations.

Henderson's view of predestination is equally strange. He argues that "we can have a predestined plan for our lives and not fulfill it" (36). Each person, he contends, has a book in heaven "with a predestined plan concerning their life" (36). But "we can either choose to discover what is in the books about us or disregard it and go our own way" (36). Again, Paul says nothing to this effect. What he does say is that all those whom God foreknew he "also predestined to be conformed to the image of his Son" (Rom. 8:29). In other words, the focus of this passage is soteriological, pertaining to our salvation from its beginning with God's foreknowledge and its consummation in our glorification.

These, says Paul, "he also called" (Rom. 8:30), which Henderson says refers to "the stage where we begin to get glimpses of what we were made for" (37). And how do we "get glimpses" of this sort? We are to "look into" our hearts (38). "When we discover the passion of our heart, we will begin to discover what is written in our books in Heaven" (38). Again, this is pure speculation based on nothing in the biblical text. To be "called" is to hear and respond to the effectual invitation of the Spirit to embrace Jesus as Lord and Savior.

To be justified, says Henderson, "is where we have been into the court-room of Heaven and every accusation the devil is using against us is silenced" (38). No, to be justified is to be declared righteous because the righteousness of Jesus himself is imputed or reckoned to us by faith (Rom. 3:23–24; 5:1). And what does Henderson make of our having also been "glorified" (Rom. 8:30)? This is not "talking about going to Heaven. It is speaking about us fully stepping into all that is written in the books of Heaven about us" (39).

To get a clear sense of the way this passage is misunderstood, Henderson says that "the most critical stage of this process for individuals all the way to nations [where are "nations" mentioned in Romans 8:29–30?], is being justified. Once we maneuver our ways through the courts of Heaven and get legal things arranged, God can freely then grant to us the passion of His heart" (40). But friends, we already "have been justified by faith" in Christ (Rom. 5:1). We are "justified by his grace as a gift, through the redemption that is in Christ Jesus" (Rom. 3:24). We don't have to "maneuver" anywhere through anything. We are declared righteous and fully accepted before God when we trust Christ for our salvation.

Hebrews 4:16

I'm not repudiating the idea that there are "courts" in heaven and that legal matters are determined there. But nowhere in the Bible are we explicitly told that to get our prayers answered we must "discover secrets" (20) inscribed in the books of heaven. Perhaps you would respond by pointing to Hebrews 4:16, where we are urged to "draw near to the throne of grace, that we may receive mercy and find grace to help in time of need."

Henderson believes this is where we find answers to help us "on a personal or family level" (46). But there is no restriction placed by the author of Hebrews on what kind of need we may have or for whom or for what reason we might pray. And note that it is to a "throne of grace," not a law court to which we draw near, with the assurance that there we find "mercy" and "grace" to help us in our time of need, not secrets written in books that we must discern and decree.

1 John 1:9

Henderson contends that since "mercy" is nowhere mentioned in this verse, forgiveness is entirely a matter of justice. Now, make no mistake. Justice has been served in the death of Jesus in our place. The legal requirements of the law have been fulfilled in his sinless life. The penal consequences of our sin have been exhausted in his suffering on the cross. But that does not mean that the forgiveness of our sins is wholly legal and not also the fruit of God's mercy and grace. It is both.

Paul says that it was because God was "rich in mercy" and had such "great love" for us that he made us alive together with Christ (Eph. 2:4). If that were not enough, the apostle again writes "when the goodness and loving kindness of God our Savior appeared, he saved us [this would include the new birth, justification, forgiveness of sins, etc.], not because of works done by us in righteousness, but according to his own mercy [!], by the washing of regeneration and renewal of the Holy Spirit, whom he poured out on us richly through Jesus Christ our Savior, so that being justified by his grace we might become heirs according to the hope of eternal life" (Titus 3:4–7). The apostle Peter concurs, attributing our new birth and salvation to God's "great mercy" (1 Peter 1:3–5).

Henderson repeatedly emphasizes repentance, and rightly so. But he does this for the wrong reasons. "Our repentance," he says, "grants God the legal right to display and show His mercy" (51). But how can this be when our repentance is itself the gift of God? We only repent because God mercifully enables us to do so, as we clearly see in such texts as Acts 5:31; 11:18; 2 Timothy 2:24–26.

Matthew 16:18–19

To demonstrate his thesis that God "can do nothing unless we give him the legal right" (55; yes, you read that correctly!), he cites the words of Jesus in Matthew 16:18–19 which speaks of the "keys of the kingdom of heaven" and the authority of the church either to "bind" or "loose." According to Henderson, "Jesus was saying that the Ecclesia [church] has a judicial responsibility to establish binding contracts with Heaven that allow God the legal right to invade and impact the planet. The Ecclesia also has the job of legally dissolving contracts with the devil that allow him to operate in the Earth. When we learn to get legal things in place, we can then see the devil expelled and God's will established" (56).

Well, no. This text is not about prayer. It is not about establishing or dissolving contracts. The person with "keys" "has the power to exclude or permit entrance (cf. Rev. 9:1–6; 20:1–3)" (D. A. Carson, *Matthew*, 370). The words translated "shall be bound in heaven" and "shall be loosed in heaven" may well be rendered, "shall have been bound in heaven" and "shall have been loosed in heaven" (a strict rendering of the future periphrastic perfects in Greek). This binding and loosing pertains to persons and their respective responses to the gospel of the kingdom. Carson explains:

Peter accomplishes this binding and loosing by proclaiming a gospel that has already been given and by making personal application on that basis.... Whatever he binds or looses will have been bound or loosed, so long as he adheres to that divinely disclosed gospel. He has no direct pipeline to heaven, still less do his decisions force heaven to comply; but he may be authoritative in binding and loosing because heaven has acted first.... Those he ushers in or excludes have already been bound or loosed by God according to the gospel already revealed and which Peter, by confessing Jesus as the Messiah, has most clearly grasped. (373)

It's not an easy text to decipher, but one thing is clear: this has nothing to do with navigating the courts of heaven and discerning secrets in the books so that we either establish or dissolve contracts and give God permission to accomplish his will.

Luke 22:31–32

This passage relates how Jesus promised to pray for Peter that his faith would not fail. Henderson believes that "Jesus went into the courts of Heaven on behalf of Peter and secured the destiny written in the books of Heaven for him" (56). As we have seen time and time again, Henderson reads into the text ideas and words that simply aren't there. Jesus asked the Father on Peter's behalf for strength to persevere, and it was granted.

There are numerous other texts cited by Henderson in defense of his view, but none of them ever say what he wants us to believe they say. His thesis is repeated throughout the book: "We must learn to operate in the courts of Heaven and grant the Lord His legal right to bless the nations and us again. It is His heart to bless us, but we must grant Him the legal right to do so" (69). Again and again, he appeals to you, the reader: "Let's grant God the legal right to fulfill the passion of His heart and what He wrote in the books before time began" (75).

A Biblical Perspective on Prayer

We read in Luke 11:1 that one of Jesus' disciples said to him, "Lord, teach us to pray." This would appear to be an excellent opportunity for Jesus to instruct us to pray as Henderson says we should. But we find nothing about operating in the courts of heaven or securing a legal verdict that would allow God to answer our prayers. Instead, Jesus tells us to address God as "Father," not Judge (which isn't to say God isn't a Judge; of course he is). See the parallel of the Lord's Prayer in Matthew 6:5–15. Throughout this latter paragraph, Jesus tells us to address God and to come to him in prayer as Father. The personal address of God as "Father" is found twice in verse 6, once in verse 8, once in verse 9, once in verse 14, and once in verse 15.

If there is any one text that ought to govern how we pray, it is Luke 11:5–13. The Father's goodness is the basis for our reassurance that persevering prayer receives an answer. Jesus makes no mention of releasing God to act or granting him permission. We receive answers to our requests because our heavenly Father, as over against "evil" people like you and me (v. 13), is good and kind and generous. That is why he is "much more" inclined to "give the Holy Spirit to those who ask him" (v. 13). In Matthew's account, the Father doesn't only give us the Holy Spirit when we ask (note well: "ask," not decree or declare or secure a verdict, but simply "ask"), but also gives us "good things."

When the early church prayed, they asked God to "grant" boldness to speak the word (Acts 4:29). It is God who "grants" to us what we need, not we who "grant" God permission to give us what he desires but would otherwise be hindered from giving. Prayer is referenced numerous times in Acts, but not once in the way that Henderson says it should be done (see 1:24; 2:42; 4:29, 31; 6:4, 6; 8:15, 22, 24; 9:11, 40; 10:2, 4, 9, 30, 31; 11:5; 12:5; 13:3; 16:25; 20:36).

Prayer is mentioned in numerous New Testament epistles, such as Romans 1:9–10; 8:26–27; 10:1; 12:12; 15:30; 1 Corinthians 7:5; 11:4–5; 14:13, 14, 15. I could continue to cite texts in 2 Corinthians where prayer is often mentioned. Paul speaks of prayer numerous times in Ephesians (see 1:15–18; 3:14–21; and 6:18). The same is true of Philippians (1:3–10, 19; 4:4–7), Colossians (1:3–4; 4:2–4), 1 Thessalonians (1:2; 5:17), 2 Thessalonians (1:11; 3:1), 1 Timothy (2:1–2, 8), just to mention a few. I'm sure I've overlooked some texts, especially those where the word *prayer* does not occur but prayers are actually being prayed. There is also James 1:5–6; 4:2–3; 5:13–18; 1 Peter 3:7; 1 John 5:14–15, 16–17; 3 John 2; Jude 20; and numerous references in the book of Revelation.

Why did I list all these texts? Simply to show that none portray the model or theology of prayer advocated by Henderson. This is a major concern of mine when it comes to my brothers and sisters in the charismatic world.

Although they regularly affirm their belief in the sufficiency of Scripture, their practice and writings often suggest they don't understand what it means or do understand and simply ignore it. The tendency to create doctrines and practices that not only are absent from Scripture but some that actually contradict what is in Scripture is deeply dangerous. I fear that the hankering after something novel and "never heard before" often drives charismatic authors and leaders. May we fully embrace the wide range of spiritual gifts set forth in the New Testament. At the same time, may we rest confident in the complete sufficiency of Scripture to teach us and provide for our every need, especially concerning prayer.

"Voices in the Courts"?

We now turn to the second half of Henderson's book where he discusses what he calls "Voices in the Courts." He contends that there are "many different voices in the courts of Heaven" and that "our job is to understand these voices and come into agreement with them" (77). Only as we "join with these voices and release our faith and agreement with them" will God's kingdom on earth be accomplished (77). If there is "a lack of manifestation of Kingdom purpose" it is because you and I "have yet to grant the Father the legal right to fulfill His passion toward us" (77).

If you ask, "Where in Scripture do we find this?" the answer is, again, nowhere. Of course, Henderson thinks otherwise, and points us to Hebrews 12:22–24:

> But you have come to Mount Zion and to the city of the living God, the heavenly Jerusalem, and to innumerable angels in festal gathering, and to the assembly of the firstborn who are enrolled in heaven, and to God, the judge of all, and to the spirit of the righteous made perfect, and to Jesus, the mediator of a new covenant, and to the sprinkled blood that speaks a better word than the blood of Abel.

I don't have space to address the numerous ways in which Henderson misunderstands and misapplies Hebrews 12. So, let's get right to his major point. He writes, "Hebrews 12:22–24 lists the voices within the court system of Heaven. There are eight voices [later he includes a ninth] mentioned that we can encounter in the courts of Heaven and are to come into agreement with" (87). And "when we come into agreement with these voices, we become a part of granting God the legal right to fulfill His passion" (87). Do you see any of this in Hebrews 12? I don't. Nowhere in Hebrews 12 are these realities described as "voices" to which we should listen.

The only place where anything remotely approaching a "voice" can be found is the reference in verse 24 to "Jesus, the mediator of a new covenant" and "the sprinkled blood that speaks a better word than the blood of Abel." Following Cain's murder of Abel, God declared that the latter's blood "is crying to me from the ground" (Gen. 4:10). Clearly, the point of this text is that Abel's death calls for justice. Cain must suffer the consequences of his deed. Earlier, in Hebrews 11:4, the author of Hebrews says that Abel, "though he died, . . . still speaks." What does this mean? Is the blood of Abel literally talking? Is Abel literally speaking to us today? No. This is obviously a vivid image designed to emphasize the lasting influence of Abel's testimony. It is Abel's faith to which we are being directed. His "blood" only "speaks" in the sense that his death is an example of the price that must often be paid for faith, loyalty, and obedience to God.

In Hebrews 12:24, the contrast is between the blood of Jesus and the blood of Abel. Whereas Abel's blood cried out for justice and penal retribution, the blood of Jesus declares forgiveness of sins and reconciliation to God. That is why "the sprinkled blood" of Jesus is "better" than "the blood of Abel."

At times, I can't help but wonder aloud where Henderson gets his ideas. For example, he believes that his (Henderson's) "literal blood" in his veins "had a voice of violence" (96). He says that "the anger that was in me had its roots in my blood that was defiled by the sins of my past generations" (96). Or could it simply be that this problem with anger was due to his fallen flesh? Instead of placing the blame on something your "past generations" may have done, take responsibility for the brokenness of your own heart and its sinful desires. Ask God for forgiveness and the power to resist the temptation to explode in rage.

Another example of such unbiblical thinking is his claim that "if God loses, it is because something legal has not been dealt with by us" (111). In another place, he says, "our financial giving, sacrifices, and offerings of ourselves create a basis for us to pray and intercede" (112). Well, no! The basis or grounds on which we pray and intercede at the throne of grace is the once-for-all finished work of Christ for us on the cross and his resurrection from the dead.

As we've already seen, Henderson has an odd view of justification. He seems to believe that God will continually impute his righteousness to us and justify us each time we repent (113) when justification is a one-time event that occurs the moment we put our trust in Christ for salvation.

Echoing a theme that is found throughout this book, Henderson argues that "if we do not take our place in the courts of Heaven, God's plan for the planet cannot come to fruition" (120). Really?

Henderson comes close to adopting a Roman Catholic view of the communion of saints when he argues that the martyrs "are still praying and interceding" (122). Interceding for whom? Surely not for us. Contrary to what Henderson believes Revelation 6:9–11 is saying, the martyrs are simply asking God when will he avenge their blood on those who took their lives. They are not praying for us or interceding for anyone.

He also interprets Hebrews 12:1 as teaching that the saints who have died for their faith "are actually in the courts releasing their voice and testimony on behalf of those of us who must now complete the work for which they gave their lives" (123). But I see nothing in the text that says this is what these "witnesses" are doing. Insofar as these "witnesses" are likely the Old Testament faithful saints just described in Hebrews 11, they bore witness or gave testimony through their lives to the grace of God and the possibilities of a life of faith. Their lives of faith are the evidence, so to speak, to which they direct our attention that God is worthy of our trust. It isn't so much that they are looking at us, but we are encouraged to look to them and their witness and, in doing so, be encouraged, strengthened, and reminded of what can be accomplished when we exercise faith in God. Simply put, these Old Testament saints bore witness through their lives of faith and perseverance, an example we are now admonished to follow. Nothing in the text would lead us to believe they "still have a voice and are releasing testimony in the courts of Heaven" (123).

Henderson still contends that "as we function in the courts from the earthly realm, we are to come into agreement with the intercession of these witnesses. Our agreement with them produces the legal right for Heaven to fulfill the reason for which they laid down their lives" (123). Again, I must repeat myself. Where is this represented in the text? I know of no text in the Bible where the church on Earth is admonished to "come into agreement" with the church that is in heaven in order for God's kingdom will to be accomplished (124).

Yet another misinterpretation is Henderson's view of Hebrews 11:39–40. There we read of the Old Testament believers who "did not receive what was promised, since God had provided something better for us, that apart from us they should not be made perfect." The failure to receive what was promised was mentioned earlier in Hebrews 11:13 and has reference to the consummation of God's redemptive purposes for his people. Their purification from sin could not be fully and finally achieved by the sacrifices of the old covenant but had to await the "better" covenant that Jesus inaugurated by which we are all, together, "made perfect."

But Henderson believes this text is telling us that "their ultimate passion cannot be fulfilled without us finishing and joining with their sacrifice to see God's agenda done" (125). However, it isn't about "us" finishing anything or "joining" with their sacrifice, but rather God bringing us into the state of moral perfection by virtue of the finished work of Christ. "The cloud of witnesses," says Henderson, "is committed to helping us fulfill our assignments in our generations [nowhere does the text say this] because without us, they will not be made perfect" (127). But they have already been made perfect, as Hebrews 12:23 clearly asserts. This perfection refers to the full and final forgiveness of sins that awaited the sacrifice of Christ on the cross.

In his appeal to God "the judge of all" (Heb. 12:23), Henderson argues that "there can be legal issues that hinder His fatherly desires being fulfilled. God will never compromise Himself as Judge in order to fulfill His fatherly desires. To do so would make Him less than God" (131). Well, of course, God never compromises his justice as Judge. But what makes him "less than God" is the belief that he is impotent and helpless to accomplish his desires and so utterly dependent on us that he would otherwise "lose" should we fail to exercise our legal rights in heaven. To say that "God cannot intervene until we give Him the legal right to do so" (134) is to reduce the omnipotent and altogether majestic God of heaven and earth to a puppet of our will.

Again, Henderson appeals to Hebrews 12:23 to argue that "the Church of the firstborn is registered in Heaven for operation in the courts of the Lord."

Yes, they are registered in heaven, their names having been written down in the Lamb's Book of Life. But where does he get the notion that they operate in the courts of the Lord? Not from Hebrews 12, that's for sure.

Once more, Hebrews 12 is cited to prove that "angels have the important task of gathering and presenting evidence. They release the necessary testimonies and evidence needed for God to render judgments" (165). I know I'm sounding like a broken record, but again, where in any text (much less Hebrews 12) does the Bible say this? Not only the angels but "all the voices in Heaven operate for this purpose, but it is our job to agree with them until legal precedents are in place" (166). These ideas are the fruit of Henderson's imagination, not the result of carefully reading the biblical text.

Why did the events of 9/11 take place? Henderson contends that it was due to our failure "to take our place as the Ecclesia and grant God the legal right to thwart the plans of the devil" (174). I simply have no words left to respond to such an outrageous claim.

I could cite a dozen or more additional instances where Henderson inserts his personal theological concepts into biblical texts. This is not exegesis, but eisegesis, a reading into text's meanings and applications that cannot be read out of the texts.

One final element in Henderson's book needs to be addressed. He often speaks of repenting for the sins of other people. One of several examples is when Henderson himself says that he "began to repent for what" his "forefathers had done" (95).

The idea that a person can and should repent on behalf of others is based largely on Old Testament texts that describe the land being defiled or corrupted by the sins of Israel. The idea is that, to overcome or reverse this judgment, we today must in some way "identify" with the people of the past and "repent" for the sins they committed. George Otis describes this "repentance" in two stages: "(1) an acknowledgement that one's affinity group (clan, city, nation, or organization) has been guilty of a specific corporate sin before God and man, and (2) a prayerful petition that God will use personal repudiation of this sin as a redemptive beachhead from which to move into the larger community" (*Informed Intercession*, 251).

But note that Otis nowhere refers here to the biblical concept of repentance. Yes, we must acknowledge the sins of the past and repudiate them, committing ourselves through the power of the Spirit not to repeat them in our experience. But this is far and away different from saying that we can "repent" for the sins of our ancestors.

Repentance, by definition, is the acknowledgment (which typically entails deep sorrow and contrition), confession of, and turning from the sins that one has committed, both in terms of what one believes and how one behaves. That being the case, it is impossible that I can repent for sins I haven't committed. However, that isn't to say that the sins of others, whether those of our ancestors or our contemporaries, are irrelevant to us. So, how do we respond to the sins of others? What is our responsibility?

First, we should acknowledge and confess such sins. We should acknowledge that our ancestors or contemporaries, with whom we are connected or related, have transgressed the law of God. Perhaps the most explicit example of this in the Bible is found in Nehemiah. There Nehemiah says:

> O LORD God of heaven, the great and awesome God who keeps covenant and steadfast love with those who love him and keep his commandments, let your ear be attentive and your eyes open, to hear the prayer of your servant that I now pray before you day and night for the people of Israel your servants, confessing the sins of the people of Israel, which we have sinned against you. Even I and my father's house have sinned. We have acted very corruptly against you and have not kept the commandments, the statutes, and the rules that you commanded your servant Moses. (Neh. 1:5–7)

A similar prayer was spoken by Daniel during the time of the Babylonian captivity (see Dan. 9:1–19). But note carefully that nowhere do either Daniel or Nehemiah "repent" for other people. They identify the sins of others. They declare that they and others in Israel have transgressed. They make no excuse for their sins. They both ask God to have mercy on themselves and the people of Israel. But that is not the same as "repenting" for the sins of others. They undoubtedly repented for their own sins by resolving to forsake their sinful ways and to obey God's revealed will. But one person can't do that in the place of another. Everyone must do this for himself or herself.

We must also remember that Nehemiah and Daniel were living under the dictates of the Mosaic covenant. The blessings and curses (see Deut. 28) for obedience or rebellion no longer apply to any other geopolitical nation-state. God does not enter into covenant with nations, but only with the "holy nation" of the church of Jesus Christ, a distinctively multiethnic, spiritual body of believers (1 Peter 2:9). We must guard against the tendency (especially seen in the broader Pentecostal-charismatic world) to apply uniquely old covenant texts with its promises and warnings to those who now live under the terms of the new covenant in Christ.

Thus, I might confess to God that "we" at my home church here in Oklahoma City have in some manner turned away from God and that "we" are rightly under his discipline. I can declare the truth regarding our transgressions, renounce them, and cry out to God on behalf of the people as a whole. But I cannot repent for what anyone else has done, only for what I have done, and then pray that God's Spirit would awaken others to likewise repent of their own sins.

Second, we should also renounce, repudiate, and disavow the sins of our ancestors or our contemporaries with whom we are in close relationship. We should make it clear by confession and behavior that we want no part of that sort of wicked behavior, that we wish never to repeat such sinful activity, and that we choose to distance ourselves from the destructive consequences that follow upon the sinful behavior of our ancestors or contemporaries. But to renounce the sins of others is not the same as repenting for the sins of others.

Third, it's important to remember that none of us is held guilty by God for the sins of our ancestors or contemporaries, unless, of course, we ourselves contributed to their sins by encouraging them to behave wickedly or by choosing to repeat in our own lives their sinful behavior. But God will not hold me guilty for the sins of my ancestors, nor will he punish or judge me for what they have done.

What, then, do we make of texts such as Exodus 20:5–6?

> You shall not bow down to them or serve them, for I the LORD your God am a jealous God, visiting the iniquity of the fathers on the children to the third and the fourth generation of those who hate me, but showing steadfast love to thousands of those who love me and keep my commandments.

Note carefully that the visitation of the iniquity of one's ancestors on subsequent generations comes only upon "those who hate me." It is only when we choose to repeat, copy, or perpetuate the sins of our ancestors that we suffer divine judgment. Likewise, it is on those who love God and keep his commandments that steadfast love comes.

Along these lines, we must take into consideration Deuteronomy 24:16 (NASB 1995): "Fathers shall not be put to death for their sons, nor shall sons be put to death for their fathers; everyone shall be put to death for his own sin" (cf. Ezek. 18:2–4, 20). The point is this: if you do not hate God, this threat is not applicable to you.

I close with a simple warning and a word of counsel: this book is not helpful, will not empower your prayer life, and should be avoided by all Christians.

My counsel is equally simple and straightforward. The most basic question anyone can ask when they hear of some strange new theory or interpretation is this: "Where is that in the Bible?" Don't simply embrace the agendas, theologies, or strategies that someone claims are justified by certain biblical texts. Examine the texts for yourself and simply ask, "Is that actually in the words of Scripture? Where in the text does he find that?" This will serve you well as you seek to understand the teaching of God's Word.

Subject Index

Scripture Index